Proportionate-type Normalized Least Mean Square Algorithms

FOCUS SERIES

Series Editor Francis Castanié

Proportionate-type Normalized Least Mean Square Algorithms

Kevin Wagner
Miloš Doroslovački

iSTE

WILEY

First published 2013 in Great Britain and the United States by ISTE Ltd and John Wiley & Sons, Inc.

ISTE Ltd
27-37 St George's Road
London SW19 4EU
UK

www.iste.co.uk

John Wiley & Sons, Inc.
111 River Street
Hoboken, NJ 07030
USA

www.wiley.com

Library of Congress Control Number: 2013937864

British Library Cataloguing-in-Publication Data
A CIP record for this book is available from the British Library
ISSN: 2051-2481 (Print)
ISSN: 2051-249X (Online)
ISBN: 978-1-84821-470-5

FSC www.fsc.org MIX Paper from responsible sources FSC® C013604

Printed and bound in Great Britain by CPI Group (UK) Ltd., Croydon, Surrey CR0 4YY

Contents

Preface

Aims of this book

The primary goal of this book is to impart additional capabilities and tools to the field of adaptive filtering. A large part of this book deals with the operation of adaptive filters when the unknown impulse response is sparse. A sparse impulse response is one in which only a few coefficients contain the majority of energy. In this case, the algorithm designer attempts to use the *a priori* knowledge of sparsity. Proportionate-type normalized least mean square (PtNLMS) algorithms attempt to leverage this knowledge of sparsity. However, an ideal algorithm would be robust and could provide superior channel estimation in both sparse and non-sparse (dispersive) channels. In addition, it would be preferable for the algorithm to work in both stationary and non-stationary environments. Taking all these factors into consideration, this book attempts to add to the state of the art in PtNLMS algorithm functionality for all these diverse conditions.

Organization of this book

Chapter 1 introduces the framework of the PtNLMS algorithm. A review of prior work performed in the field of adaptive filtering is presented.

Chapter 2 describes classic techniques used to analyze the steady-state and transient regimes of the least mean square (LMS) algorithm.

In Chapter 3, a general methodology is presented for analyzing steady-state and transient analysis of an arbitrary PtNLMS algorithm for white input signals. This chapter builds on the previous chapter and examines that the usability and limitations of assuming the weight deviations are Gaussian.

In Chapter 4, several new algorithms are discussed which attempt to choose a gain at any time instant that will minimize user-defined criteria, such as mean square output error and mean square weight deviation. The solution to this optimization problem results in a water-filling algorithm. The algorithms described are then tested in a wide variety of input as well as impulse scenarios.

In Chapter 5, an analytic expression for the conditional probability density function of the weight deviations, given the preceding weight deviations, is derived. This joint conditional probability density function is then used to derive the steady-state joint probability density function for weight deviations under different gain allocation laws.

In Chapter 6, a modification of the μ-law PNLMS algorithm is introduced. Motivated by minimizing the mean square error (MSE) at all times, the adaptive step-size algorithms described in this chapter are shown to exhibit robust convergence properties.

In Chapter 7, the PtNLMS algorithm is extended from real-valued signals to complex-valued signals. In addition, several simplifications of the complex PtNLMS algorithm are proposed and so are their implementations. Finally, complex water-filling algorithms are derived.

In Chapter 8, the computational complexities of algorithms introduced in this book are compared to classic algorithms such as the normalized least mean square (NLMS) and proportionate normalized least mean square (PNLMS) algorithms.

Notation

The following notation is used throughout this book. Vectors are denoted by boldface lowercase letters, such as $\mathbf{x}$. All vectors are column vectors unless explicitly stated otherwise. Scalars are denoted by Roman or Greek letters, such as x or ν. The ith component of vector $\mathbf{x}$ is given by x_i. Matrices are denoted by boldface capital letters, such as $\mathbf{A}$. The (i, j)th entry of any matrix $\mathbf{A}$ is denoted as $[\mathbf{A}]_{ij} \equiv a_{ij}$. We frequently encounter time-varying vectors in this book. A vector at time k is given by $\mathbf{x}(k)$. For notational convenience, this time indexing is often suppressed so that the notation $\mathbf{x}$ implies $\mathbf{x}(k)$. Additionally, we use the definitions $\mathbf{x}^+ \equiv \mathbf{x}(k+1)$ and $\mathbf{x}^- \equiv \mathbf{x}(k-1)$ to represent the vector $\mathbf{x}$ at times $k+1$ and $k-1$, respectively.

For vector $\mathbf{a}$ with length L, we define the function $\mathbf{Diag}\{\mathbf{a}\}$ as an $L \times L$ matrix whose diagonal entries are the L elements of $\mathbf{a}$ and all other entries are zero. For matrix $\mathbf{A}$, we define the function $\mathbf{diag}\{\mathbf{A}\}$ as a column vector containing the L diagonal entries from $\mathbf{A}$. For matrices, $\mathrm{Re}\{\mathbf{A}\}$ and $\mathrm{Im}\{\mathbf{A}\}$ represent the real and imaginary parts of the complex matrix $\mathbf{A}$.

The list of notation is given below.

$\mathbf{x}$	a vector
x	a scalar
$\mathbf{A}$	a matrix
x_i	the ith entry of vector $\mathbf{x}$
$[\mathbf{A}]_{ij} \equiv a_{ij}$	the (i, j)th entry of any matrix $\mathbf{A}$
$\mathbf{Diag}\{\mathbf{a}\}$	a diagonal matrix whose diagonal entries are the elements of vector $\mathbf{a}$
$\mathbf{diag}\{\mathbf{A}\}$	a column vector whose entries are the diagonal elements of matrix $\mathbf{A}$
$\mathbf{I}$	identity matrix
$E\{\mathbf{x}\}$	expected value of random vector $\mathbf{x}$

$.^T$	matrix transposition
$.^H$	complex transposition (Hermitian transposition)
$.^*$	complex conjugation
$\odot$	the Hadamard product
$\text{Im}\{\mathbf{A}\}$	imaginary part of complex matrix $\mathbf{A}$
$\text{Re}\{\mathbf{A}\}$	real part of complex matrix $\mathbf{A}$
$\|\|\mathbf{x}\|\|^2$	squared Euclidean norm of the vector $\mathbf{x}$
$\|\|\mathbf{x}\|\|^2_{\mathbf{W}}$	$\mathbf{x}^T\mathbf{W}\mathbf{x}$ for column vector $\mathbf{x}$ and positive definite matrix $\mathbf{W}$
$\text{Tr}\{\mathbf{A}\}$	trace of the matrix $\mathbf{A}$

Acronyms

The following acronyms are used in this book.

AEPNLMS	adaptive ϵ-proportionate normalized least mean square
AMPNLMS	adaptive μ-proportionate normalized least mean square
APAF	affine projection adaptive filter
ASPNLMS	adaptive segmented proportionate normalized least mean square
cCWF	complex colored water-filling
cLMS	complex least mean square
cMPNLMS	complex μ-proportionate normalized least mean square
cNLMS	complex normalized least mean square
cPNLMS	complex proportionate normalized least mean square
cPtAP	complex proportionate-type affine projection
cPtNLMS	complex proportionate-type normalized least mean square
CWF	colored water-filling
cWF	complex water-filling
DCT	discrete cosine transform
DCT-cPtNLMS	discrete cosine transform complex proportionate-type normalized least mean square
DCT-LMS	discrete cosine transform least mean square
DCT-NLMS	discrete cosine transform normalized least mean square
DCT-PNLMS	discrete cosine transform proportionate-type normalized least mean square
DCT-WF	discrete cosine transform water-filling
DFT	discrete Fourier transform
DWT	discrete wavelet transform
EPNLMS	ϵ-proportionate normalized least mean square
Haar-cPtNLMS	Haar complex proportionate-type normalized least mean square

Haar-NLMS	Haar normalized least mean square
Haar-PNLMS	Haar proportionate-type normalized least mean square
Haar-WF	Haar water-filling
IAF-PNLMS	individual activation factor proportionate normalized least mean square
IIPNLMS	improved improved proportionate normalized least mean square
IPNLMS	improved proportionate normalized least mean square
LMS	least mean square
MMSE	minimum mean square error
MPNLMS	μ-proportionate normalized least mean square
MSE	mean square error
MSWD	mean square weight deviation
MWD	mean weight deviation
NLMS	normalized least mean square
PDF	probability distribution function
PNLMS	proportionate normalized least mean square
PNLMS++	proportionate normalized least mean square plus plus
PtLMS	proportionate-type least mean square
PtNLMS	proportionate-type normalized least mean square
RLS	recursive least squares
SNR	signal-to-noise ratio
SO-NLMS	self-orthogonalizing normalized least mean square
SO-PNLMS	self-orthogonalizing proportionate normalized least mean square
SO-WF	self-orthogonalizing water-filling
SPNLMS	segmented proportionate normalized least mean square
TD-CPtNLMS	transform domain complex proportionate-type normalized least mean square
VOIP	voice over IP
WD	weight deviation
WF	water-filling

1

Introduction to PtNLMS Algorithms

The objective of this chapter is to introduce proportionate-type normalized least mean square (PtNLMS) algorithms in preparation for performing analysis of these algorithms in subsequent chapters. In section 1.1, we begin by presenting applications for PtNLMS algorithms as the motivation for why analysis and design of PtNLMS algorithms is a worthwhile cause. In section 1.2, a historical review of relevant algorithms and literature is given. This review is by no means exhaustive; however, it should serve the needs of this work by acting as a foundation for the analysis that follows. In section 1.3, standard notation and a unified framework for representing PtNLMS algorithms are presented. This notation and framework will be used throughout the remainder of this book. Finally, with this standardized notation and framework in hand, we present several PtNLMS algorithms in section 1.4. The chosen PtNLMS algorithms will be referenced frequently throughout this work.

1.1. Applications motivating PtNLMS algorithms

Historically, PtNLMS algorithms have found use in network echo cancellation applications as a method for reducing the presence of delayed copies of the original signal, i.e. echoes. For instance, in many telephone communication systems the network consists of two types of wire segments: a four-wire central network and a two-wire local network [MIN 06]. A converting device, called a hybrid, is needed at the junction of the two-wire to four-wire segments. When a far-end user talks a portion of the signal is reflected back to the far-end listener, due to the impedance mismatch in the hybrid as shown in Figure 1.1. This type of echo is called electric echo or circuit echo. An adaptive filter can be used to estimate the impulse response of the hybrid and remove the echo caused by the hybrid.

In modern telephone networks, greater delays increase the need for echo cancellation. Specifically, these communication networks have driven the need for faster converging echo cancellation algorithms when the echo path is sparse. A sparse echo path is that in which a large percentage of the energy is distributed to only a few coefficients. Conversely, a dispersive echo path has distributed most of its energy more or less evenly across all of the coefficients. Examples of a dispersive impulse response and a sparse impulse response are shown in Figures 1.2a and 1.2b, respectively. While most network echo path cancelers have echo path lengths in the order of 64 ms, the active part of the echo path is usually only about 4–6 ms long [GAY 98], hence the echo path is sparse. The active part of an echo path corresponds to the coefficients of the echo path that contain the majority of the energy. When the impulse response is sparse, PtNLMS algorithms can offer improved performance relative to standard algorithms such as the least mean square (LMS) and normalized least mean square (NLMS) [HAY 02].

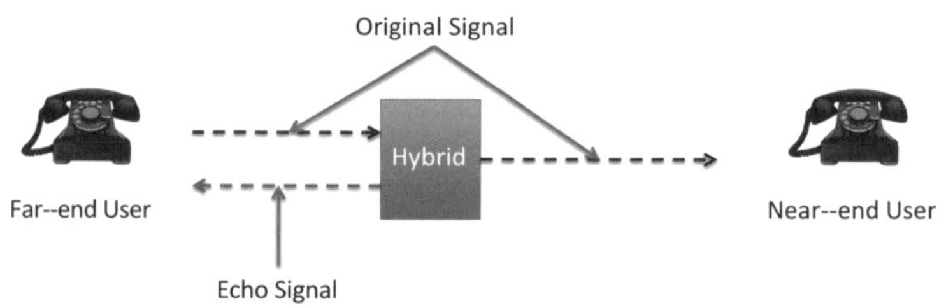

Figure 1.1. *Telephone echo example*

Another application for PtNLMS has been spawned by the emergence of Voice over IP (VOIP) as an important and viable alternative to circuit switched networks. In these systems, longer delays are introduced due to packetization [SON 06]. In addition, echoes can be created during the transition from traditional telephone circuits to IP-based telephone networks [MIN 06].

The advent of telephone communication via satellite has motivated the search for a better way to eliminate echoes [WEI 77]. The distortion caused by echo suppressors is particularly noticeable on satellite-routed connections.

Let us also mention that modern applications of echo cancellation include acoustic underwater communication where the impulse response is often sparse [STO 09], television signals where the delay can be significant due to satellite communication [SCH 95], high-definition television terrestrial transmission that requires equalization due to inter-symbol interference caused by multi-path channels exhibiting sparse behavior [FAN 05], and applications where the impulse response is sparse in the transform domain [DEN 07].

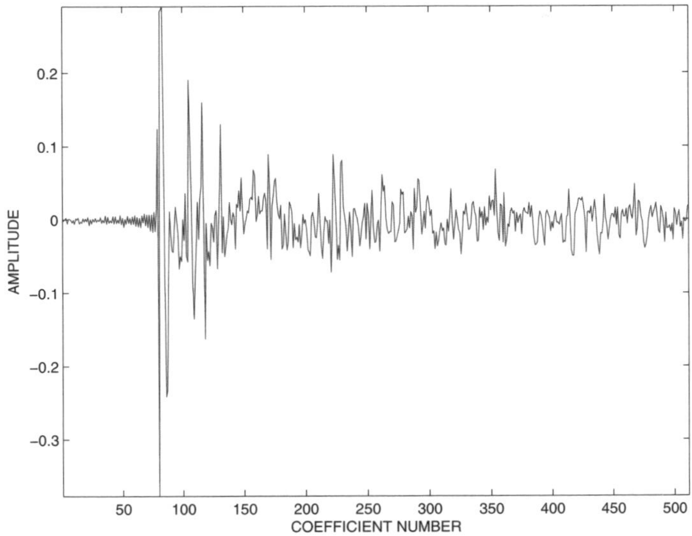

a) Dispersive impulse response

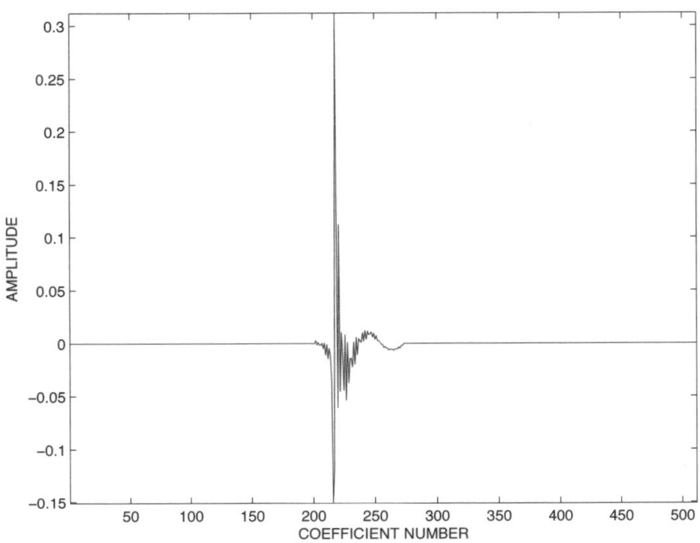

b) Sparse impulse response

Figure 1.2. *Dispersive and sparse impulse responses*

When examining these applications as well as others like them, several questions regarding the desired performance of the PtNLMS algorithms need to be answered in order to design an algorithm for the intended application. For instance, we need to know what the required convergence of the algorithm needs to be. We also need to know the computational complexity that the application can support as well as what level of steady-state bias can be tolerated. To address these questions we need to understand the underlying mechanics of each PtNLMS algorithm as well as what factors control how the algorithms perform. Therefore, we intend to analyze PtNLMS algorithms to find out what factors influence the convergence, steady-state performance, and what the implementation cost of possible improvements in terms of computational complexity is. In doing so, a better understanding of what influences the performance of PtNLMS algorithms is provided. Answering these questions will allow us to design algorithms that perform their desired tasks more efficiently.

1.2. Historical review of existing PtNLMS algorithms

In the past, adaptive filtering algorithms such as the LMS and NLMS have been examined extensively [HAY 02]. These algorithms offer low computational complexity and proven robustness. The LMS and NLMS algorithms share the property of the adaptive weights being updated in the direction of the input vector. These algorithms perform favorably in most adaptive filtering situations.

The LMS and NLMS algorithms fall within the larger class of PtNLMS algorithms. PtNLMS algorithms can update the adaptive filter coefficients such that some coefficients are favored. That is, some coefficients receive more emphasis during the update process. Because of this fact, the PtNLMS algorithms are better suited to deal with sparse impulse responses.

An example of a PtNLMS algorithm is the proportionate normalized least mean square (PNLMS) algorithm [DUT 00]. This algorithm updates the adaptive filter coefficients by assigning a gain proportional to the magnitude of the current coefficient estimates. This approach improves the initial convergence rates. However, this gain adaptation scheme causes the PNLMS algorithm to suffer from slow convergence of small coefficients, and as a result the time needed to reach steady-state error is increased compared to the NLMS algorithm. The PNLMS algorithm has been shown to outperform the LMS and NLMS algorithms when operating on a sparse impulse response. Currently, any analytical model to describe learning curve convergence of the PNLMS algorithm does not exist [SON 06].

Another weakness of the PNLMS algorithm is that when the impulse response is dispersive, the algorithm converges much slower than the NLMS algorithm. To remedy this issue the PNLMS++ was proposed [GAY 98]. The PNLMS++ algorithm solves this issue by alternating between the NLMS and PNLMS algorithms on each sample period of the algorithm. The improved PNLMS (IPNLMS) was introduced to build upon the PNLMS++ algorithm [BEN 02]. The IPNLMS attempts to exploit the shape of the estimated echo, instead of blindly alternating between the PNLMS and NLMS algorithms as is done in the PNLMS++ algorithm. The IPNLMS algorithm performs better than the NLMS and PNLMS algorithms no matter what the nature of the impulse response.

In the following, the improved IPNLMS (IIPNLMS) algorithm was proposed [CUI 04]. This algorithm attempted to identify active and inactive regions of the echo path impulse response. Active regions received updates more in-line with the NLMS methodology, while inactive regions received gains based upon the PNLMS methodology. In this way, the IIPNLMS was able to outperform the IPNLMS algorithm. The idea of applying gain selectively to active and inactive regions was explored previously in the so-called partial update algorithms. These algorithms, motivated by reducing computational complexity while improving performance, update a subset of all the coefficients during each sampling period. Examples of partial update NLMS algorithms can be found in [TAN 02] and [NAY 03].

Another set of algorithms was designed by seeking a condition to achieve the fastest overall convergence. Initially, the steepest descent algorithm was optimized and then the resulting deterministic algorithm was cast into the stochastic framework. It can be shown that the total number of iterations for overall convergence is minimized when all of the coefficients reach the ϵ-vicinity of their true values simultaneously (where ϵ is some small positive number). This approach results in the μ-law PNLMS (MPNLMS) [DEN 05]. The MPNLMS algorithm addresses the issue of assigning too much update gain to large coefficients, which occurs in the PNLMS algorithms.

The ϵ-law PNLMS (EPNLMS) [WAG 06] algorithm is a second implementation of the same philosophy used to generate the MPNLMS algorithm. This algorithm gives the minimum gain possible to all of the coefficients with magnitude less than ϵ. It assumes that the impulse response is sparse and contains many small magnitude coefficients [DEN 06]. The EPNLMS outperforms the MPNLMS algorithm in many cases, however the MPNLMS algorithm's performance is more robust regarding the choice of algorithm parameters, as well as input signal and unknown system characteristics, than the EPNLMS algorithm.

The individual activation factor PNLMS (IAF-PNLMS) algorithm was introduced in [DAS 10]. The standard PNLMS algorithm performance depends on some predefined parameters controlling proportionality activation through a minimum gain that is common for all of the coefficients. In contrast, the IAF-PNLMS algorithm computes a separate minimum gain for each coefficient. This time varying minimum gain is called the activation factor and has the following characteristics: (1) an individual activation factor is used for each adaptive filter coefficient; (2) each individual activation factor is computed in terms of the past and current values of the corresponding coefficient magnitude, thereby each activation factor presents some inherent memory associated with its corresponding coefficient magnitude; (3) the individual activation factors do not rely on the proportionality and initialization parameters, since they are no longer in the proposed formulation. As a consequence, the convergence features of the IAF-PNLMS algorithm are improved relative to the NLMS and PNLMS algorithms.

1.3. Unified framework for representing PtNLMS algorithms

We begin by introducing a unified framework for representing PtNLMS algorithms. All signals are real-valued throughout this chapter and the majority of this book. It will be stated explicitly if the signals under examination are complex. Let us assume there is some input signal denoted as $\mathbf{x}(k)$ for time k that excites an unknown system with impulse response $\mathbf{w}$. Let the output of the system be $y(k) = \mathbf{w}^T\mathbf{x}(k)$, where $\mathbf{x}(k) = [x(k), x(k-1), \ldots, x(k-L+1)]^T$ and L is the length of the filter. The measured output of the system, $d(k)$, contains measurement noise $v(k)$ and is equal to the sum of $y(k)$ and $v(k)$. The impulse response of the system is estimated with the adaptive filter coefficient vector (also called weight vector), $\hat{\mathbf{w}}(k)$, which also has length L. The outputs of the adaptive filters is given by $\hat{y}(k) = \hat{\mathbf{w}}^T(k)\mathbf{x}(k)$. The error signal $e(k)$ between the outputs of the adaptive filters $\hat{y}(k)$ and $d(k)$ drives the adaptive algorithm. A diagram of this processing scheme is shown in Figure 1.3. The weight deviation vector is given by $\mathbf{z}(k) = \mathbf{w} - \hat{\mathbf{w}}(k)$.

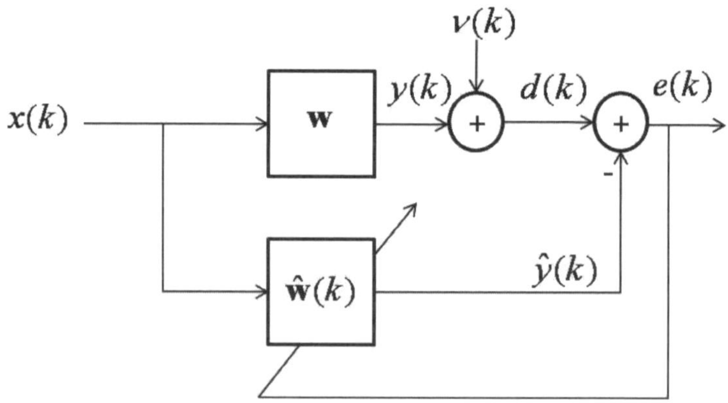

Figure 1.3. *Adaptive filtering "system identification" configuration*

The PtNLMS algorithm is shown in Table 1.1. Here, β is the fixed step-size parameter. The term $F[|\hat{w}_l(k)|, k]$, with $l \in \{1, 2, \ldots, L\}$, governs how each coefficient is updated and we refer to this term as the control law. In the case when $F[|\hat{w}_l(k)|, k]$ is less than $\gamma_{\min}$, the quantity $\gamma_{\min}$ is used to set the minimum gain a coefficient can receive. The constant δ_p, where $\delta_p \geq 0$, is important in the beginning of learning when all of the coefficients are zero and together with ρ, where $\rho \geq 0$, prevent the very small coefficients from stalling. $\mathbf{G}(k) = \mathbf{Diag}\{g_1(k), \ldots, g_L(k)\}$ is the time-varying step-size control diagonal matrix. The constant δ is typically a small positive number used to avoid division by zero if the inputs are zero, that is when $\mathbf{x}(k) = \mathbf{0}$.

$\mathbf{x}(k)$	$= [x(k), x(k-1), \ldots, x(k-L+1)]^T$
$\hat{y}(k)$	$= \mathbf{x}^T(k)\hat{\mathbf{w}}(k)$
$e(k)$	$= d(k) - \hat{y}(k)$
$F[\lvert\hat{w}_l(k)\rvert, k]$	= Specified by the user
$\gamma_{\min}(k)$	$= \rho \max\{\delta_p, F[\lvert\hat{w}_1(k)\rvert, k], \ldots, F[\lvert\hat{w}_L(k)\rvert, k]\}$
$\gamma_l(k)$	$= \max\{\gamma_{\min}(k), F[\lvert\hat{w}_l(k)\rvert, k]\}$
$g_l(k)$	$= \frac{\gamma_l(k)}{\frac{1}{L}\sum_{i=1}^{L}\gamma_i(k)}$
$\mathbf{G}(k)$	$= \mathbf{Diag}\{g_1(k), \ldots, g_L(k)\}$
$\hat{\mathbf{w}}(k+1)$	$= \hat{\mathbf{w}}(k) + \frac{\beta\mathbf{G}(k)\mathbf{x}(k)e(k)}{\mathbf{x}^T(k)\mathbf{G}(k)\mathbf{x}(k)+\delta}$

Table 1.1. *PtNLMS algorithm with time-varying step-size matrix*

Some common examples of the term $F[|\hat{w}_l(k)|, k]$ are $F[|\hat{w}_l(k)|, k] = 1$ and $F[|\hat{w}_l(k)|, k] = |\hat{w}_l(k)|$, which result in the NLMS and PNLMS algorithms, respectively.

Assuming that the impulse response being estimated is sparse, the PtNLMS algorithms begin by setting $\hat{\mathbf{w}}(0) = \mathbf{0}$. These algorithms rely on the fact that the true system impulse response $\mathbf{w}$ is sparse and most coefficients are zero, therefore the initial estimate $\hat{\mathbf{w}}(0) = \mathbf{0}$ is correct for most of the estimated weights. In the following, the weights that differ from zero should be driven toward their true values as quickly as possible to speed up convergence. The question, as proposed in [DEN 05], then becomes how to determine when an estimated coefficient's true value is non-zero and how to assign gain to all of the coefficients in a manner that increases the convergence rate of the overall algorithm. These two issues give rise to the question of switching criteria within the context of the overall control law. The control law determines how to assign gain to each of the estimated coefficients. This process can be broken into separate steps for most algorithms:

1) The first step does switching in order to separate the estimated coefficients into two categories: those that are near to their true values and those that are not.

2) The second step of the overall control law determines how to assign gain once the coefficients have been separated into two categories based on the switching criterion.

In general, we want to assign the minimal possible gain to all of the coefficients that are near their true values. This law is common throughout almost all of the PtNLMS algorithms. The various algorithms addressed mainly differ in how they assign gain to the estimated coefficients that are not near their optimal values. That is, the algorithms vary in the specification of the function $F[|\hat{w}_l(k)|, k]$.

1.4. Proportionate-type NLMS adaptive filtering algorithms

In this section, mathematical representations of several PtNLMS algorithms are presented in further detail.

1.4.1. *Proportionate-type least mean square algorithm*

The first algorithm we examine is the PtLMS algorithm. Strictly speaking, the PtLMS algorithm is not a PtNLMS algorithm because the update term for the weight deviation is not normalized by the input signal power. However, the PtLMS algorithm serves as a building block toward the PtNLMS algorithms. The PtLMS adaptive filtering algorithm is presented in Table 1.2. When we set $\mathbf{G}(k) = \mathbf{I}$ for all k, where $\mathbf{I}$ is the identity matrix, then the PtLMS algorithm reduces to the widely known LMS [HAY 02] algorithm.

$\mathbf{x}(k)$	$= [x(k), x(k-1), \ldots, x(k-L+1)]^T$
$\hat{y}(k)$	$= \mathbf{x}^T(k)\hat{\mathbf{w}}(k)$
$e(k)$	$= d(k) - \hat{y}(k)$
$\hat{\mathbf{w}}(k+1)$	$= \hat{\mathbf{w}}(k) + \beta\mathbf{G}(k)\mathbf{x}(k)e(k)$

Table 1.2. *PtLMS algorithm with time-averaging step-size matrix*

1.4.2. *PNLMS algorithm*

The Proportionate NLMS algorithm was first proposed in [DUT 00]. The control law for these algorithms assigns a gain proportionate to the magnitude of the estimated coefficients,

$$F[|\hat{w}_l(k)|, k] = |\hat{w}_l(k)|, \ 1 \leq l \leq L. \qquad [1.1]$$

The motivation for this algorithm is based on knowledge that the impulse response is sparse. Therefore it is desired to adapt coefficients with large magnitudes faster than those that are at or near zero.

1.4.3. *PNLMS++ algorithm*

The PNLMS++ algorithm introduced in [GAY 98] is a combination of the PNLMS and NLMS algorithms. For instance, one implementation of the PNLMS++

algorithm is to alternate between the NLMS and PNLMS gains logic every iteration. This implementation is shown here:

$$F[|\hat{w}_l(k)|, k] = \begin{cases} |\hat{w}_l(k)|, \ 1 \leq l \leq L, & \text{if } k \text{ is odd,} \\ 1, & \text{if } k \text{ is even.} \end{cases}$$

An alternative implementation of the PNLMS++ algorithm is to alternate between the NLMS and PNLMS algorithms every Mth iteration.

1.4.4. *IPNLMS algorithm*

The improved PNLMS (IPNLMS) was introduced in [BEN 02] and has the following control law:

$$F[|\hat{w}_l(k)|, k] = (1 - \alpha_{\text{IPNLMS}})\frac{||\hat{\mathbf{w}}(k)||_1}{L} + (1 + \alpha_{\text{IPNLMS}})|\hat{w}_l(k)|, \qquad [1.2]$$

where $||\hat{\mathbf{w}}(k)||_1 = \sum_{j=1}^{L} |\hat{w}_j(k)|$ is the L_1 norm of the vector $\hat{\mathbf{w}}(k)$ and $-1 \leq \alpha_{\text{IPNLMS}} \leq 1$. The algorithm uses $\rho = 0$, that is the minimum gain logic introduced in Table 1.1, which in this case, is unnecessary. The components of the time-varying gain matrix are given by:

$$\begin{aligned} g_l(k) &= \frac{F[|\hat{w}_l(k)|, k]}{||F[|\hat{w}_l(k)|, k]||_1} \\ &= \frac{(1 - \alpha_{\text{IPNLMS}})}{2L} + (1 + \alpha_{\text{IPNLMS}})\frac{|\hat{w}_l(k)|}{2||\hat{\mathbf{w}}(k)||_1}. \end{aligned} \qquad [1.3]$$

However in practice, to avoid division by zero, especially at the beginning of adaptation when the estimated coefficients are all close to zero, a slightly modified form of the time-varying gain matrix is used:

$$g_l(k) = \frac{(1 - \alpha_{\text{IPNLMS}})}{2L} + (1 + \alpha_{\text{IPNLMS}})\frac{|\hat{w}_l(k)|}{2||\hat{\mathbf{w}}(k)||_1 + \epsilon_{\text{IPNLMS}}}, \qquad [1.4]$$

where ϵ_{IPNLMS} is a small positive number. Note for $\alpha_{\text{IPNLMS}} = -1$ this algorithm reduces to the NLMS algorithm and for $\alpha_{\text{IPNLMS}} = 1$ the IPNLMS algorithm behaves like the PNLMS algorithm.

1.4.5. *IIPNLMS algorithm*

In the following, the improved IPNLMS (IIPNLMS) algorithm was given in [CUI 04]. The components of the time-varying gain matrix for the IIPNLMS algorithm are given by:

$$
\begin{aligned}
F[|\hat{w}_l(k)|, k] &= |\hat{w}_l(k)| \\
\gamma_{\min}(k) &= \rho \max\{\delta_p, F[|\hat{w}_1(k)|, k], \ldots, F[|\hat{w}_L(k)|, k]\} \\
\gamma_l(k) &= \max\{\gamma_{\min}(k), F[|\hat{w}_l(k)|, k]\} \\
\gamma'_l(k) &= \frac{1 - \alpha_{\text{IIPNLMS } l}(k)}{2} + \frac{1 + \alpha_{\text{IIPNLMS } l}(k)}{2}\gamma_l(k) \\
g_l(k) &= \frac{\gamma'_l(k)}{\frac{1}{L}\sum_{l=1}^{L}\gamma'_l(k)}.
\end{aligned}
$$

The term $\alpha_{\text{IIPNLMS } l}(k)$ is unique to the IIPNLMS algorithm and is described as follows. First, the objective of the IIPNLMS algorithm was to derive a rule to locate the "active" portion of the echo path in order to further improve performance. In the IPNLMS, the parameter α_{IPNLMS} was fixed for the whole echo path coefficients. Second, in the IIPNLMS version, α_{IIPNLMS} is allowed to vary as:

$$
\alpha_{\text{IIPNLMS } l}(k) = \begin{cases} \alpha_{1 \text{ IIPNLMS}}, \text{ when } \gamma_l(k) > \gamma_{\text{IIPNLMS}} \max\limits_l \gamma_l(k) \\ \alpha_{2 \text{ IIPNLMS}}, \text{ when } \gamma_l(k) < \gamma_{\text{IIPNLMS}} \max\limits_l \gamma_l(k) \end{cases}
$$

where γ_{IIPNLMS} is a parameter used to control the threshold in order to locate the "active" portion.

1.4.6. *IAF-PNLMS algorithm*

The IAF-PNLMS algorithm was introduced in [DAS 10]. The IAF-PNLMS algorithm proceeds in the following manner:

$$
\begin{aligned}
F[|\hat{w}_l(k)|, k] &= |\hat{w}_l(k)| \\
\psi_l(k) &= \begin{cases} \frac{1}{2}F[|\hat{w}_l(k)|, k] + \frac{1}{2}\gamma_l(k-1), & k = mL \\ & m = 1, 2, 3, \ldots \\ \psi_l(k-1), & \text{otherwise} \end{cases} \\
\gamma_l(k) &= \max\{\psi_l(k), F[|\hat{w}_l(k)|, k]\}.
\end{aligned}
$$

Typically, $\psi_l(0)$ is initialized to some small positive constant for all of the coefficients.

In contrast to the other PNLMS-type algorithms, such as the PNLMS and IPNLMS, the IAF-PNLMS algorithm transfers part of the inactive coefficient gains via $\psi_l(k)$ to the active coefficient gains [DAS 10], and, as a consequence, has the following properties:

1) It provides better ("truly proportionate") gain distribution compared with the PNLMS and IPNLMS algorithms.

2) It slows down the convergence speed of the small coefficients.

Point (1) leads to an improvement in the convergence speed as well as in tracking ability, enabling the IAF-PNLMS algorithm to outperform both the PNLMS and IPNLMS algorithms for impulse responses with high sparseness. Moreover, the point (2) is undesirable, arising from the fact that the IAF-PNLMS algorithm transfers gains from the inactive coefficients to the active coefficients over the whole adaptation process.

1.4.7. *MPNLMS algorithm*

The control law for the MPNLMS algorithm assigns a gain proportional to the logarithm of the estimated coefficients [DEN 05, DEN 06] as follows:

$$F[|\hat{w}_l(k)|, k] = \ln(1 + \mu|\hat{w}_l(k)|),\ 1 \leq l \leq L, \qquad [1.5]$$

where $\mu = 1/\epsilon$. The parameter ϵ is used to define when a coefficient is considered to be converged. For instance, a coefficient could be considered to have converged if it is within the ϵ-vicinity of its true value.

1.4.8. *EPNLMS algorithm*

The EPNLMS algorithm uses switching [DEN 06]. The switching criterion for this algorithm is based on the magnitude of the estimated coefficients. If the coefficient magnitude is less than ϵ, the minimum possible gain is assigned. Otherwise the gain assigned to the coefficients is proportional to the natural logarithm of the magnitude of the coefficient as shown here:

$$F[|\hat{w}_l(k)|, k] = \begin{cases} 0 & \text{if } |\hat{w}_l(k)| < \epsilon \\ \ln\left(\frac{|\hat{w}_l(k)|}{\epsilon}\right) & \text{if } |\hat{w}_l(k)| \geq \epsilon. \end{cases}$$

This algorithm tries to limit the resources (update gain) applied to the coefficients that have reached the ϵ-vicinity of their assumed true values of zero (sparsity).

1.5. Summary

In this chapter, an introduction to PtNLMS algorithms was given. The chapter started by presenting applications that motivate the design and analysis of PtNLMS algorithms. Classic examples of applications for PtNLMS algorithms such as telephone echo cancellation were discussed as well as more recent applications such as VOIP and acoustic underwater communication. Then a unified framework for representing PtNLMS algorithms was presented, followed by several examples of PtNLMS algorithms. Key strengths and weaknesses of each PtNLMS algorithm were also discussed.

2

LMS Analysis Techniques

After the introduction of the LMS algorithm, several underlying theories were developed in order to predict the performance of the algorithm. In this chapter, a review of LMS analysis techniques are presented. The first LMS analysis technique reviewed in this chapter relies on the small adaptation step-size assumption. This assumption results in a recursion for the weight deviation vector that has constant coefficients. The second LMS analysis technique reviewed in this chapter assumes that the input signal is an independent Gaussian vector random process that is also independent of the measurement noise. In this case, the recursion for the weight deviation vector is an equation with random coefficients. Note that other techniques have been used to analyze the convergence of LMS algorithms such as ordinary differential equations introduced in [BEN 80]. We do not examine these other techniques.

2.1. LMS analysis based on small adaptation step-size

In this section, we review techniques that have been used to analyze LMS filters in both the steady-state and transient regimes. The LMS theory presented here assumes a small step-size β and was developed by Kushner [KUS 84] and Haykin [HAY 02].

2.1.1. *Statistical LMS theory: small step-size assumptions*

ASSUMPTION 2.1.– The input $\mathbf{x}(k)$ and weight deviation vector $\mathbf{z}(k)$ are independent.

This is a reasonable assumption when β is sufficiently small, that is when $\mathbf{z}(k)$ fluctuates much slower than $\mathbf{x}(k)$ [HAY 02, SAY 03]. In this case, the LMS estimator acts as a low-pass filter with a low cutoff frequency.

ASSUMPTION 2.2.– The measurement noise $v(k)$ is a stationary white process with zero-mean, variance σ_v^2, and it is independent of the input.

2.1.2. *LMS analysis using stochastic difference equations with constant coefficients*

In this section, we will review the transient and steady-state analysis as presented by [HAY 02]. We begin with the transient analysis of the LMS algorithm and conclude with the steady-state analysis of the LMS algorithm. The transient analysis presented here focuses on finding three quantities: the mean weight deviation (MWD) recursion, the mean square weight deviation (MSWD) recursion and the mean square error (MSE) recursion. Now we will examine each of these quantities.

2.1.2.1. *Transient analysis of the LMS algorithm: MWD recursion*

The weight deviation recursion is obtained by starting with the weight vector recursion for the LMS algorithm:

$$\hat{\mathbf{w}}(k+1) = \hat{\mathbf{w}}(k) + \beta \mathbf{x}(k)e(k). \tag{2.1}$$

Next the error term is expressed in terms of the weight deviation vector as:

$$e(k) = \mathbf{x}^T(k)[\mathbf{w} - \hat{\mathbf{w}}(k)] + v(k) = \mathbf{x}^T(k)\mathbf{z}(k) + v(k). \tag{2.2}$$

Now the weight deviation recursion can be formed by substituting equation [2.1] into the definition of the weight deviation $\mathbf{z}(k+1) = \mathbf{w} - \hat{\mathbf{w}}(k+1)$ and replacing the error term with the term given in equation [2.2] to form:

$$\mathbf{z}(k+1) = \mathbf{z}(k) - \beta \mathbf{x}(k)\mathbf{x}^T(k)\mathbf{z}(k) - \beta \mathbf{x}(k)v(k). \tag{2.3}$$

Taking the expectation of the weight deviation recursion yields:

$$\begin{aligned} E\{\mathbf{z}(k+1)\} &= E\{\mathbf{z}(k)\} - \beta E\{\mathbf{x}(k)\mathbf{x}^T(k)\mathbf{z}(k)\} - E\{\beta \mathbf{x}(k)v(k)\} \\ &= (\mathbf{I} - \beta \mathbf{R})E\{\mathbf{z}(k)\}, \end{aligned} \tag{2.4}$$

where $\mathbf{R} = E\{\mathbf{x}(k)\mathbf{x}^T(k)\}$.

The term $E\{\mathbf{x}(k)\mathbf{x}^T(k)\mathbf{z}(k)\}$ was calculated by using assumption 2.1. Since the input signal is independent of the weight deviation the following expectation can be expressed as:

$$E\{\mathbf{x}(k)\mathbf{x}^T(k)\mathbf{z}(k)\} = E[E\{\mathbf{x}(k)\mathbf{x}^T(k)\}\mathbf{z}(k)] = \mathbf{R}E\{\mathbf{z}(k)\}. \tag{2.5}$$

Similarly, by enacting assumption 2.2 the expectation $E\{\beta \mathbf{x}(k)v(k)\}$ is zero.

It turns out that the MWD at time $k+1$ can be expressed in terms of the true weight vector $\mathbf{w}$ by the equation:

$$E\{\mathbf{z}(k+1)\} = (\mathbf{I} - \beta \mathbf{R})^{k+1}E\{\mathbf{z}(0)\} = (\mathbf{I} - \beta \mathbf{R})^{k+1}\mathbf{w}. \tag{2.6}$$

The term $\mathbf{z}(0) = \mathbf{w} - \hat{\mathbf{w}}(0)$. Throughout this chapter it is assumed that the initial estimate $\hat{\mathbf{w}}(0) = \mathbf{0}$. Hence, the weight deviation at time zero reduces the true weight vector.

2.1.2.1.1. Coordinate change

To study the conditions that result in the stability of equation [2.4], it is convenient to introduce a coordinate change. Beause the covariance matrix $\mathbf{R}$ is real and symmetric, we can perform an eigendecomposition to produce the relation:

$$\mathbf{R} = \mathbf{Q}\mathbf{\Lambda}\mathbf{Q}^T, \tag{2.7}$$

where $\mathbf{\Lambda}$ is a diagonal matrix and $\mathbf{Q}$ an orthonormal matrix such that $\mathbf{Q}\mathbf{Q}^T = \mathbf{Q}^T\mathbf{Q} = \mathbf{I}$. Note that the ith diagonal entry of $\mathbf{\Lambda}$ is denoted by λ_i and represents the ith eigenvalue of the matrix $\mathbf{R}$.

Let us now introduce the transformed quantity $\dot{\mathbf{z}} = \mathbf{Q}^T\mathbf{z}$. Hence equation [2.4] can now be rewritten as:

$$E\{\dot{\mathbf{z}}(k+1)\} = (\mathbf{I} - \beta\mathbf{\Lambda})E\{\dot{\mathbf{z}}(k)\}. \tag{2.8}$$

2.1.2.1.2. MWD stability condition

Examining equation [2.8] we see that stability of $E\{\dot{\mathbf{z}}(k+1)\}$ can be guaranteed if $|1-\beta\lambda_i| < 1$ for all $i = 1, 2, \ldots, L$, that is the algorithm is guaranteed to converge. Next, let us consider $\lambda_{\max}$ be the largest eigenvalue. Then using the fact that $\beta > 0$ and $\lambda_i > 0$ for all i, the stability condition can be rewritten as:

$$0 < \beta < \frac{2}{\lambda_{\max}}. \tag{2.9}$$

This condition guarantees that the LMS filter converges in the mean [HAY 02].

2.1.2.2. *Transient analysis of the LMS algorithm: MSWD recursion*

In [HAY 02], the MSWD recursion is analyzed by first performing the coordinate change procedure discussed in section 2.1.2.1.1 on [2.3] and then replacing the resulting equation with the stochastic equation given by:

$$\dot{\mathbf{z}}(k+1) = [\mathbf{I} - \beta\mathbf{\Lambda}]\dot{\mathbf{z}}(k) - \beta\dot{\mathbf{x}}(k)v(k). \tag{2.10}$$

Kushner [KUS 84] has shown that for small step-size, the solution of the original difference equation [2.3] is close to the solution of [2.10]. We can write the vector recursion in component-wise form as:

$$\dot{z}_i(k+1) = (1-\beta\lambda_i)\dot{z}_i(k) - \beta\dot{x}_i(k)v(k). \tag{2.11}$$

This recursion can be expressed in terms of all the prior weight deviations as:

$$\dot{z}_i(k+1) = (1-\beta\lambda_i)^{k+1}\dot{w}_i - \beta\sum_{l=0}^{k}(1-\beta\lambda_i)^{k-l}\dot{x}_i(l)v(l), \quad [2.12]$$

where we used the definition $\dot{z}_i(0) = \dot{w}_i$. Next the square weight deviation can be formed by squaring the previous expression:

$$\begin{aligned}\dot{z}_i^2(k+1) &= (1-\beta\lambda_i)^{2(k+1)}\dot{w}_i^2 \\ &+\beta^2\sum_{l=0}^{k}\sum_{j=0}^{k}(1-\beta\lambda_i)^{(2k-l-j)}\dot{x}_i(l)v(l)\dot{x}_i(j)v(j) \\ &-2\beta(1-\beta\lambda_i)^{k+1}\dot{w}_i\sum_{l=0}^{k}(1-\beta\lambda_i)^{k-l}\dot{x}_i(l)v(l).\end{aligned} \quad [2.13]$$

Next the expectation of $\dot{z}_i^2(k+1)$ is formed. This process results in:

$$E\{\dot{z}_i^2(k+1)\} = (1-\beta\lambda_i)^{2(k+1)}\dot{w}_i^2 + \beta^2\sum_{l=0}^{k}(1-\beta\lambda_i)^{2(k-l)}\lambda_i\sigma_v^2, \quad [2.14]$$

where we have employed the facts that the noise is white, zero-mean and independent of the input signal, and the transformed input signal has covariance matrix $\mathbf{\Lambda}$. Using the definition of the geometric series it is possible to rewrite the term:

$$\sum_{l=0}^{k}(1-\beta\lambda_i)^{2(k-l)} = \frac{1-(1-\beta\lambda_i)^{2(k+1)}}{\beta\lambda_i(2-\lambda_i\beta)}. \quad [2.15]$$

Hence the recursion for the mean square deviation for the ith weight becomes:

$$E\{\dot{z}_i^2(k+1)\} = (1-\beta\lambda_i)^{2(k+1)}\left[\dot{w}_i^2 - \frac{\beta\sigma_v^2}{2-\lambda_i\beta}\right] + \frac{\beta\sigma_v^2}{2-\lambda_i\beta}. \quad [2.16]$$

Using the previous expression it is possible to write the MSWD recursion at time $k+1$ in terms of the impulse response, $\dot{\mathbf{w}}$, as:

$$E||\dot{\mathbf{z}}(k+1)||^2 = E||\dot{\mathbf{w}}||^2_{\mathbf{F}^{k+1}} + \sum_{l=0}^{k}\beta^2\sigma_v^2\mathrm{Tr}(\mathbf{F}^l\mathbf{\Lambda}), \quad [2.17]$$

where $\mathbf{F} = (\mathbf{I} - \beta\mathbf{\Lambda})^2$. The condition for convergence in this case is given by $\beta < 2/\lambda_{\max}$.

2.1.2.3. *Transient analysis of the LMS algorithm: relationship of MSWD to MSE*

The MSE at time k is given by the equation:

$$\begin{aligned} J(k) &= E\{e^2(k)\} \\ &= E\{[\mathbf{x}^T(k)\mathbf{z}(k) + v(k)]^2\} \\ &= E\{\mathbf{z}^T(k)\mathbf{x}(k)\mathbf{x}^T(k)\mathbf{z}(k) + 2\mathbf{x}^T(k)\mathbf{z}(k)v(k) + v^2(k)\}. \end{aligned} \quad [2.18]$$

The first term in this expression can be replaced by $E\{\mathbf{z}^T(k)\mathbf{R}\mathbf{z}(k)\}$ by applying assumption 2.1. Applying assumption 2.2 results in the second term becoming zero and the last term being equal to σ_v^2. Hence the MSE can be expressed as:

$$E\{e^2(k)\} \approx \sigma_v^2 + E\{\mathbf{z}^T(k)\mathbf{R}\mathbf{z}(k)\}. \quad [2.19]$$

Substituting $\dot{\mathbf{z}} = \mathbf{Q}^T\mathbf{z}$ into this expression yields:

$$E\{e^2(k)\} \approx \sigma_v^2 + E\{\dot{\mathbf{z}}^T(k)\mathbf{\Lambda}\dot{\mathbf{z}}(k)\} = \sigma_v^2 + \sum_{j=1}^{L} \lambda_i E\{\dot{z}_i^2(k)\}. \quad [2.20]$$

Hence using [2.20] and [2.16] we can calculate the MSE at all times.

2.1.2.4. *Steady-state analysis of the LMS algorithm*

By taking the limits as k approaches infinity of [2.6], [2.16] and [2.20] and assuming the stability condition given in [2.9] holds, then it is straightforward to calculate the MWD, MSWD and MSE in steady-state.

First, the MWD in steady-state is zero. This implies that the estimated impulse response approaches the true impulse response in the mean. Next the ith component of MSWD becomes:

$$E\{\dot{z}_i^2(\infty)\} = \frac{\beta\sigma_v^2}{2 - \beta\lambda_i} \quad [2.21]$$

in steady-state. And finally the MSE in steady-state is given by:

$$J(\infty) = \sigma_v^2 + \beta\sigma_v^2 \sum_{j=1}^{L} \frac{\lambda_j}{2 - \beta\lambda_j}. \quad [2.22]$$

Hence, the MSE for the LMS algorithm decays to the value given by equation [2.22].

Finally, we introduce misadjustment, which is a quantity used to measure the ratio of the steady-state value of the excess MSE to the minimum MSE. The excess MSE is the difference between the MSE at time k and the minimum MSE. The minimum MSE is the variance of the noise, σ_v^2. For the LMS algorithm the misadjustment is given by:

$$\mathcal{M} = \frac{J(\infty) - \sigma_v^2}{\sigma_v^2} = \beta \sum_{j=1}^{L} \frac{\lambda_j}{2 - \beta\lambda_j}. \qquad [2.23]$$

Note that it is possible to reduce the steady-state quantities to simpler forms by making more assumptions. For instance, we could assume that the input signal was independently and identically distributed (i.i.d.), which would reduce steady-state MSE to:

$$J(\infty) = \sigma_v^2 + \beta\sigma_v^2 L \frac{\lambda}{2 - \beta\lambda},$$

where $\lambda_i = \lambda$ for all i.

2.2. LMS analysis based on independent input signal assumptions

In the previous section, the LMS theory assuming a small step-size was examined. The strengths of this theory include the fact that there is no assumption made about the input signal and, therefore, the theory should be robust under a wide variety of input signals. A weakness of this theory is that the small step-size assumption implies the theory will not work for large values of the step-size parameter. In this section, the small step-size assumption is removed. Instead the input signal is assumed to be an independent Gaussian random vector process. We begin by presenting the assumptions that will be applied in this section.

2.2.1. *Statistical LMS theory: independent input signal assumptions*

ASSUMPTION 2.3.– The input signal, $\mathbf{x}(k)$, is an independent, identically distributed, Gaussian vector process with zero-mean and covariance $\mathbf{R} = E\{\mathbf{x}(k)\mathbf{x}(k)^T\}$.

This assumption allows the calculation of fourth-order terms of the input signal.

In addition, assumption 2.2 specifies the properties of the measurement noise, $v(k)$.

2.2.2. *LMS analysis using stochastic difference equations with stochastic coefficients*

Replacing the weight deviation recursion [2.3] with the stochastic equation given by [2.10] simplifies analysis. However, this substitution results in erroneous results when compared with simulations due to the fact that fourth-order terms of the input signal present when squaring [2.3] are disregarded in the treatment of the approximate system. A more thorough treatment was presented by [SAY 03]. We will present the findings here. We begin by noting that the treatment of the MWD is the same in both sets of work, therefore we will not discuss the MWD in this section.

2.2.2.1. *Transient analysis of the LMS algorithm: MSWD recursion revisited*

In this section, we seek the MSWD recursion. However, in order to find the MSWD it will prove helpful to first find a more general recursion for $E||\mathbf{z}(k+1)||^2_{\mathbf{\Sigma}}$, where $\mathbf{\Sigma}$ is an arbitrary positive definite diagonal matrix. We will refer to this recursion as the weighted variance recursion.

We begin by writing the weighted variance at time $k+1$ in terms of the weighted variance at time k. Substituting equation [2.3] into $||\mathbf{z}(k+1)||^2_{\mathbf{\Sigma}}$ yields:

$$\begin{aligned}
||\mathbf{z}(k+1)||^2_{\mathbf{\Sigma}} = {} & ||\mathbf{z}(k)||^2_{\mathbf{\Sigma}} - \beta||\mathbf{z}(k)||^2_{\mathbf{x}(k)\mathbf{x}^T(k)\mathbf{\Sigma}} - \beta||\mathbf{z}(k)||^2_{\mathbf{\Sigma}\mathbf{x}(k)\mathbf{x}^T(k)} \\
& +\beta^2||\mathbf{z}(k)||^2_{\mathbf{x}(k)\mathbf{x}^T(k)\mathbf{\Sigma}\mathbf{x}(k)\mathbf{x}^T(k)} \\
& +\beta^2\mathbf{z}^T(k)\mathbf{x}(k)v(k)||\mathbf{x}(k)||^2_{\mathbf{\Sigma}} + \beta^2||\mathbf{x}(k)||^2_{\mathbf{\Sigma}}\mathbf{x}^T(k)\mathbf{z}(k)v(k) \\
& +\beta^2 v^2(k)||\mathbf{x}(k)||^2_{\mathbf{\Sigma}} \\
& -\beta v(k)\mathbf{z}^T(k)\mathbf{\Sigma}\mathbf{x}(k) - \beta v(k)\mathbf{x}^T(k)\mathbf{\Sigma}\mathbf{z}(k).
\end{aligned} \quad [2.24]$$

The next step is to consider the expectation of both sides of equation [2.24]. The cross terms involving $v(k)$ vanish due to assumption 2.2, that is the noise terms are zero-mean and independent of the input signal. Hence, we can write:

$$\begin{aligned}
E\left\{||\mathbf{z}(k+1)||^2_{\mathbf{\Sigma}}\right\} = {} & E\left\{||\mathbf{z}(k)||^2_{\mathbf{\Sigma}}\right\} - \beta E\left\{||\mathbf{z}(k)||^2_{\mathbf{x}(k)\mathbf{x}^T(k)\mathbf{\Sigma}}\right\} \\
& - \beta E\left\{||\mathbf{z}(k)||^2_{\mathbf{\Sigma}\mathbf{x}(k)\mathbf{x}^T(k)}\right\} \\
& + \beta^2 E\left\{||\mathbf{z}(k)||^2_{\mathbf{x}(k)\mathbf{x}^T(k)\mathbf{\Sigma}\mathbf{x}(k)\mathbf{x}^T(k)}\right\} \\
& + \beta^2 E\left\{v^2(k)||\mathbf{x}(k)||^2_{\mathbf{\Sigma}}\right\}.
\end{aligned} \quad [2.25]$$

This equality can be written more compactly by introducing the quantity:

$$\mathbf{\Sigma}' = \mathbf{\Sigma} - \beta\mathbf{x}(k)\mathbf{x}^T(k)\mathbf{\Sigma} - \beta\mathbf{\Sigma}\mathbf{x}(k)\mathbf{x}^T(k) + \beta^2\mathbf{x}(k)\mathbf{x}^T(k)\mathbf{\Sigma}\mathbf{x}(k)\mathbf{x}^T(k). \quad [2.26]$$

Then, we can write:

$$E\left\{||\mathbf{z}(k+1)||^2_{\mathbf{\Sigma}}\right\} = E\left\{||\mathbf{z}(k)||^2_{\mathbf{\Sigma}'}\right\} + \beta^2\sigma_v^2 E\left\{||\mathbf{x}(k)||^2_{\mathbf{\Sigma}}\right\}, \quad [2.27]$$

where in the second term we applied the independence of the noise and the input.

2.2.2.1.1. Independence assumption

At this point, we apply assumption 2.1 that states that the input signal and weight deviations can be considered independent. This allows us to write:

$$E\left\{||\mathbf{z}(k)||^2_{\mathbf{\Sigma}'}\right\} = E\left\{||\mathbf{z}(k)||^2_{E\{\mathbf{\Sigma}'\}}\right\}, \quad [2.28]$$

where

$$E\left\{\mathbf{\Sigma}'\right\} = \mathbf{\Sigma} - \beta E\left\{\mathbf{x}(k)\mathbf{x}^T(k)\right\}\mathbf{\Sigma} - \beta\mathbf{\Sigma}E\left\{\mathbf{x}(k)\mathbf{x}^T(k)\right\} + \beta^2 E\left\{\mathbf{x}(k)\mathbf{x}^T(k)\mathbf{\Sigma}\mathbf{x}(k)\mathbf{x}^T(k)\right\}. \quad [2.29]$$

2.2.2.1.2. Coordinate change

The evaluation of the moments in [2.29] can be simplified with a change of coordinates. We apply the similar coordinate transformations to the transformations used in the section 2.1.2.1.1, namely $\dot{\mathbf{z}}(k) = \mathbf{Q}^T\mathbf{z}(k)$, $\dot{\mathbf{x}}(k) = \mathbf{Q}^T\mathbf{x}(k)$ and $\dot{\mathbf{\Sigma}} = \mathbf{Q}^T\mathbf{\Sigma}\mathbf{Q}$.

After making these changes of variable, the variance relation [2.27] maintains the same form. For instance, it is easy to show that:

$$||\dot{\mathbf{z}}(k)||^2 = \dot{\mathbf{z}}^T(k)\dot{\mathbf{z}}(k) = \mathbf{z}^T(k)\mathbf{Q}\mathbf{Q}^T\mathbf{z}(k) = ||\mathbf{z}(k)||^2.$$

Therefore the variance relation becomes:

$$E\left\{||\dot{\mathbf{z}}(k+1)||^2_{\dot{\mathbf{\Sigma}}}\right\} = E\left\{||\dot{\mathbf{z}}(k)||^2_{E\{\dot{\mathbf{\Sigma}}'\}}\right\} + \beta^2\sigma_v^2 E\left\{||\dot{\mathbf{x}}(k)||^2_{\dot{\mathbf{\Sigma}}}\right\}, \quad [2.30]$$

where

$$E\left\{\dot{\mathbf{\Sigma}}'\right\} = \dot{\mathbf{\Sigma}} - \beta E\left\{\dot{\mathbf{x}}(k)\dot{\mathbf{x}}^T(k)\right\}\dot{\mathbf{\Sigma}} - \beta\dot{\mathbf{\Sigma}}E\left\{\dot{\mathbf{x}}(k)\dot{\mathbf{x}}^T(k)\right\} + \beta^2 E\left\{\dot{\mathbf{x}}(k)\dot{\mathbf{x}}^T(k)\dot{\mathbf{\Sigma}}\dot{\mathbf{x}}(k)\dot{\mathbf{x}}^T(k)\right\}. \quad [2.31]$$

With this transformation in place we will now calculate the expectation:

$$E\left\{\dot{\mathbf{x}}(k)\dot{\mathbf{x}}(k)^T\dot{\mathbf{\Sigma}}\dot{\mathbf{x}}(k)\dot{\mathbf{x}}(k)^T\right\}.$$

Since $\dot{\mathbf{x}}$ is a real-valued Gaussian random vector with zero-mean and diagonal covariance $\mathbf{\Lambda}$, the fourth moment is well known [HAY 02] and is given by:

$$E\left\{\dot{\mathbf{x}}(k)\dot{\mathbf{x}}(k)^T\dot{\mathbf{\Sigma}}\dot{\mathbf{x}}(k)\dot{\mathbf{x}}(k)^T\right\} = \mathbf{\Lambda}\mathrm{Tr}(\dot{\mathbf{\Sigma}}\mathbf{\Lambda}) + 2\mathbf{\Lambda}\dot{\mathbf{\Sigma}}\mathbf{\Lambda}.$$

Hence, [2.31] simplifies to:

$$E\left\{\dot{\mathbf{\Sigma}}'\right\} = \dot{\mathbf{\Sigma}} - \beta\dot{\mathbf{\Sigma}}\mathbf{\Lambda} - \beta\mathbf{\Lambda}\dot{\mathbf{\Sigma}} + \beta^2\left[\mathbf{\Lambda}\mathrm{Tr}(\dot{\mathbf{\Sigma}}\mathbf{\Lambda}) + 2\mathbf{\Lambda}\dot{\mathbf{\Sigma}}\mathbf{\Lambda}\right]. \qquad [2.32]$$

2.2.2.1.3. Linear vector relation

Using the fact that $\mathbf{\Lambda}$ and $\dot{\mathbf{\Sigma}}$ are diagonal matrices, it is possible to write [2.30] in a more compact form. Note that since $\mathbf{\Lambda}$ and $\dot{\mathbf{\Sigma}}$ are diagonal this implies that $E\left\{\dot{\mathbf{\Sigma}}'\right\}$ is diagonal too. First, define $\boldsymbol{\lambda} = \mathbf{diag}(\mathbf{\Lambda})$ and $\dot{\boldsymbol{\sigma}} = \mathbf{diag}(\dot{\mathbf{\Sigma}})$. Using these definitions it is possible to write [2.32] as a vector recursion:

$$E\left\{\dot{\boldsymbol{\sigma}}'\right\} = (\mathbf{I} - 2\beta\mathbf{\Lambda} + 2\beta^2\mathbf{\Lambda}^2)\dot{\boldsymbol{\sigma}} + \beta^2\boldsymbol{\lambda}\boldsymbol{\lambda}^T\dot{\boldsymbol{\sigma}},$$

which can be written as:

$$E\left\{\dot{\boldsymbol{\sigma}}'\right\} = \mathbf{F}\dot{\boldsymbol{\sigma}},$$

where

$$\mathbf{F} = \mathbf{I} - 2\beta\mathbf{\Lambda} + 2\beta^2\mathbf{\Lambda}^2 + \beta^2\boldsymbol{\lambda}\boldsymbol{\lambda}^T.$$

Now we can rewrite [2.30] as:

$$E\left\{||\dot{\mathbf{z}}(k+1)||^2_{\mathbf{Diag}(\dot{\boldsymbol{\sigma}})}\right\} = E\left\{||\dot{\mathbf{z}}(k)||^2_{\mathbf{Diag}(\mathbf{F}\dot{\boldsymbol{\sigma}})}\right\} + \beta^2\sigma_v^2\lambda^T\dot{\boldsymbol{\sigma}}. \qquad [2.33]$$

By choosing $\dot{\boldsymbol{\sigma}} = \mathbf{1}$, where $\mathbf{1} = [1, 1, \ldots, 1]^T$, the MSWD at time $k+1$ can be expressed in terms of the impulse response as:

$$E\left\{||\dot{\mathbf{z}}(k+1)||^2\right\} = E\left\{||\dot{\mathbf{w}}||^2_{\mathbf{Diag}(\mathbf{F}^{k+1}\mathbf{1})}\right\} + \beta^2\sigma_v^2\sum_{l=0}^{k}\lambda^T\mathbf{F}^l\mathbf{1}. \qquad [2.34]$$

This expression also allows us to calculate the MSE at any time using [2.20].

2.2.2.1.4. MSWD stability condition

To ensure mean square stability we require that $\mathbf{F}$ is a stable matrix. It has been shown in [SAY 03] and [HAY 91] that this condition can be satisfied if:

$$\frac{1}{2}\sum_{i=1}^{L}\frac{\beta\lambda_i}{1-\beta\lambda_i} < 1. \quad [2.35]$$

A separate proof of this same claim is given next.

The difference equation describing the evolution of the MSWD error is:

$$\begin{bmatrix} E\left\{(z_1^+)^2\right\} \\ \vdots \\ E\left\{(z_L^+)^2\right\} \end{bmatrix} = \mathbf{F}^T \begin{bmatrix} E\left\{z_1^2\right\} \\ \vdots \\ E\left\{z_L^2\right\} \end{bmatrix} + \beta^2\sigma_v^2\boldsymbol{\lambda}, \quad [2.36]$$

where

$$\mathbf{F} = \mathbf{F}^T = \mathbf{I} - 2\beta\mathbf{\Lambda} + 2\beta^2\mathbf{\Lambda}^2 + \beta^2\boldsymbol{\lambda}\boldsymbol{\lambda}^T.$$

The stability of the MSWD error is guaranteed if and only if all eigenvalues of $\mathbf{F}$, $\vartheta(\mathbf{F})$, satisfy:

$$-1 < \vartheta(\mathbf{F}) < 1.$$

Since

$$\mathbf{F} = (\mathbf{I} - \beta\mathbf{\Lambda})^2 + \beta^2\mathbf{\Lambda}^2 + \beta^2\boldsymbol{\lambda}\boldsymbol{\lambda}^T$$

is non-negative definite, $\vartheta(\mathbf{F}) > -1$ is satisfied.

Note that if $\mathbf{v}$ and α are an eigenvector and eigenvalue of $\mathbf{F}$, then $\mathbf{v}$ and $\alpha - 1$ are an eigenvector and eigenvalue of $\mathbf{F} - \mathbf{I}$:

$$\mathbf{F}\mathbf{v} = \alpha\mathbf{F} \implies (\mathbf{F} - \mathbf{I})\mathbf{v} = \mathbf{F}\mathbf{v} - \mathbf{v} = \alpha\mathbf{v} - \mathbf{v} = (\alpha - 1)\mathbf{v}.$$

Therefore, to show $\vartheta(\mathbf{F}) < 1$ we can equivalently show $\vartheta(\mathbf{F} - \mathbf{I}) < 0$. Next, we define:

$$\begin{aligned}
\mathbf{G} &\equiv \mathbf{F} - \mathbf{I} = -2\beta\mathbf{\Lambda} + 2\beta^2\mathbf{\Lambda}^2 + \beta^2\boldsymbol{\lambda}\boldsymbol{\lambda}^T \\
&= -2\beta\mathbf{\Lambda}(\mathbf{I} - \beta\mathbf{\Lambda}) + \beta^2\boldsymbol{\lambda}\boldsymbol{\lambda}^T \\
&= \mathbf{\Lambda}^{\frac{1}{2}}(\mathbf{I} - \beta\mathbf{\Lambda})^{\frac{1}{2}} \\
&\times \left[-2\beta\mathbf{I} + \beta^2(\mathbf{I} - \beta\mathbf{\Lambda})^{-\frac{1}{2}}\mathbf{\Lambda}^{-\frac{1}{2}}\boldsymbol{\lambda}\boldsymbol{\lambda}^T\mathbf{\Lambda}^{-\frac{1}{2}}(\mathbf{I} - \beta\mathbf{\Lambda})^{-\frac{1}{2}}\right](\mathbf{I} - \beta\mathbf{\Lambda})^{\frac{1}{2}}\mathbf{\Lambda}^{\frac{1}{2}} \\
&= \mathbf{\Lambda}^{\frac{1}{2}}(\mathbf{I} - \beta\mathbf{\Lambda})^{\frac{1}{2}}\mathbf{H}(\mathbf{I} - \beta\mathbf{\Lambda})^{\frac{1}{2}}\mathbf{\Lambda}^{\frac{1}{2}},
\end{aligned}$$

where

$$\mathbf{H} \equiv \left[-2\beta\mathbf{I} + \beta^2(\mathbf{I}-\beta\mathbf{\Lambda})^{-\frac{1}{2}}\mathbf{\Lambda}^{-\frac{1}{2}}\boldsymbol{\lambda}\boldsymbol{\lambda}^T\mathbf{\Lambda}^{-\frac{1}{2}}(\mathbf{I}-\beta\mathbf{\Lambda})^{-\frac{1}{2}}\right]. \quad [2.37]$$

The matrices $\mathbf{G}$ and $\mathbf{H}$ are congruent matrices (i.e. for some arbitrary matrix $\mathbf{A}$, $\mathbf{G} = \mathbf{AHA}^T$). Sylvester's law of inertia states that two congruent symmetric matrices with real entries have the same numbers of positive, negative and zero eigenvalues [SYL 52]. Hence to show that all eigenvalues of $\mathbf{G}$ are negative implies that all eigenvalues of $\mathbf{H}$ are negative and vice-versa. By inspection one eigenvector of $\mathbf{H}$ is $(\mathbf{I}-\beta\mathbf{\Lambda})^{-1/2}\mathbf{\Lambda}^{-1/2}\boldsymbol{\lambda}$, which yields:

$$\left[-2\beta\mathbf{I} + \beta^2(\mathbf{I}-\beta\mathbf{\Lambda})^{-\frac{1}{2}}\mathbf{\Lambda}^{-\frac{1}{2}}\boldsymbol{\lambda}\boldsymbol{\lambda}^T(\mathbf{I}-\beta\mathbf{\Lambda})^{-\frac{1}{2}}\mathbf{\Lambda}^{-\frac{1}{2}}\right](\mathbf{I}-\beta\mathbf{\Lambda})^{-\frac{1}{2}}\mathbf{\Lambda}^{-\frac{1}{2}}\boldsymbol{\lambda}$$
$$= \left[-2\beta + \beta^2\boldsymbol{\lambda}^T(\mathbf{I}-\beta\mathbf{\Lambda})^{-1}\mathbf{\Lambda}^{-1}\boldsymbol{\lambda}\right](\mathbf{I}-\beta\mathbf{\Lambda})^{-\frac{1}{2}}\mathbf{\Lambda}^{-\frac{1}{2}}\boldsymbol{\lambda}. \quad [2.38]$$

Therefore, the eigenvector:

$$(\mathbf{I}-\beta\mathbf{\Lambda})^{-\frac{1}{2}}\mathbf{\Lambda}^{-\frac{1}{2}}\boldsymbol{\lambda}$$

has the eigenvalue:

$$-2\beta + \beta^2\boldsymbol{\lambda}^T(\mathbf{I}-\beta\mathbf{\Lambda})^{-1}\mathbf{\Lambda}^{-1}\boldsymbol{\lambda}.$$

The other $L-1$ eigenvectors are perpendicular to the eigenvector:

$$(\mathbf{I}-\beta\mathbf{\Lambda})^{-\frac{1}{2}}\mathbf{\Lambda}^{-\frac{1}{2}}\boldsymbol{\lambda}.$$

Let us denote these $L-1$ eigenvectors as:

$$\left[(\mathbf{I}-\beta\mathbf{\Lambda})^{-\frac{1}{2}}\mathbf{\Lambda}^{-\frac{1}{2}}\boldsymbol{\lambda}\right]^{\perp}.$$

Multiplying $\mathbf{H}$ with these eigenvectors yields:

$$\left[-2\beta\mathbf{I} + \beta^2(\mathbf{I}-\beta\mathbf{\Lambda})^{-\frac{1}{2}}\mathbf{\Lambda}^{-\frac{1}{2}}\boldsymbol{\lambda}\boldsymbol{\lambda}^T(\mathbf{I}-\beta\mathbf{\Lambda})^{-\frac{1}{2}}\mathbf{\Lambda}^{-\frac{1}{2}}\right]\left[(\mathbf{I}-\beta\mathbf{\Lambda})^{-\frac{1}{2}}\mathbf{\Lambda}^{-\frac{1}{2}}\boldsymbol{\lambda}\right]^{\perp}$$
$$= -2\beta\left[(\mathbf{I}-\beta\mathbf{\Lambda})^{-\frac{1}{2}}\mathbf{\Lambda}^{-\frac{1}{2}}\boldsymbol{\lambda}\right]^{\perp}. \quad [2.39]$$

On the basis of this result, the other $L-1$ eigenvalues have value -2β that is always negative.

To guarantee that all eigenvalues are negative we need only to require that:

$$\begin{aligned} 0 &> -2\beta + \beta^2 \boldsymbol{\lambda}^T (\mathbf{I} - \beta\boldsymbol{\Lambda})^{-1} \boldsymbol{\Lambda}^{-1} \boldsymbol{\lambda} \\ \implies & \beta^2 \sum_{i=1}^{L} \frac{\lambda_i}{(1 - \beta\lambda_i)} < 2\beta \\ \implies & \frac{1}{2} \sum_{i=1}^{L} \frac{\beta\lambda_i}{(1 - \beta\lambda_i)} < 1. \end{aligned}$$

This is the result given in equation [2.35].

It turns out that this condition also ensures convergence in the mean, that is $E\{\dot{\mathbf{z}}(\infty)\} = \mathbf{0}$. In the case when the input is also i.i.d., that is $\lambda_i = \lambda \; \forall \; i$, then the stability condition can be reduced to:

$$\beta < \frac{1}{\lambda(\frac{L}{2} + 1)}. \qquad [2.40]$$

2.2.2.2. *LMS steady-state revisited*

Using the MSWD recursion given by [2.34] in the limit as k approaches infinity results in the relation:

$$E\left\{||\dot{\mathbf{z}}(\infty)||^2\right\} = \beta^2\sigma_v^2 \lambda^T (\mathbf{I} - \mathbf{F})^{-1} \mathbf{1} = \frac{\beta\sigma_v^2 \sum_{j=1}^{L} \frac{1}{1-\beta\lambda_j}}{2 - \beta \sum_{j=1}^{L} \frac{\lambda_j}{1-\beta\lambda_j}}. \qquad [2.41]$$

This implies the MSE in steady-state is given by:

$$J(\infty) = \sigma_v^2 + \frac{\beta\sigma_v^2 \sum_{j=1}^{L} \frac{\lambda_j}{1-\beta\lambda_j}}{2 - \beta \sum_{j=1}^{L} \frac{\lambda_j}{1-\beta\lambda_j}} \qquad [2.42]$$

and the misadjustment is:

$$\mathcal{M} = \frac{\beta \sum_{j=1}^{L} \frac{\lambda_j}{1-\beta\lambda_j}}{2 - \beta \sum_{j=1}^{L} \frac{\lambda_j}{1-\beta\lambda_j}}. \qquad [2.43]$$

2.3. Performance of statistical LMS theory

We now examine the performance of the statistical LMS theory developed in [HAY 02] and [SAY 03]. In Figures 2.1 and 2.2, the convergence curve of the LMS algorithm obtained by Monte Carlo simulation is compared to the convergence curve derived from the statistical LMS theory presented in [HAY 02] and [SAY 03]. In

Figure 2.1, $\beta = 0.0005$, while in Figure 2.2 $\beta = 0.0001$. In both cases, the input signal is white and has power $\sigma_x^2 = 1$, the noise has power $\sigma_v^2 = 10^{-4}$ and the sparse impulse response depicted in Figure 1.2b was employed. A total of 10 Monte Carlo trials were averaged together to produce the simulation curve. For large values of β the independent input theory agrees more with the simulation than the small step-size theory. For smaller values of β both theories agree well with the simulation.

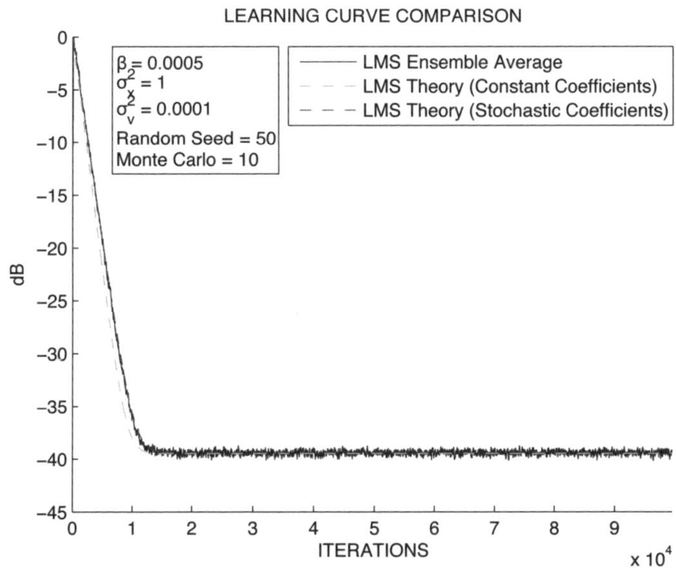

Figure 2.1. *Convergence analysis of LMS algorithm ($\beta = 0.0005$)*

In Figure 2.3, the steady-state MSE using the small step-size theory and the independent input theory are compared to the simulated steady-state MSE as a function of β. The vertical line represents the cutoff value of β given in [2.40], which the LMS algorithm will still converge. For small values of β the steady-state value generated by both the small step-size theory and the independent input theory match the simulated steady-state MSE. As β increases, independent input theory matches the simulation much better than the small step-size theory. Finally, the LMS algorithm remains stable for values of β less than the theorized stability limit.

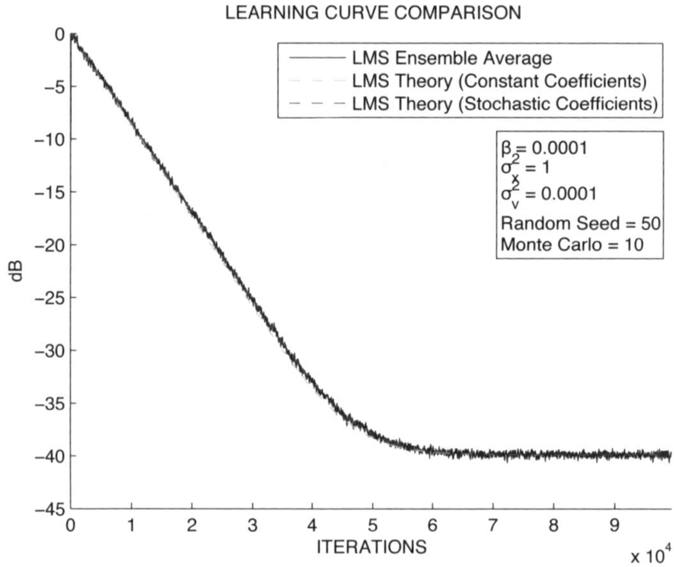

Figure 2.2. *Convergence analysis of LMS algorithm ($\beta = 0.0001$)*

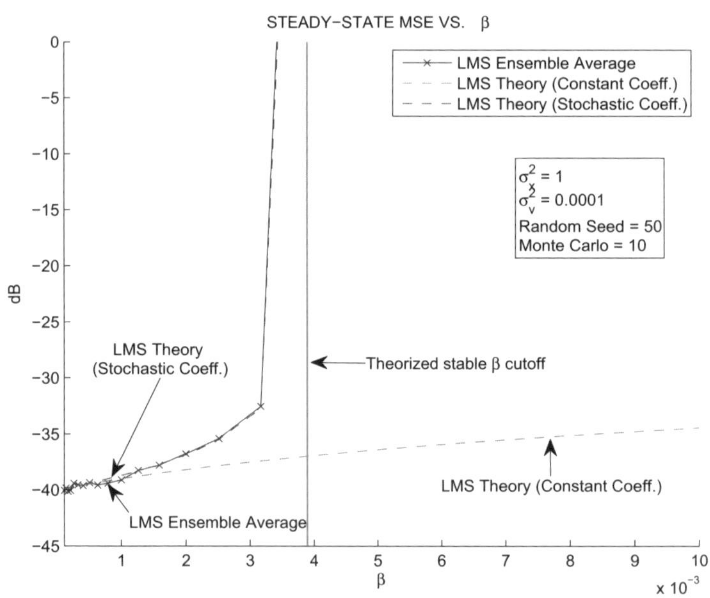

Figure 2.3. *Steady-state MSE vs. β*

2.4. Summary

This chapter presented a review of LMS analysis techniques used to predict and measure the performance of the LMS algorithm. Two analysis techniques were employed to analyze the LMS algorithm. The first LMS analysis technique reviewed in this chapter relied on the small adaptation step-size assumption. This assumption results in a recursion for the weight deviation vector, which has constant coefficients. The second LMS analysis technique reviewed in this chapter assumed that the input signal is an independent Gaussian vector random process that is also independent of the measurement noise. In this case, the recursion for the weight deviation vector is an equation with random coefficients.

In addition, the analysis performed under both sets of assumptions examined the LMS algorithms' performance in the transient and steady-state regimes of convergence. The transient regime analysis developed expressions for the MWD, MSWD and MSE. The steady-state analysis of the LMS examined the MSE and misalignment. Finally, simulations were used to compare the performance of the LMS algorithm to the theory developed in the chapter.

3

PtNLMS Analysis Techniques

In this chapter, we analyze the transient and steady-state properties of two PtNLMS algorithms for the white input. One initial goal of our research was to analyze the PNLMS algorithm in both the steady-state and transient regimes. Currently, an analytical model to describe the transient and steady-state properties of the PNLMS algorithm does not exist [SON 06]. In the process of analyzing the PNLMS algorithm, we also examined a simplified version of the algorithm named the simplified PNLMS. The simplified algorithm served the purposes of testing the validity of certain assumptions employed and easing the analysis.

In addition, in this chapter, we will present analysis with a diverse number of assumptions being applied. Removing assumptions renders the analysis mathematically more difficult in exchange for obtaining more accurate modeling. We will point out the implications of assumptions as we proceed.

This chapter is organized as follows. First, a general approach will be described and then the simplified PNLMS algorithm will be analyzed, followed by the analysis of the PNLMS algorithm. As we proceed, some results in each section can be applied to later algorithms. These results will be pointed out as needed.

3.1. Transient analysis of PtNLMS algorithm for white input

In this section, the theory for analyzing the transient regime of the PtNLMS is presented. This analysis involves generating deterministic recursions for the MWD, MSWD, and MSE as a function time, so that these quantities can be evaluated at any given time.

3.1.1. *Link between MSWD and MSE*

In addition to assumptions 2.1 and 2.2, we introduce the following assumption:

ASSUMPTION 3.1.– The input signal $x(k)$ is a stationary white Gaussian random process with zero-mean and variance σ_x^2.

This implies that the covariance matrix, $\mathbf{R}$, is a diagonal matrix with $[\mathbf{R}]_{ii} = \sigma_x^2$ for all i. The more general case of a colored input signal can be transformed into a system with a diagonal covariance matrix through a coordinate change as shown in sections 2.1.2.1.1 and 2.2.2.1.2, and the results presented here can be extended to this system. However, it should be noted that the input signal to the transformed system is not necessarily i.i.d. and care should be taken when applying the presented results.

In the case of zero-mean white stationary input, [2.19] can be written as:

$$J(k) \approx \sigma_v^2 + \sigma_x^2 \sum_{i=1}^{L} E\left\{z_i^2(k)\right\}. \quad [3.1]$$

Hence, in order to calculate the MSE, we need to find the expected value of the square WDs $z_i^2(k)$.

3.1.2. *Recursive calculation of the MWD and MSWD for PtNLMS algorithms*

At this stage, we calculate the recursive forms of the MWD and the MSWD for an arbitrary PtNLMS algorithm. We can represent the WD at time $k+1$ in terms of the prior WD at time k using the recursion for the estimated optimal coefficient vector. We assume that the input vector, $\mathbf{x}(k)$, contains input values in the delay line, that is $x_i(k) = x(k-i+1)$, for $i = 1, 2, \ldots, L$.

Using the time-index dropping notation, the WD recursion for any PtNLMS algorithm in component-wise form is given by:

$$z_i^+ = z_i - \frac{\beta g_i x_i \sum_{j=1}^{L} x_j z_j}{\sum_{j=1}^{L} x_j^2 g_j + \delta} - \frac{\beta g_i x_i v}{\sum_{j=1}^{L} x_j^2 g_j + \delta}. \quad [3.2]$$

The component-wise form of the square of the WD is given by:

$$\begin{aligned}(z_i^+)^2 = z_i^2 &- \frac{2\beta g_i x_i \sum_{j=1}^{L} x_j z_j z_i}{\sum_{j=1}^{L} x_j^2 g_j + \delta} - \frac{2\beta g_i x_i v z_i}{\sum_{j=1}^{L} x_j^2 g_j + \delta} \\ &+ \frac{\beta^2 g_i^2 x_i^2 \sum_{j=1}^{L} \sum_{m=1}^{L} x_j x_m z_j z_m}{(\sum_{j=1}^{L} x_j^2 g_j + \delta)^2} + \frac{\beta^2 g_i^2 x_i^2 v^2}{(\sum_{j=1}^{L} x_j^2 g_j + \delta)^2} \\ &+ \frac{2\beta^2 g_i^2 x_i^2 \sum_{j=1}^{L} x_j z_j v}{(\sum_{j=1}^{L} x_j^2 g_j + \delta)^2}.\end{aligned} \quad [3.3]$$

At this point, equations [3.2] and [3.3] are general to all PtNLMS algorithms.

3.1.2.1. *MWD calculation*

The MWD can be found recursively from the prior time step by:

$$\begin{aligned} E\left\{z_i^+\right\} &= E\left\{z_i\right\} - \beta E\left\{g_i \sum_{j=1}^{L}\left(E\left\{\frac{x_i x_j}{\sum_{j=1}^{L} g_j x_j^2 + \delta}\middle|\mathbf{z}\right\} z_j\right)\right\} \\ &= E\left\{z_i\right\} - E\left\{\beta_i^{(0)} g_i z_i\right\}, \end{aligned} \qquad [3.4]$$

where

$$\beta_i^{(0)} = E\left\{\beta \frac{x_i^2}{\sum_{j=1}^{L} g_j x_j^2 + \delta}\middle|\mathbf{z}\right\}$$

and it can be calculated approximately as:

$$\beta_i^{(0)} \approx \frac{\beta}{g_i}\left[1 - b\sqrt{\frac{\pi}{2\sigma_x^2}} e^{\frac{b^2}{2\sigma_x^2}} \operatorname{erfc}\left(\frac{b}{\sqrt{2\sigma_x^2}}\right)\right], \qquad [3.5]$$

where $b^2 = \sigma_x^2(L - g_i)/g_i$ as shown in section A1.1. Note that the conditional expectation in [3.4] is zero when $i \neq j$, that is

$$E\left\{\frac{x_i x_j}{\sum_{j=1}^{L} g_j x_j^2 + \delta}\middle|\mathbf{z}\right\} = 0, \quad \forall\, i \neq j,$$

since the probability of

$$\frac{|x_i x_j|}{\sum_{j=1}^{L} g_j x_j^2 + \delta}$$

and the probability of

$$\frac{-|x_i x_j|}{\sum_{j=1}^{L} g_j x_j^2 + \delta}$$

are same. We can calculate the term $E\left\{g_i z_i \beta_i^{(0)}\right\}$ explicitly by making the assumption that the variances of z_i are small, such that when we calculate the term $\beta_i^{(0)}$, we can replace z_i with their means and have

$$\beta_i^{(0)} \approx \beta_i^{(0)}|_{\mathbf{z}=E\{\mathbf{z}\}} = \hat{\beta}_i^{(0)}. \qquad [3.6]$$

Now we can rewrite

$$E\left\{g_i z_i \beta_i^{(0)}\right\} \approx E\left\{g_i z_i\right\} \hat{\beta}_i^{(0)}. \qquad [3.7]$$

3.1.2.2. *MSWD calculation*

Next, we calculate the expectation of the square WD:

$$E\left\{(z_i^+)^2\right\} = E\left\{z_i^2\right\} - 2\beta E\left\{g_i z_i \sum_{j=1}^{L} E\left\{\frac{x_i x_j}{\sum_{j=1}^{L} g_j x_j^2 + \delta}\middle|\mathbf{z}\right\} z_j\right\}$$

$$+ \beta^2 E\left\{g_i^2 \sum_{j=1}^{L} E\left\{\frac{x_i^2 x_j^2}{(\sum_{j=1}^{L} g_j x_j^2 + \delta)^2}\middle|\mathbf{z}\right\} z_j^2\right\}$$

$$+ \beta^2 \sigma_v^2 E\left\{g_i^2 E\left\{\frac{x_i^2}{(\sum_{j=1}^{L} g_j x_j^2 + \delta)^2}\middle|\mathbf{z}\right\}\right\}$$

$$= E\left\{z_i^2\right\} - 2E\left\{g_i z_i^2 \beta_i^{(0)}\right\} + E\left\{g_i^2 \sum_{j=1}^{L} \beta_{i,j}^{(1)} z_j^2\right\}$$

$$+ \sigma_v^2 E\left\{g_i^2 \beta_i^{(2)}\right\}, \qquad [3.8]$$

where

$$\beta_{i,j}^{(1)} = E\left\{\frac{\beta^2 x_i^2 x_j^2}{(\sum_{j=1}^{L} g_j x_j^2 + \delta)^2}\middle|\mathbf{z}\right\}$$

and

$$\beta_i^{(2)} = E\left\{\frac{\beta^2 x_i^2}{(\sum_{j=1}^{L} g_j x_j^2 + \delta)^2}\middle|\mathbf{z}\right\}.$$

It can be derived that $\beta_{i,j}^{(1)}$ is approximately $\beta_i^{(0)}\beta_j^{(0)}$ for $i \neq j$ as shown in appendix A1.2. The approximate calculation for $\beta_i^{(2)}$ can also be done (see section A1.3) and is given by:

$$\beta_i^{(2)} \approx \frac{\beta^2}{2g_i^2}\left[\sqrt{\frac{\pi}{2\sigma_x^2}}e^{\frac{b^2}{2\sigma_x^2}} \operatorname{erfc}\left(\frac{b}{\sqrt{2\sigma_x^2}}\right)\left(\frac{1}{b} + \frac{b}{\sigma_x^2}\right) - \frac{1}{\sigma_x^2}\right]. \qquad [3.9]$$

The expectations involving the conditional expectations can be done similarly, as in the case of $\beta_i^{(0)}$, see [3.6] and [3.7].

At this point, in order to go further, we need to calculate terms such as $E\{g_i z_i\}$, $E\{g_i z_i^2\}$, $E\{g_i^2 z_j^2\}$ and $E\{g_i^2\}$. Since these terms involve the gain function g_i, the specific algorithm being used needs to be known to perform the expectation. We will delay this analysis for the time being and focus on steady-state next.

3.2. Steady-state analysis of PtNLMS algorithm: bias and MSWD calculation

The steady-state MWD and MSWD for a PtNLMS algorithm can be calculated by setting

$$E\left\{z_i^+\right\} = E\left\{z_i\right\}$$

and

$$E\left\{(z_i^+)^2\right\} = E\left\{z_i^2\right\},$$

respectively. The following assumption is also employed.

ASSUMPTION 3.2.– The denominator term in [3.2] and [3.3], $\sum_{j=1}^{L} x_j^2 g_j + \delta$, is assumed to be constant and equal to $E\{\sum_{j=1}^{L} x_j^2 g_j + \delta\} = L\sigma_x^2 + \delta$.

For $L >> \sqrt{2\sum_{i=1}^{L} g_i^2}$, the standard deviation of the term $\sum_{j=1}^{L} x_j^2 g_j + \delta$ becomes much smaller than the expected value [DOR 06]. Hence, we say that the denominator term is approximately constant. This condition is satisfied for large values of L and g that have at least several tens of significant entries.

Using recursions [3.4] and [3.8] for the MWD and MSWD, respectively, and assumption 3.2, yields in the steady-state regime:

$$E\left\{g_i z_i\right\} = 0 \qquad [3.10]$$

$$0 = -2E\left\{g_i z_i^2\right\} + \beta_0 E\left\{g_i^2(2z_i^2 + \sum_{j=1}^{L} z_j^2)\right\} + \beta_0 \frac{\sigma_v^2}{\sigma_x^2} E\left\{g_i^2\right\}, \qquad [3.11]$$

where

$$\beta_0 = \frac{\beta\sigma_x^2}{\sigma_x^2 L + \delta}$$

and the following substitutions have been made:

$$\hat{\beta}_i^{(0)} \leftrightarrow \beta_0 \qquad [3.12]$$

$$\hat{\beta}_{i,i}^{(1)} \leftrightarrow 3\beta_0^2$$

$$\hat{\beta}_{i,j}^{(1)} \leftrightarrow \beta_0^2,\ i \neq j$$

$$\hat{\beta}_i^{(2)} \leftrightarrow \frac{\beta_0^2}{\sigma_x^2}.$$

The analysis that follows could be performed also by using $\hat{\beta}_i^{(0)}$, $\hat{\beta}_{i,j}^{(1)}$ and $\hat{\beta}_i^{(2)}$.

To calculate the expectations in these expressions, we assume that the gain can be expanded in a Taylor series about the zero WD as:

$$g_i(\mathbf{z}) \approx g_i(\mathbf{0}) + \sum_{j=1}^{L} \nabla g_{ij}(\mathbf{0}) z_j,$$

where $\nabla g_{ij}(\cdot)$ is the gradient of the ith gain with respect to WD z_j. Next, we assume that only ∇g_{ii} are significantly different from zero and $\nabla g_{ij} \approx 0$ if $i \neq j$. This assumption was based on calculating the gradient for numerous algorithms and then recognizing that the off-diagonal terms of the gradient matrix $\nabla \mathbf{G}$, $[\nabla \mathbf{G}]_{ij} = \nabla g_{ij}$, were much smaller than the diagonal terms. Simulation results depicting the gradient will be presented in following sections when discussing specific algorithms. Under this assumption, we can express

$$\begin{aligned} E\{g_i z_i\} &\approx E\{[g_i(\mathbf{0}) + \nabla g_{ii}(\mathbf{0}) z_i] z_i\} \\ &= g_i(\mathbf{0}) E\{z_i\} + \nabla g_{ii}(\mathbf{0}) E\{z_i^2\}. \end{aligned} \quad [3.13]$$

This expression along with [3.10] implies that the steady-state bias can be related to the steady-state MSWD in the following manner:

$$E\{z_i\} = -\frac{\nabla g_{ii}(\mathbf{0})}{g_i(\mathbf{0})} E\{z_i^2\}.$$

A consequence of this relationship is that the steady-state bias only tends to zero when there is no noise. In simulations of the PNLMS algorithm, we have seen that this bias does exist. For example, the WD of a coefficient having the true value -0.14 is shown in Figure 3.1. We can clearly see a bias exists. The parameters used to generate this curve were $\sigma_x^2 = 1$, $\sigma_v^2 = 10^{-2}$, and $\beta = 1.8$. The used echo path impulse response is the same as the response in Figure 1.2(b).

To calculate the expectations in [3.11] we need the following expressions for $E\{z_i^3\}$ and $E\{z_i^4\}$:

$$E\{z_i^3\} = 3E\{z_i\} E\{z_i^2\} - 2E\{z_i\}^3$$

$$E\{z_i^4\} = 3E\{z_i^2\}^2 - 2E\{z_i\}^4.$$

These expressions can be derived by assuming that in steady-state, $z_i = u_i + E\{z_i\}$, where u_i is a zero-mean Gaussian random variable. These expressions use the knowledge that a steady-state bias exists.

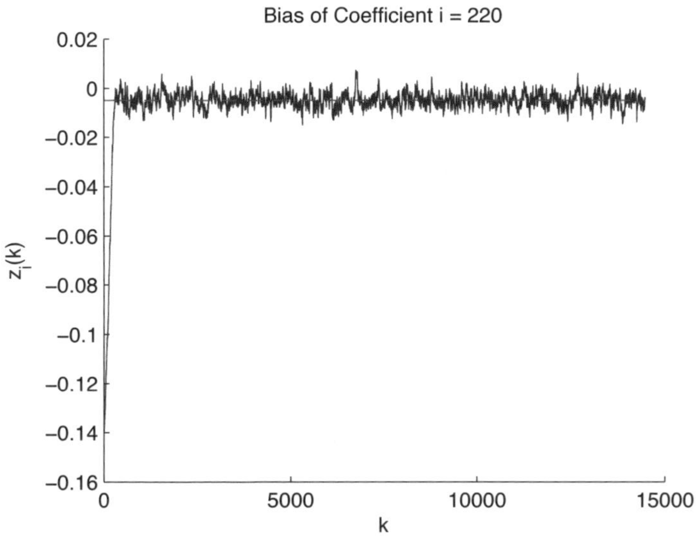

Figure 3.1. *Simulated weight deviation of a coefficient with true value −0.14*

Next, we calculate $E\left\{g_i z_i^2\right\}$, $E\left\{g_i^2 z_j^2\right\}$ and $E\left\{g_i^2\right\}$ as:

$$E\left\{g_i z_i^2\right\} \approx g_i(\mathbf{0})E\left\{z_i^2\right\} - 3\frac{\nabla g_{ii}^2(\mathbf{0})}{g_i(\mathbf{0})}E\left\{z_i^2\right\}^2 + 2\frac{\nabla g_{ii}^4(\mathbf{0})}{g_i^3(\mathbf{0})}E\left\{z_i^2\right\}^3 \qquad [3.14]$$

$$E\left\{g_i^2 z_j^2\right\} \approx \begin{cases} g_i^2(\mathbf{0})E\left\{z_j^2\right\} - \nabla g_{ii}^2(\mathbf{0})E\left\{z_i^2\right\}E\left\{z_j^2\right\}, \ i \neq j \\ g_i^2(\mathbf{0})E\left\{z_i^2\right\} - 3\nabla g_{ii}^2(\mathbf{0})E\left\{z_i^2\right\}^2 \\ +4\frac{\nabla g_{ii}^4(\mathbf{0})}{g_i^2(\mathbf{0})}E\left\{z_i^2\right\}^3 - 2\frac{\nabla g_{ii}^6(\mathbf{0})}{g_i^4(\mathbf{0})}E\left\{z_i^2\right\}^4, \ i = j \end{cases} \qquad [3.15]$$

$$E\left\{g_i^2\right\} \approx g_i^2(\mathbf{0}) - \nabla g_{ii}^2(\mathbf{0})E\left\{z_i^2\right\}. \qquad [3.16]$$

If we place these expectations into [3.11] and ignore all terms involving $E\left\{z_i^2\right\}^2$ and $E\left\{z_i^2\right\}^3$, this results in

$$\alpha_i E\left\{z_i^2\right\} - \sum_{j\neq i} E\left\{z_j^2\right\} \approx \frac{\sigma_v^2}{\sigma_x^2}, \ i = 1, 2, \ldots, L, \qquad [3.17]$$

where we define

$$\alpha_i = \frac{2g_i(\mathbf{0}) - 3\beta_0 g_i^2(\mathbf{0})}{\beta_0\left[g_i^2(\mathbf{0}) - \nabla g_{ii}^2(\mathbf{0})E\left\{z_i^2\right\}\right]}.$$

We can solve the system of equations in [3.17] using the matrix inversion lemma [WOO 50]. Equation [3.17] can be rewritten in the following form:

$$\left(\mathbf{Diag}\{\boldsymbol{\alpha}\} + \mathbf{I} - \mathbf{1}\mathbf{1}^T\right) E\{\mathbf{z} \odot \mathbf{z}\} = \frac{\sigma_v^2}{\sigma_x^2}\mathbf{1}, \qquad [3.18]$$

where $\boldsymbol{\alpha} = [\alpha_1, \alpha_2, \ldots, \alpha_L]^T$, $\mathbf{1}$ is the vector of 1s, and $E\{\mathbf{z} \odot \mathbf{z}\} = [E\{z_1^2\}, E\{z_2^2\}, \ldots, E\{z_L^2\}]^T$. Defining $\mathbf{A} = \mathbf{Diag}\{\boldsymbol{\alpha}\} + \mathbf{I}$ and applying the matrix inversion lemma to [3.18], yields:

$$E\{\mathbf{z} \odot \mathbf{z}\} = \left(\mathbf{A}^{-1} + \frac{\mathbf{A}^{-1}\mathbf{1}\mathbf{1}^T\mathbf{A}^{-1}}{1 - \sum_{j=1}^{L}\frac{1}{\alpha_j+1}}\right)\frac{\sigma_v^2}{\sigma_x^2}\mathbf{1}. \qquad [3.19]$$

Rewriting [3.19] in component-wise form and performing a few algebraic manipulations, it is possible to show that the solution to [3.17] is given by:

$$E\{z_i^2\} = \frac{\frac{1}{1+\alpha_i}}{1 - \sum_{j=1}^{L}\frac{1}{1+\alpha_j}}\frac{\sigma_v^2}{\sigma_x^2}.$$

We make one final assumption that β_0 is small and therefore we can rewrite α_i as:

$$\alpha_i \approx \frac{2g_i(\mathbf{0})}{\beta_0\left[g_i^2(\mathbf{0}) - \nabla g_{ii}^2(\mathbf{0})E\{z_i^2\}\right]}.$$

Next, we can write

$$E\{z_i^2\} \approx \frac{\beta_0\left[g_i(\mathbf{0}) - \frac{\nabla g_{ii}(\mathbf{0})}{g_i(\mathbf{0})}E\{z_i^2\}\right]}{2 - \beta_0 L + \beta_0\sum_{j=1}^{L}\frac{\nabla g_{jj}(\mathbf{0})}{g_j(\mathbf{0})}E\{z_j^2\}}\frac{\sigma_v^2}{\sigma_x^2}.$$

If we let

$$c = \frac{\beta_0}{2 - \beta_0 L + \beta_0\sum_{j=1}^{L}\frac{\nabla g_{jj}(\mathbf{0})}{g_j(\mathbf{0})}E\{z_j^2\}}\frac{\sigma_v^2}{\sigma_x^2}, \qquad [3.20]$$

then we can express $E\{z_i^2\}$ as:

$$E\{z_i^2\} \approx \frac{c g_i(\mathbf{0})}{1 + c\frac{\nabla g_{ii}^2(\mathbf{0})}{g_i(\mathbf{0})}}. \qquad [3.21]$$

By replacing $E\{z_j^2\}$ in [3.20] by [3.21] we can numerically solve for c and finally get $E\{z_i^2\}$ through [3.21].

3.3. Convergence analysis of the simplified PNLMS algorithm

The simplified PNLMS algorithm, as its name suggests, makes several assumptions in order to simplify the PNLMS algorithm from the standpoint of trying to analyze and predict its performance. The calculation of the gain for the simplified PNLMS algorithm is given in Table 3.1. The simplified PNLMS algorithm avoids the usage of the maximum function that is employed in the PNLMS, MPNLMS and EPNLMS algorithms.

$$
\begin{aligned}
\mathbf{x}(k) &= [x(k), x(k-1), \ldots, x(k-L+1)]^T \\
\hat{y}(k) &= \mathbf{x}^T(k)\hat{\mathbf{w}}(k) \\
e(k) &= d(k) - \hat{y}(k) \\
F[|\hat{w}_l(k)|, k] &= \rho + |\hat{w}_l(k)| \\
g_l(k) &= \frac{F[|\hat{w}_l(k)|,k]}{\frac{1}{L}\sum_{i=1}^{L} F[|\hat{w}_i(k)|,k]} \\
\mathbf{G}(k) &= \mathbf{Diag}\{g_1(k), \ldots, g_L(k)\} \\
\hat{\mathbf{w}}(k+1) &= \hat{\mathbf{w}}(k) + \frac{\beta \mathbf{G}(k)\mathbf{x}(k)e(k)}{\mathbf{x}^T(k)\mathbf{G}(k)\mathbf{x}(k)+\delta}
\end{aligned}
$$

Table 3.1. *Simplified PNLMS algorithm*

For comparison purposes, we plot the simplified PNLMS algorithm learning curve performance versus the PNLMS algorithm learning curve performance in Figure 3.2. The following parameters were used in these simulations: $\sigma_x^2 = 1$, $\sigma_v^2 = 10^{-4}$, $\rho = 0.01$, $\delta_p = 0.01$, $\delta = 10^{-4}$, $L = 512$ and $\beta = 0.1$ as well as the impulse response shown in Figure 1.2(b). The input signal was white zero-mean Gaussian noise. In this case, the simplified PNLMS has better MSE performance for a large portion of the transient regime.

3.3.1. *Transient theory and results*

Now, as the gain function used by the simplified PNLMS algorithm has been introduced, we can analyze the transient regime of the simplified PNLMS algorithm by applying the theory developed in section 3.1.2.

3.3.1.1. *Product of gain and WD expectations*

To calculate the MWD and MSWD, we will find the following expectations: $E\{g_i z_i\}$, $E\{g_i z_i^2\}$, $E\{g_i^2 z_i^2\}$ and $E\{g_i^2\}$. Note that we assume $E\{g_i^2 z_j^2\} \approx E\{g_i^2\} E\{z_j^2\}$ if $i \neq j$, that is g_i^2 and z_j^2 are approximately uncorrelated. We begin by assuming that the ith component of the WD at time k has a normal distribution with mean $\mu_i(k)$ and variance $\sigma_i^2(k)$, that is

$$z_i(k) \sim \mathcal{N}\left[\mu_i(k), \sigma_i^2(k)\right].$$

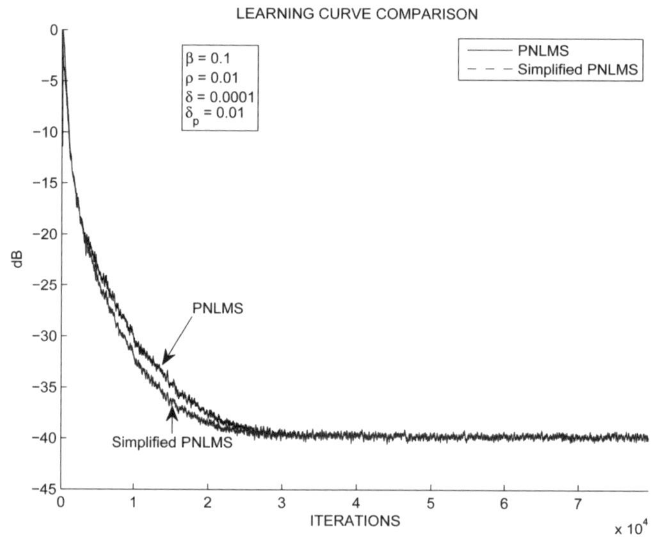

Figure 3.2. *Learning curve comparison of the simplified PNLMS and PNLMS algorithms*

We will try to support this assumption using simulations. In Figures 3.3 and 3.4, we plot histograms (empirical estimates of probability density functions) for coefficient 20 and coefficient 1 at times $k = 10, 100, 400$ and 2,952, respectively. For comparison purposes, we have also plotted a Gaussian curve with mean and variance estimated from the data. These plots were generated by 10,000 Monte Carlo runs of the simplified PNLMS algorithm. We recorded the value of the coefficients at times $k = 10, 100, 400$ and 2,952 for each Monte Carlo trial. The impulse response had length $L = 50$ and was the unit sample function shifted by 20 sampling periods. That is, $w_i = 1$ for $i = 20$ and 0 for all other coefficients. We used the following parameters in these simulations: $\beta = 0.1$, $\sigma_x^2 = 1$ $\sigma_v^2 = 10^{-4}$, $\rho = 0.01$ and $\delta = 10^{-4}$. The measurement noise used in the simulation was Gaussian. Coefficient 20 was chosen to generate the histogram because it was the location of the impulse response, while coefficient 1 was the location of a zero.

Examining these figures, we see that after several iterations, the coefficients have histograms that are approximately Gaussian in shape. Initially, the histograms are not Gaussian. When using a real-world echo impulse response, the histograms have a similar appearance, the difference being Gaussianity is observed after more iterations of the simplified PNLMS algorithm. These results give us some basis for assuming that the WD has a Gaussian probability distribution function (PDF). Also note that the mean of coefficient 20 shifts from a value of approximately 0–1 as time passes. This is expected as the algorithm converges in time.

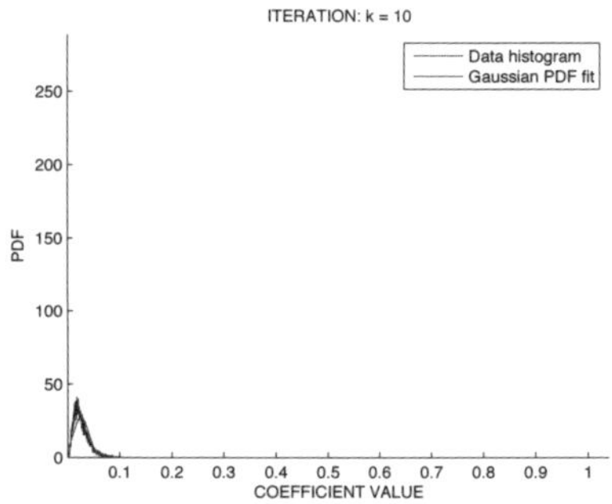

a) Empirical and Gaussian PDFs for coefficient 20 at iteration $k = 10$

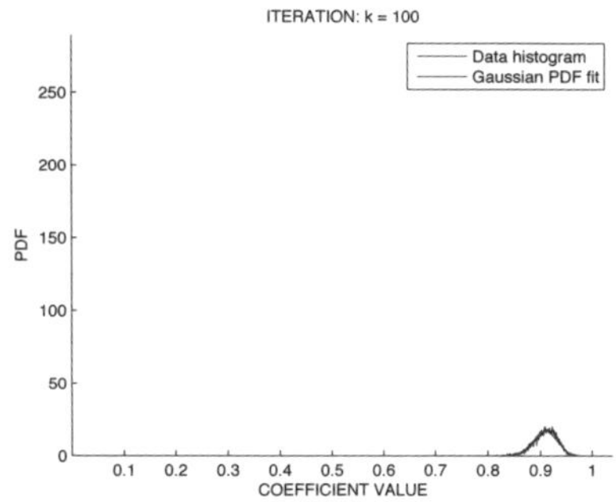

b) Empirical and Gaussian PDFs for coefficient 20 at iteration $k = 100$

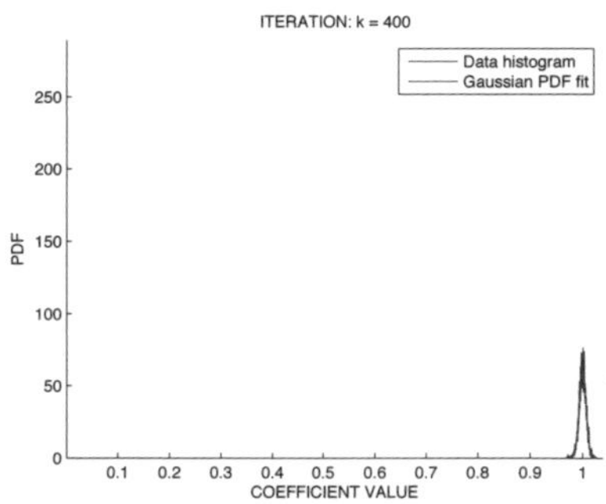

c) Empirical and Gaussian PDFs for coefficient 20 at iteration $k = 400$

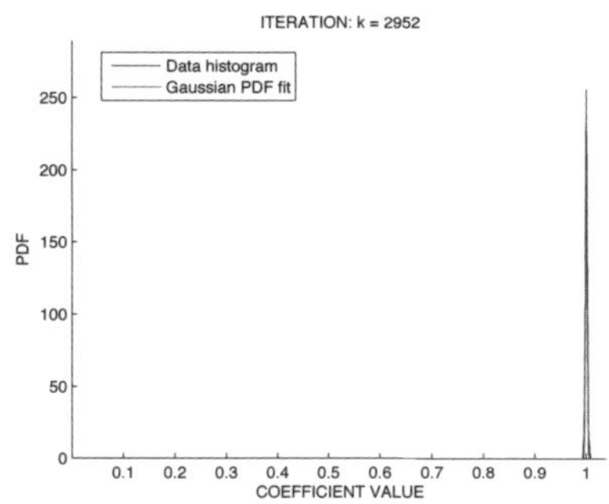

d) Empirical and Gaussian PDFs for coefficient 20 at iteration $k = 2,952$

Figure 3.3. *Histograms and Gaussian PDF fits for coefficient 20 at iterations* $k = 10, 100, 400$ *and 2,952 using the unit sample impulse response and simplified PNLMS algorithm*

Next, we plot the MSE versus iteration in Figure 3.5. This is to show that the steady-state has been reached. As a final test of Gaussianity, we have performed Lilliefors test [CON 80] and plotted the results in Figures 3.6 and 3.7 for coefficient 20 and 1, respectively. The Lilliefors test is a variant of the Kolmogorov–Smirnov test. The Kolmogorov–Smirnov statistic provides a means of testing whether a set of observations comes from a completely specified continuous distribution, however if one or more of the distribution parameters are estimated from the data, the Kolmogorov–Smirnov test is no longer valid. The Lilliefors test provides a means of determining whether a set of observations comes from a normal distribution when the mean and variance are unknown and must be estimated from the data [LIL 67]. In these figures, we have plotted three curves versus time. The first curve being the output of the Lilliefors test where 1 indicates Gaussianity has been rejected with a 5% significance level and 0 indicates Gaussianity has not been rejected. Note that just because the Lilliefors test has not rejected the hypothesis of Gaussianity, this does not guarantee the distribution is Gaussian. The second curve is the Lilliefors test statistic and the last curve is the Lilliefors test critical value. The Lilliefors test statistic needs to be less than the critical value to avoid rejection. As can be seen in these two figures, as the algorithm approaches steady-state, Gaussianity is no longer rejected. In the transient regime, Gaussianity is rejected implying that our Gaussian assumption of the WD is closer to reality as the algorithm proceeds with time.

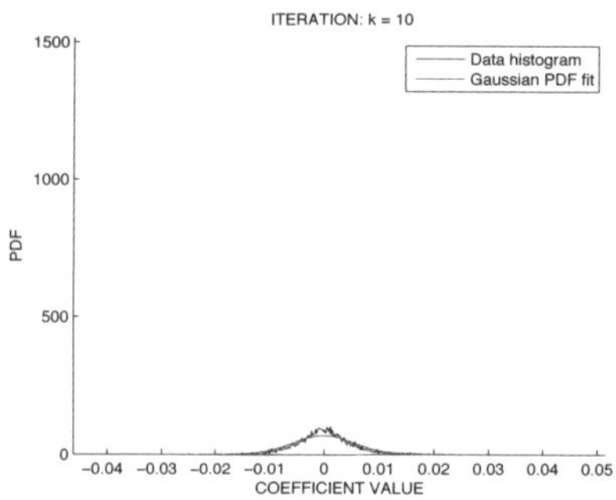

a) Empirical and Gaussian PDFs for coefficient 1 at iteration $k = 10$

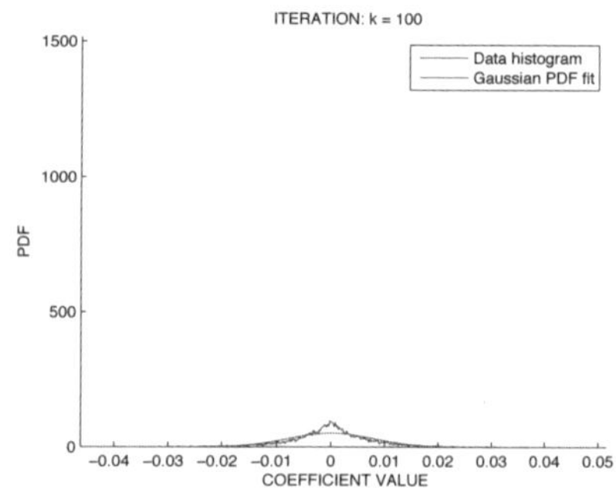

b) Empirical and Gaussian PDFs for coefficient 1 at iteration $k = 100$

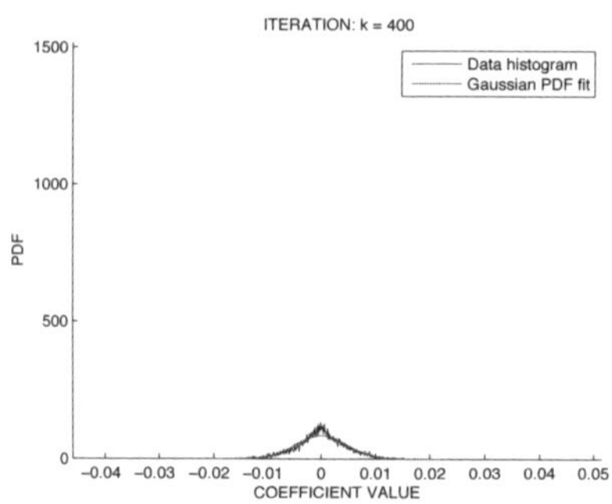

c) Empirical and Gaussian PDFs for coefficient 1 at iteration $k = 400$

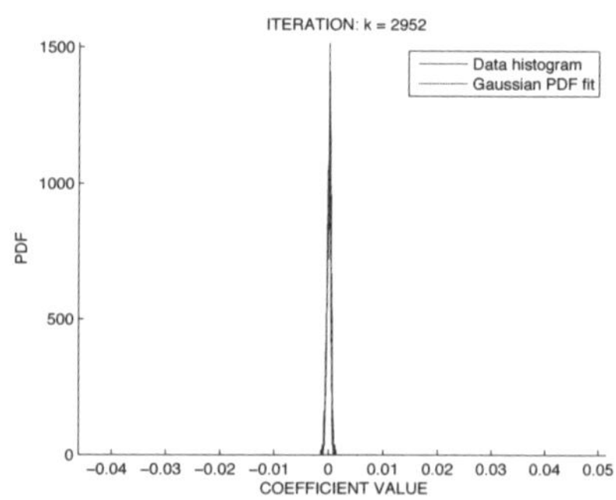

d) Empirical and Gaussian PDFs for coefficient 1 at iteration $k = 2{,}952$

Figure 3.4. *Histograms and Gaussian PDF fits for coefficient 1 at iterations* $k = 10, 100, 400$ *and 2,952 using the unit sample impulse response and simplified PNLMS algorithm*

With the assumption that the WDs are Gaussian random variables, we are now in a position to calculate the expected value of various gain and WD products. One final assumption is that the expectation of the ratio is equal to the ratio of expectations. For example,

$$E\{g_i\} = E\left\{\frac{(\rho + |\hat{w}_i|)}{\frac{1}{L}\sum_{j=1}^{L}(\rho + |\hat{w}_j|)}\right\} \approx \frac{E\{(\rho + |\hat{w}_i|)\}}{E\left\{\frac{1}{L}\sum_{j=1}^{L}(\rho + |\hat{w}_j|)\right\}}. \quad [3.22]$$

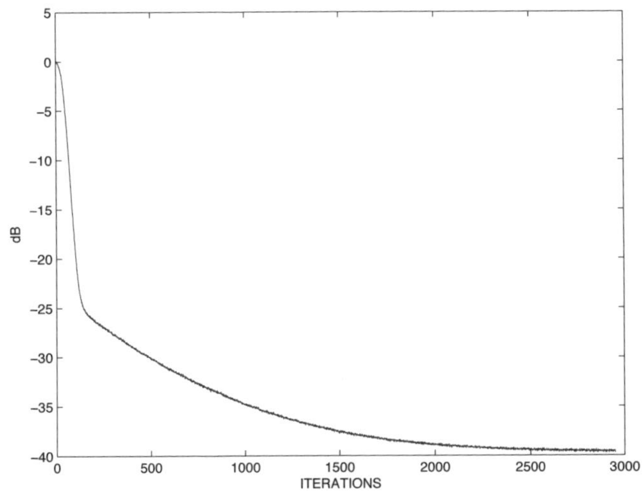

Figure 3.5. *Simplified PNLMS MSE*

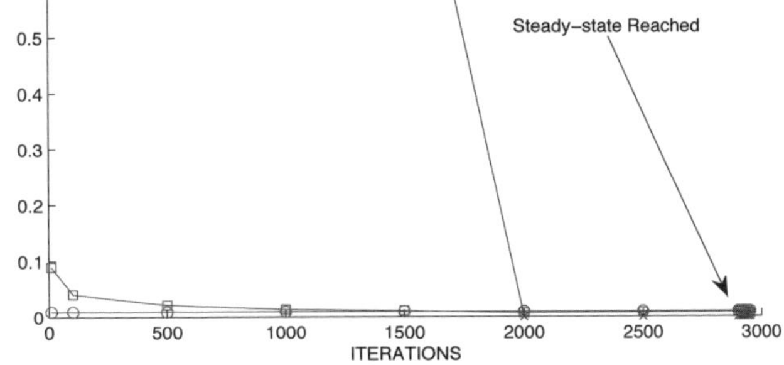

Figure 3.6. *Result of Lilliefors test for coefficient 20*

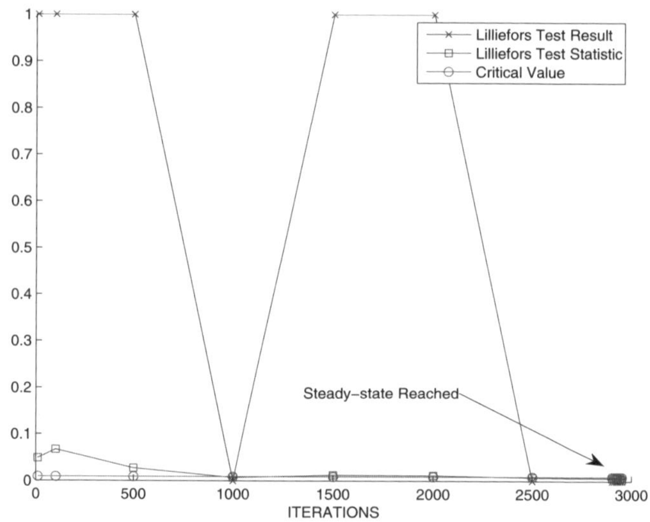

Figure 3.7. *Result of Lilliefors test for coefficient 1*

After this assumption, what remains to be calculated is $E\{\rho + |\hat{w}_i|\}$, $E\{(\rho + |\hat{w}_i|)z_i\}$, $E\{(\rho + |\hat{w}_i|)z_i^2\}$, $E\left\{(\rho + |\hat{w}_i|)^2 z_i^2\right\}$ and $E\left\{(\rho + |\hat{w}_i|)^2\right\}$. Each of these expectations can be found. Now we show each expectation after applying the assumption that the WD is a Gaussian random variable. For notational convenience, we let $\mu_i = \mu$, $w_i = w$, $\hat{w}_i = \hat{w}$, $z_i = z$ and $\sigma_i = \sigma$, so we can write

$$E\{\rho + |\hat{w}|\} = \rho + \frac{2}{\sqrt{2\pi\sigma^2}}\left[\sqrt{\frac{\pi\sigma^2}{2}}(\mu - w)\text{erf}\left(\frac{\mu - w}{\sqrt{2\sigma^2}}\right) + \sigma^2 e^{-\frac{(\mu-w)^2}{2\sigma^2}}\right]$$

$$E\{(\rho + |\hat{w}|)z\} = \rho\mu + \frac{2}{\sqrt{2\pi\sigma^2}}\left[\sqrt{\frac{\pi\sigma^2}{2}}(\mu^2 - \mu w + \sigma^2)\text{erf}\left(\frac{\mu - w}{\sqrt{2\sigma^2}}\right)\right.$$
$$\left. + \sigma^2 \mu e^{-\frac{(\mu-w)^2}{2\sigma^2}}\right]$$

$$E\left\{(\rho + |\hat{w}|)z^2\right\} = \rho(\mu^2 + \sigma^2) + \frac{2}{\sqrt{2\pi\sigma^2}}\left[\sqrt{\frac{\pi\sigma^2}{2}}(\mu^3 - \mu^2 w + 3\mu\sigma^2 - \sigma^2 w)\right.$$
$$\left. \times \text{ erf}\left(\frac{\mu - w}{\sqrt{2\sigma^2}}\right) + \sigma^2(\mu^2 + 2\sigma^2)e^{-\frac{(\mu-w)^2}{2\sigma^2}}\right]$$

$$E\left\{(\rho + |\hat{w}|)^2\right\} = \rho^2 + \frac{4\rho}{\sqrt{2\pi\sigma^2}}\left[\sqrt{\frac{\pi\sigma^2}{2}}(\mu - w)\text{erf}\left(\frac{\mu - w}{\sqrt{2\sigma^2}}\right)\right.$$
$$\left. + \sigma^2 e^{-\frac{(\mu-w)^2}{2\sigma^2}}\right] + w^2 - 2w\mu + \sigma^2 + \mu^2$$

$$E\left\{(\rho+|\hat{w}|)^2 z^2\right\}=\rho^2(\mu^2+\sigma^2)+\frac{4\rho}{\sqrt{2\pi\sigma^2}}\left[\sqrt{\frac{\pi\sigma^2}{2}}(\mu^3-\mu^2 w+3\mu\sigma^2-\sigma^2 w)\right.$$
$$\left.\times\ \mathrm{erf}\left(\frac{\mu-w}{\sqrt{2\sigma^2}}\right)+\sigma^2(\mu^2+2\sigma^2)e^{-\frac{(\mu-w)^2}{2\sigma^2}}\right]$$
$$+w^2(\mu^2+\sigma^2)-2w\mu(\mu^2+3\sigma^2)+\mu^4+6\mu^2\sigma^2+3\sigma^4. \quad [3.23]$$

This approach has been named the non-separable approach. The non-separable approach uses the terms $\beta_i^{(0)}$, $\beta_{i,j}^{(1)}$ and $\beta_i^{(2)}$ directly and does not use the approximations given in [3.12].

3.3.1.2. *Separability of gain and WD*

For comparison purposes, we examine the implications of assuming the WD and gain are independent. The theory that results from this assumption is referred to as the separable approach theory. With separability, assumed expectations of the form $E\{h_1(g_i)h_2(z_j)\}$ are equal to $E\{h_1(g_i)\}E\{h_2(z_j)\}$ for all i and j and arbitrary functions h_1 and h_2. The argument for this assumption is that g_i is a function of $\hat{w}_i = w_i - z_i$ and it is dominated by w_i when z_i is small. In addition, the assumption is made that $E\{g_i^2\} \approx E\{g_i\}^2$. This assumption is reasonable when z_i is small. The separable approach uses the approximations given in [3.12] in place of $\beta_i^{(0)}$, $\beta_{i,j}^{(1)}$ and $\beta_i^{(2)}$.

In the separable case, the MWD and MSWD are given by (after also assuming $\sum_{j=1}^{L} g_j x_j^2 + \delta = L\sigma_x^2 + \delta$):

$$E\{z_i^+\}=E\{z_i\}-\beta_o E\{g_i\}E\{z_i\} \quad [3.24]$$
$$E\{(z_i^+)^2\}=E\{z_i^2\}-2\beta_o E\{g_i\}E\{z_i^2\}$$
$$+\beta_o^2(E\{g_i\})^2\left(\sum_{j=1}^{L}E\{z_j^2\}+2E\{z_i^2\}\right)+\frac{\beta_o^2\sigma_v^2}{\sigma_x^2}(E\{g_i\})^2, \quad [3.25]$$

respectively. At this point what remains to be found is $E\{g_i\}$. This term can be expressed as:

$$E\{g_i\}=E\left\{\frac{F_i}{\frac{1}{L}\sum_j F_j}\right\}\approx\frac{\rho+E\{|\hat{w}_i|\}}{\frac{1}{L}\sum_j(\rho+E\{|\hat{w}_j|\})}. \quad [3.26]$$

The recursions in [3.24] and [3.25] are initialized by setting $E\{z_i(0)\} = w_i$ and $E\{z_i^2(0)\} = w_i^2$.

3.3.1.3. *Transient analysis results*

In this section, we compare the learning curve generated by simulation versus the theory developed in this section for the simplified PNLMS algorithm. In the simulations and figures that are shown, the following parameters have been chosen: $L = 512$, $\sigma_x^2 = 1$ $\sigma_v^2 = 10^{-4}$, $\delta = 10^{-4}$, $\rho = 0.01$, and the impulse response used is shown in Figure 1.2(b). We have developed a metric to quantitatively measure how well the theory fits the ensemble averaged results. The metric is given by:

$$C = \frac{\sum_k |E\left\{e_T^2(k)\right\} - E\left\{e_{MC}^2(k)\right\}|}{\sum_k E\left\{e_{MC}^2(k)\right\}},$$

where $E\left\{e_T^2(k)\right\}$ is the MSE [3.1] generated by the theory at time k and $E\left\{e_{MC}^2(k)\right\}$ is the squared output error generated by the ensemble average at time k. The term in the denominator is used in an attempt to make the metric independent of the input signal power.

We compare the performance of the separable approach theory versus the non-separable approach theory. The performance of the separable approach theory is shown in Figures 3.8 and 3.9 using a log and linear scale, respectively. The linear scale has been plotted to compare theory to simulation results during the transient regime of convergence. The result when using the non-separable approach theory is shown in Figures 3.10 and 3.11 using a log and linear scale, respectively. The non-separable approach theory performs slightly better than the separable approach theory.

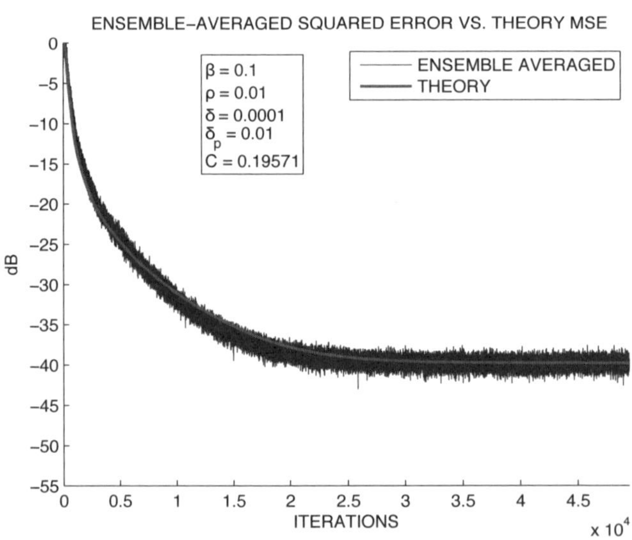

Figure 3.8. *Learning curve of simplified PNLMS algorithm using separable approach (log scale)*

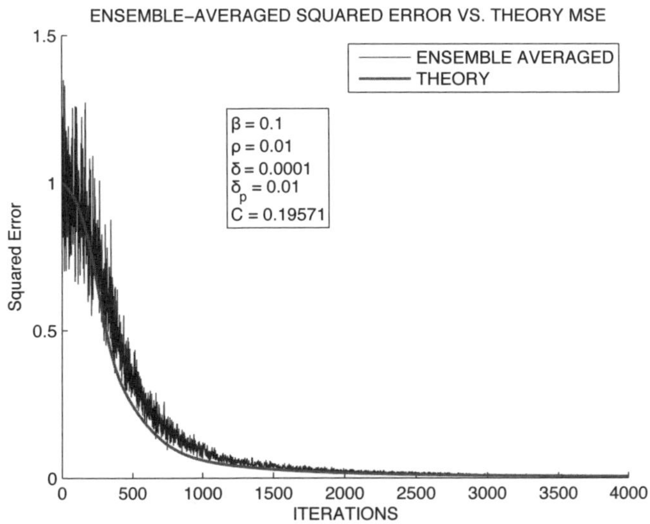

Figure 3.9. *Learning curve of simplified PNLMS algorithm using separable approach (linear scale)*

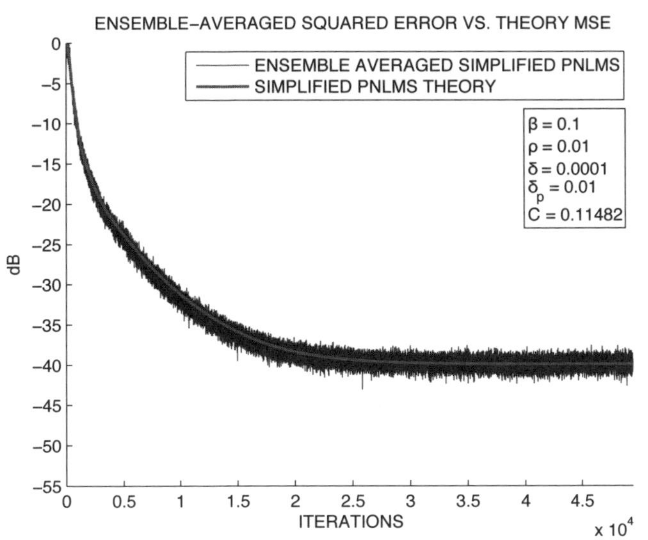

Figure 3.10. *Learning curve of simplified PNLMS algorithm using non-separable approach (log scale)*

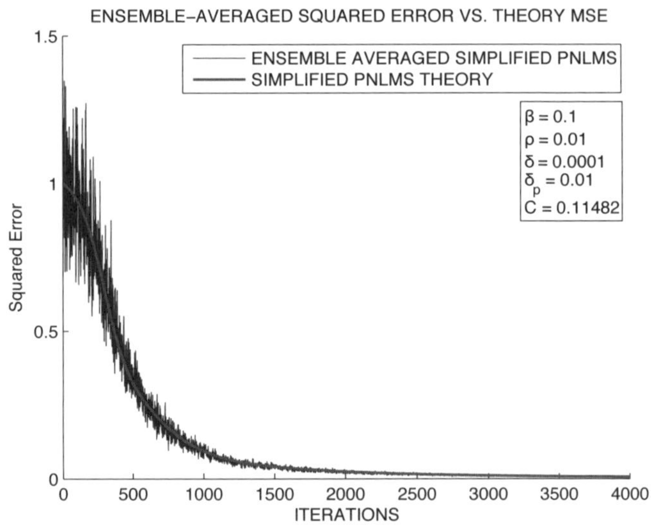

Figure 3.11. *Learning curve of simplified PNLMS algorithm using non-separable approach (linear scale)*

3.3.2. *Steady-state theory and results*

3.3.2.1. *Calculation of gradient terms*

All that remains to be calculated is the gradient of the gain $\nabla g_{ij}(\mathbf{0})$ for different values of i and j. To begin, we represent the gain as:

$$g_i(\mathbf{z}) = \frac{\rho + |w_i - z_i|}{D},$$

where

$$D = \rho L + \sum_{j=1}^{L} |w_j - z_j|.$$

Taking the derivative of the gain with respect to each component of the WD it can be shown that the gradient is given by:

$$\frac{\partial g_i}{\partial z_k} = \begin{cases} \frac{\rho+|w_i-z_i|}{D^2}\mathrm{sgn}(w_k - z_k), & i \neq k \\ \frac{\rho+|w_i-z_i|}{D^2}\mathrm{sgn}(w_i - z_i) - \frac{\mathrm{sgn}(w_i-z_i)}{D}, & i = k \end{cases} \quad [3.27]$$

where the sign operator is defined as $\mathrm{sgn}(x) = 1$ if $x > 0$, $\mathrm{sgn}(x) = 0$ if $x = 0$, and $\mathrm{sgn}(x) = -1$ if $x < 0$.

In Figure 3.12, we plot the $|\nabla g_{ik}(\mathbf{0})|$ for $k = 201, 202, \ldots, 273$, $i = 201, 202, \ldots, 273$. The echo path impulse response is the response given in Figure 1.2(b) and $\rho = 0.01$. The chosen values for i and k are in the support of the impulse response. As seen in the figure, the terms with $i = k$ are the most significant. Note that all combinations of (i, k) not displayed here resulted in a gradient with value zero.

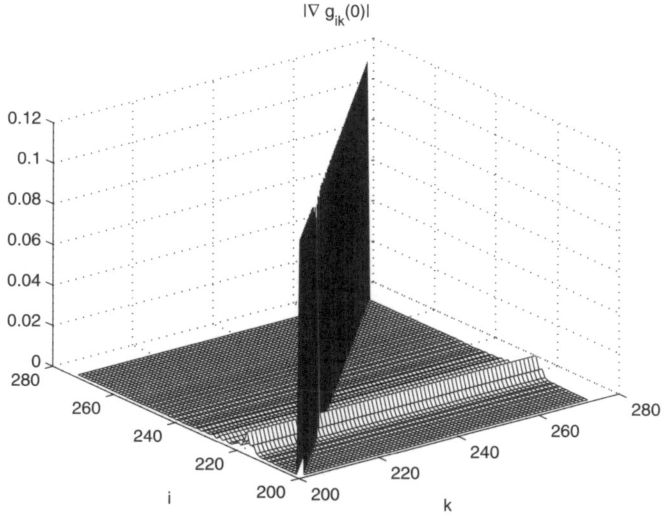

Figure 3.12. *Absolute value of gradient*

3.3.2.2. *steady-state results*

In Figure 3.13, we plot the simulated and theoretical steady-state MSE for various values of β. These curves were generated with an SNR set to 20 dB (i.e. $\sigma_v^2 = 10^{-2}$). A total of 100 Monte Carlo trials were used to generate the simulated results. In addition, $\rho = 0.01$ and $\delta = 0.0001$. The theory performs well for values of $\beta < 1$.

3.4. Convergence analysis of the PNLMS algorithm

We now attempt to extend the analysis to the PNLMS algorithm. The main difference between the simplified PNLMS algorithm and PNLMS algorithm is the usage of the max function when calculating the time-varying update gain matrix by the PNLMS algorithm. The PNLMS algorithm is given in Table 1.1 and [1.1].

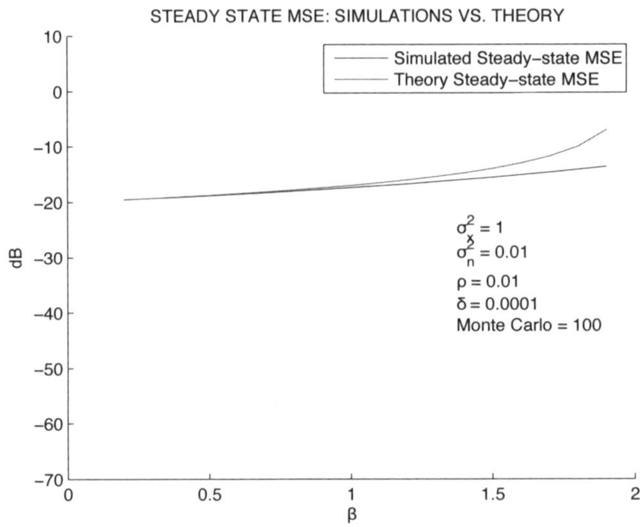

Figure 3.13. *Theoretical and simulated steady-state MSE as a function of* β

3.4.1. *Transient theory and results*

3.4.1.1. *Recursive calculation of the MWD and MSWD*

We start by placing the expression for the gain of the PNLMS algorithm into the recursions developed for the MWD [3.4] and MSWD [3.8], which are general to all PtNLMS algorithms. At this point, we need to find the following expectations: $E\{g_i z_i\}$, $E\{g_i z_i^2\}$, $E\{g_i^2 z_i^2\}$ and $E\{g_i^2\}$. Note that we assume, as before, $E\{g_i^2 z_j^2\} = E\{g_i^2\} E\{z_j^2\}$ if $i \neq j$. As we did when analyzing the simplified PNLMS, we assume that the expectation of the ratio is equal to the ratio of expectations, for example

$$E\{g_i\} = E\left\{\frac{\max\{\gamma_{\min}, |\hat{w}_i|\}}{\frac{1}{L}\sum_{j=1}^{L}\max\{\gamma_{\min}, |\hat{w}_j|\}}\right\} \approx \frac{E\{\max\{\gamma_{\min}, |\hat{w}_i|\}\}}{E\left\{\frac{1}{L}\sum_{j=1}^{L}\max\{\gamma_{\min}, |\hat{w}_j|\}\right\}}. [3.28]$$

After this assumption, the following terms will be calculated:

$$E\left\{\max\{\gamma_{\min}, |\hat{w}_i|\}\right\}$$

$$E\left\{\max\{\gamma_{\min}, |\hat{w}_i|\} z_i\right\}$$

$$E\left\{\max\{\gamma_{\min}, |\hat{w}_i|\} z_i^2\right\}$$

$$E\left\{\max^2\{\gamma_{\min}, |\hat{w}_i|\} z_i^2\right\}$$

$$E\left\{\max^2\{\gamma_{\min}, |\hat{w}_i|\}\right\}.$$

Each of these expectations can be found by assuming that the WD is Gaussian with distribution $z_i \sim \mathcal{N}\left[\mu_i, \sigma_i^2\right]$. As an example, we will show the calculation of the term $E\left\{\max\{\gamma_{\min}, |\hat{w}_i|\}\right\}$ in detail and list the others.

We begin by recognizing that $\hat{w}_i = w_i - z_i$, which implies that $\hat{w}_i$ is Gaussian with distribution $\hat{w}_i \sim \mathcal{N}\left[m_i, \sigma_i^2\right]$ where $m_i = w_i - \mu_i$. Then after dropping the subscripts for notational convenience and writing $m_i = m$, $\sigma_i = \sigma$, $w_i = w$, $\hat{w}_i = \hat{w}$, $z_i = z$ and $\gamma_{\min} = a$. It is assumed that $\max\{\mathbf{w}\} \equiv |\mathbf{w}|_{\max}$ is much larger than δ_p and

$$a \approx \rho \max\{\delta_p, |\mathbf{w}|_{\max}\} = \rho|\mathbf{w}|_{\max}.$$

The above approximation is valid after a short initial adaptation period. Next, we can write

$$E\left\{\max\{a, |\hat{w}|\}\right\} = \int_{-a}^{a} \frac{a}{\sqrt{2\pi\sigma^2}} e^{-\frac{(\hat{w}-m)^2}{2\sigma^2}} dx + \int_{a}^{\infty} \frac{\hat{w}}{\sqrt{2\pi\sigma^2}} e^{-\frac{(\hat{w}-m)^2}{2\sigma^2}} dx - \int_{-\infty}^{-a} \frac{\hat{w}}{\sqrt{2\pi\sigma^2}} e^{-\frac{(\hat{w}-m)^2}{2\sigma^2}} dx. \quad [3.29]$$

These integrals are well known and can be looked up in numerous tables. Following the same strategy, we can calculate all of the desired expectations. A list of the required expectations is shown below:

$$E\left\{\max\{a, |\hat{w}|\}\right\} = \sqrt{\frac{\sigma^2}{2\pi}} \left[e^{-\frac{(a+m)^2}{2\sigma^2}} + e^{-\frac{(a-m)^2}{2\sigma^2}}\right] + \frac{a+m}{2} \text{erf}\left(\frac{a+m}{\sqrt{2\sigma^2}}\right) + \frac{a-m}{2} \text{erf}\left(\frac{a-m}{\sqrt{2\sigma^2}}\right) \quad [3.30]$$

$$E\left\{\max\{a, |\hat{w}|\} z\right\} = \sqrt{\frac{\sigma^2}{2\pi}} (w-m) \left[e^{-\frac{(a+m)^2}{2\sigma^2}} + e^{-\frac{(a-m)^2}{2\sigma^2}}\right] + \frac{w(a+m) - am - \sigma^2 - m^2}{2} \text{erf}\left(\frac{a+m}{\sqrt{2\sigma^2}}\right) + \frac{w(a-m) - am + \sigma^2 + m^2}{2} \text{erf}\left(\frac{a-m}{\sqrt{2\sigma^2}}\right) \quad [3.31]$$

$$E\left\{\max\{a,|\hat{w}|\}z^2\right\}$$
$$= \sqrt{\frac{\sigma^2}{2\pi}}(w^2 - 2wm + m^2 + 2\sigma^2)\left[e^{-\frac{(a+m)^2}{2\sigma^2}} + e^{-\frac{(a-m)^2}{2\sigma^2}}\right]$$
$$+\frac{w^2(a+m) - 2w(am+\sigma^2+m^2) + a\sigma^2 + am^2 + 3\sigma^2 m + m^3}{2}\text{erf}\left(\frac{a+m}{\sqrt{2\sigma^2}}\right)$$
$$+\frac{w^2(a-m) - 2w(am-\sigma^2-m^2) + a\sigma^2 + am^2 - 3\sigma^2 m - m^3}{2}\text{erf}\left(\frac{a-m}{\sqrt{2\sigma^2}}\right) \quad [3.32]$$

$$E\left\{\max^2\{a,|\hat{w}|\}z^2\right\} =$$
$$\sqrt{\frac{\sigma^2}{2\pi}}\left[w^2(a-m) - 2w(-m^2 - 2\sigma^2 + am)\right.$$
$$\left. + am^2 - 5\sigma^2 m + 3\sigma^2 a - m^3\right] e^{-\frac{(a+m)^2}{2\sigma^2}}$$
$$+\sqrt{\frac{\sigma^2}{2\pi}}\left[w^2(a+m) - 2w(m^2 + 2\sigma^2 + am)\right.$$
$$\left. + am^2 + 5\sigma^2 m + 3\sigma^2 a + m^3\right] e^{-\frac{(a-m)^2}{2\sigma^2}}$$
$$+\frac{1}{2}\left[w^2(a^2 - \sigma^2 - m^2) - 2w(-3\sigma^2 m - m^3 + a^2 m) + a^2(\sigma^2 + m^2)\right.$$
$$\left. - 3\sigma^4 - 6\sigma^2 m^2 - m^4\right] \text{erf}\left(\frac{a+m}{\sqrt{2\sigma^2}}\right)$$
$$+\frac{1}{2}\left[w^2(a^2 - \sigma^2 - m^2) - 2w(-3\sigma^2 m - m^3 + a^2 m) + a^2(\sigma^2 + m^2)\right.$$
$$\left. - 3\sigma^4 - 6\sigma^2 m^2 - m^4\right] \text{erf}\left(\frac{a-m}{\sqrt{2\sigma^2}}\right)$$
$$+ w^2(\sigma^2 + m^2) - 2w(3m\sigma^2 + m^3) + 3\sigma^4 + 6\sigma^2 m^2 + m^4 \quad [3.33]$$

$$E\left\{\max^2\{a,|\hat{w}|\}\right\} = \sqrt{\frac{\sigma^2}{2\pi}}\,[a-m]\,e^{-\frac{(a+m)^2}{2\sigma^2}} + \sqrt{\frac{\sigma^2}{2\pi}}\,[a+m]\,e^{-\frac{(a-m)^2}{2\sigma^2}}$$
$$+\frac{a^2 - \sigma^2 - m^2}{2}\left[\text{erf}\left(\frac{a+m}{\sqrt{2\sigma^2}}\right) + \text{erf}\left(\frac{a-m}{\sqrt{2\sigma^2}}\right)\right] + \sigma^2 + m^2. \quad [3.34]$$

Placing these expressions into [3.4] and [3.8] allows us to recursively estimate the MWD and MSWD at all times.

3.4.1.2. *Transient analysis results*

Now we compare the theoretical expectations to actual results from Monte Carlo simulations. In the simulations and figures that are shown, the following parameters have been chosen unless specified otherwise: $L = 512$, $\sigma_x^2 = 1$, $\sigma_v^2 = 10^{-4}$, $\rho = 0.01$ and $\delta = 10^{-4}$. In Figures 3.14 and 3.15, we plot the ensemble averaged learning curve and the learning curve predicted by the theory for $\beta = 0.1$ using a log and linear scale, respectively. Similarly, in Figures 3.16 and 3.17, we plot the ensemble averaged learning curve and the learning curve predicted by the theory for $\beta = 1.0$ using a log and linear scale, respectively. Both figures used the measured echo path impulse response given in Figure 1.2(b). Note that the non-separable approach was employed in these figures. The separable approach offered significantly degraded performance when analyzing the PNLMS algorithm. The quantitative measure C introduced in section 3.3.1.3 was used here to measure how well the theory fits the ensemble averaged results. We see that for small values of β, the theory matches the simulation quite well. As β is increased, the assumptions are less applicable and the theoretical predictions are less reliable.

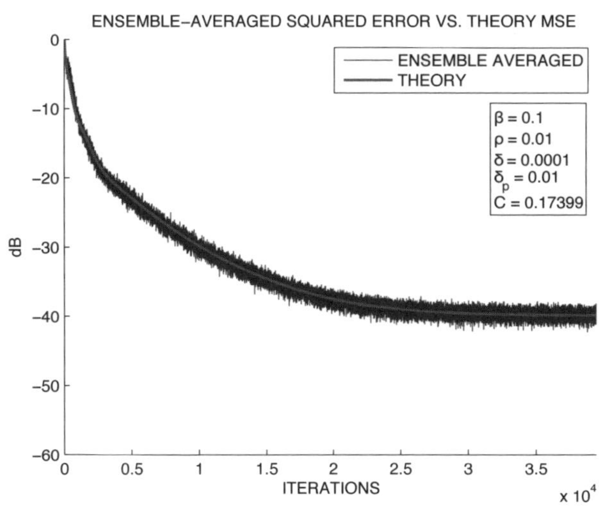

Figure 3.14. *Theoretical and experimental learning curve of PNLMS algorithm for $\beta = 0.1$ and a measured echo path impulse response (log scale)*

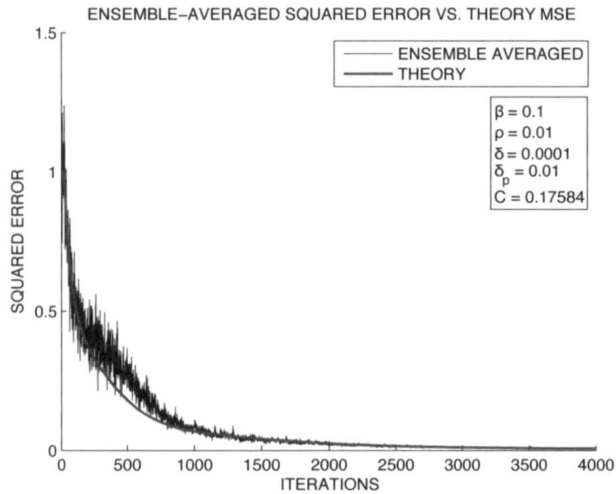

Figure 3.15. *Theoretical and experimental learning curve of PNLMS algorithm for $\beta = 0.1$ and a measured echo path impulse response (linear scale)*

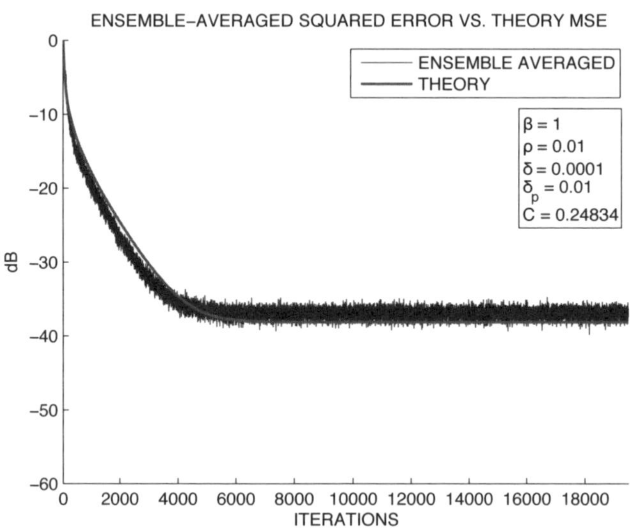

Figure 3.16. *Theoretical and experimental learning curve of PNLMS algorithm for $\beta = 1$ and a measured echo path impulse response (log scale)*

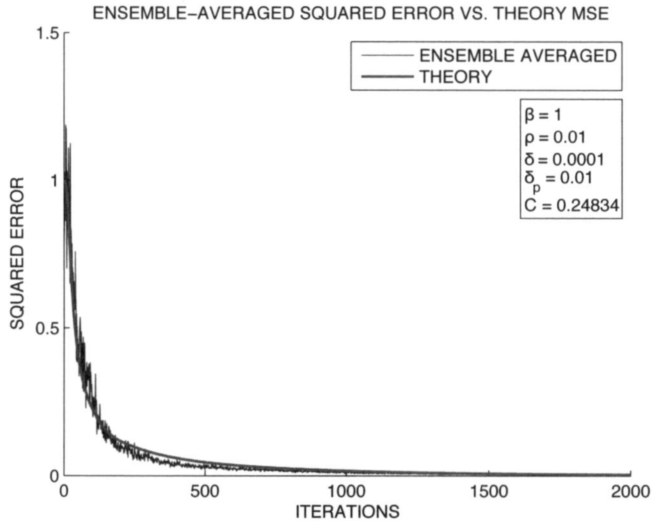

Figure 3.17. *Theoretical and experimental learning curve of PNLMS algorithm for $\beta = 1$ and a measured echo path impulse response (linear scale)*

3.4.2. *Steady-state theory and results*

3.4.2.1. *Calculation of gain gradient terms*

All that remains to be calculated is the gradient of the gain $\nabla g_{ik}(\mathbf{0})$ for different values of i and k. To begin, we represent the gain as:

$$g_i(\mathbf{z}) = \frac{\max\{\rho|w_M - z_M|, |w_i - z_i|\}}{D},$$

where

$$D = \sum_{j \in \mathcal{D}_a} |w_j - z_j| + \rho|w_M - z_M||\mathcal{D}_a^c|.$$

The index M corresponds to the element of $\mathbf{w}$ with the largest magnitude. $\mathcal{D}_a$ is a set of active coefficient indices, i.e. the indices that satisfy $|w_j - z_j| > \rho|w_M - z_M|$. $\mathcal{D}_a^c$ is the complement of $\mathcal{D}_a$ and $|\mathcal{D}_a^c|$ is the number of elements in the set $\mathcal{D}_a^c$ (cardinality of $\mathcal{D}_a^c$). An example of a gradient term for $i \in \mathcal{D}_a$ and $k = i$ evaluated at $\mathbf{z} = \mathbf{0}$ is given by:

$$\nabla g_{ii}(\mathbf{0}) = \frac{-\frac{|w_i|}{w_i} D_0 - |w_i|}{D_0^2},$$

where $D_0 = D|_{\mathbf{z}=\mathbf{0}}$.

In Figure 3.18, we plot the $|\nabla g_{ik}(\mathbf{0})|$ for $k = 201, 202, \ldots, 273$ and $i = 201, 202, \ldots, 273$. The echo path impulse response is the response given in Figure 1.2(b). As seen in the figure, the terms with $i = k$ are the most significant. In addition, all combinations of (i, k) for which the gradient is not displayed result in gradient values of zero.

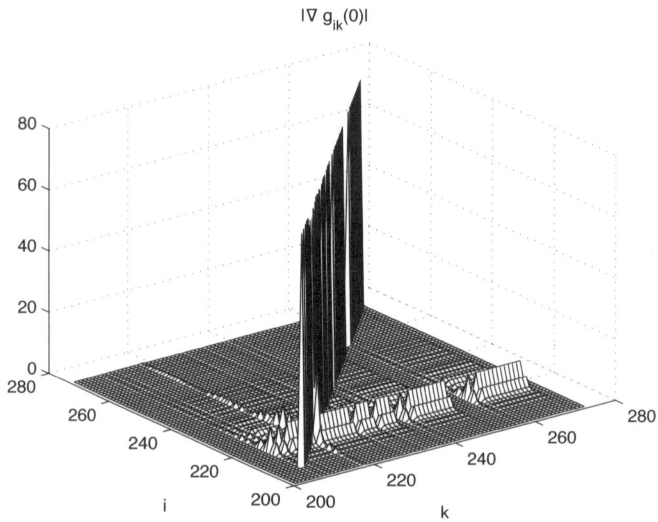

Figure 3.18. *Absolute value of gradient*

3.4.2.2. *Algorithm steady-state results*

In Figure 3.19, we plot the simulated and theoretical steady-state MSE for various values of β. These curves were generated with an SNR set to 20 dB (i.e. $\sigma_v^2 = 10^{-2}$). A total of 20 Monte Carlo trials were used to generate the simulated results. The theory performs well for values of $\beta < 1.2$.

3.5. Summary

This chapter extends the techniques used to analyze the LMS algorithm to the PtNLMS algorithm. The analysis of the transient and steady-state regimes of the PtNLMS algorithm requires calculating various expectations of the product of the WD and the gain. In general, the gain can be a nonlinear function of the WD, which makes the calculation of the expectation of the product of the WD and the gain mathematically intractable. Because of this limitation, this chapter builds the framework for analyzing an arbitrary PtNLMS algorithm and then focuses on a thorough analysis of the simplified PNLMS and PNLMS algorithms.

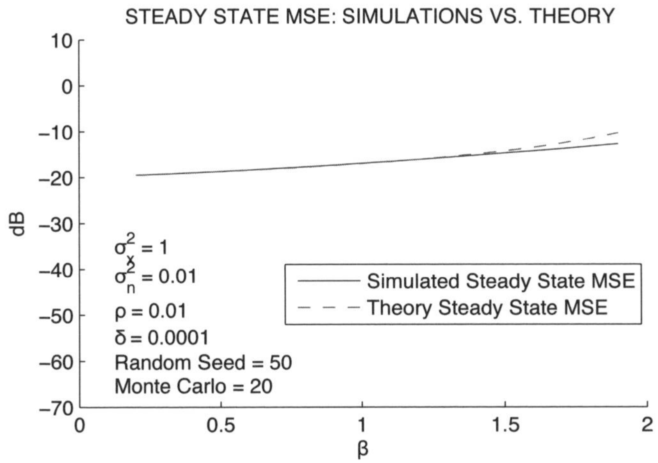

Figure 3.19. *Theoretical and simulated steady-state MSE as a function of β*

The simplified PNLMS algorithm linearizes the calculation of the gain function used in the PNLMS algorithm by replacing the max function used in the PNLMS algorithm by a linear function of the magnitude of the estimated WD. The simplified algorithm served the purposes of testing the validity of certain assumptions employed and easing the analysis. Next, the PNLMS algorithm was analyzed. The analysis presented in this chapter relied on a diverse number of assumptions being applied. After removing some assumptions the analysis became mathematically more difficult, but provided greater accuracy of modeling.

Finally, the theoretical expectations for transient and steady-state behavior of MSE were compared to numerical simulations of the simplified PNLMS and PNLMS algorithms. The simulations confirmed that the theory matches the algorithm behavior.

4

Algorithms Designed Based on Minimization of User-Defined Criteria

In this chapter, several new PtNLMS algorithms are presented. While each of these algorithms uses diverse assumptions and have diverse forms, the commonality between these new algorithms is the approach that was taken in their derivation. Specifically, all of the algorithms presented in this chapter attempt to find an optimal gain such that a user-defined criterion is minimized. First, we assume white input and derive two PtNLMS algorithms that use gain allocation minimizing the MSE in the next iteration with respect to the current MSE. Next, again for white input, we derive a PtNLMS algorithm based on minimization of the MSE modeled by exponential functions. Then, we assume colored input and derive a PtNLMS algorithm by minimizing the MSWD. For this algorithm, we give a suboptimal implementation that reduces computational complexity.

4.1. PtNLMS algorithms with gain allocation motivated by MSE minimization for white input

In the past, *ad hoc* methods have been used to choose gains in PtNLMS algorithms without strong theoretical underpinnings. In this section, a theoretical framework and motivation for adaptively choosing gains is presented, such that the MSE will be minimized at any given time. Note that due to [3.1], minimizing the MSE is reduced to minimization of the sum of the MSWDs. As a result of this approach, a new optimal PtNLMS algorithm is introduced. A computationally simplified version of the theoretical optimal algorithm is derived as well. Both of these algorithms require knowledge of the MSWDs. Feasible implementations, which estimate the MSWDs, are presented. The performance of these new feasible algorithms is compared to the performance of standard adaptive algorithms, when operating with sparse, non-sparse, and time-varying impulse responses, when the input signal is white. Specifically, we consider the transient and steady-state MSEs of each algorithm.

4.1.1. *Optimal gain calculation resulting from MMSE*

In this section, we seek the optimal gain at each time step k. Our approach to this problem is to minimize the MSE with respect to the gain under two constraints. The two constraints that are to be satisfied are $g_i(k) \geq 0 \;\forall\; i, k$ and $\sum_{i=1}^{L} g_i(k) = L \;\forall\; k$. The considered criterion is the minimization of the MSE.

The recursions for the WD and the square of the WD are given by [3.2] and [3.3], respectively.

In addition to assumptions 2.1, 2.2, 3.1 and 3.2 we use the following assumption:

ASSUMPTION 4.1.– The gain g_i is a deterministic function of time.

This assumption facilitates analysis and provides an upper bound on the performance of the algorithm.

Next, we use assumption 3.2 and define $\beta_a = \beta/(\sigma_x^2 L + \delta)$. This allows us to rewrite the WD recursion in [3.2] as:

$$z_i^+ = z_i - \beta_a g_i x_i \sum_{j=1}^{L} x_j z_j - \beta_a g_i x_i v. \qquad [4.1]$$

Note this approximation has transformed the PtNLMS algorithm into a proportionate-type least mean square (PtLMS) algorithm. This approximation will be used again in Chapters 5 and 7. At this point, we attempt to find the optimal gain at each time step k by optimizing our user-defined criterion with respect to the gain.

The criterion we try to minimize is the MSE at time $k+1$. The MSE at time k is given in [3.1]. Note that $J(k)$ is the approximate MSE at instant k [HAY 02].

Now the expectations of the WD and square WD are given by:

$$E\{z_i^+\} = E\{z_i\} - \beta_a \sigma_x^2 g_i E\{z_i\} \qquad [4.2]$$

$$E\{z_i^{+2}\} = E\{z_i^2\} - 2\beta_a \sigma_x^2 g_i E\{z_i^2\} + \beta_a^2 \sigma_x^4 g_i^2 \left(2E\{z_i^2\} + \sum_{j=1}^{L} E\{z_j^2\} \right) + \beta_a^2 \sigma_x^2 \sigma_v^2 g_i^2. \qquad [4.3]$$

Note that [4.2] and [4.3] become [3.24] and [3.25] after replacing g_i with $E\{g_i\}$ and taking care that $\beta_0 = \beta_a \sigma_x^2$. We make the following definitions for notational convenience:

$$c_i = 2\beta_a \sigma_x^2 E\left\{z_i^2\right\}$$

$$q_i = 2\beta_a^2 \sigma_x^4 \left(2E\left\{z_i^2\right\} + \sum_{j=1}^{L} E\left\{z_j^2\right\} + \frac{\sigma_v^2}{\sigma_x^2}\right).$$

Next, we assume that $E\left\{z_i^2\right\}$ are known, and we try to find the optimal gain by minimizing $J^+ = \sigma_v^2 + \sigma_x^2 \sum_{i=1}^{L} E\left\{z_i^{+2}\right\}$ for all k, with respect to the gain and impose the constraint $\sum_{j=1}^{L} g_j = L$. We can recast this problem as an optimization problem in the form

$$\min_{\mathbf{g}} \frac{J^+ - \sigma_v^2}{\sigma_x^2} - \sum_{j=1}^{L} E\left\{z_j^2\right\} = -\mathbf{c}^T\mathbf{g} + \frac{1}{2}\mathbf{g}^T\mathbf{Q}\mathbf{g},$$

such that $g_i \geq 0 \,\forall\, i$ and $\mathbf{1}^T\mathbf{g} = L$, where $\mathbf{g} = [g_1, g_2, \ldots, g_L]^T$, $\mathbf{c} = [c_1, c_2, \ldots, c_L]^T$ and $\mathbf{Q} = \mathbf{Diag}\{q_1, q_2, \ldots, q_L\}$.

Next, for convenience, we make the substitution $g_i = s_i^2$ (s_i is real) and incorporate the constraint into the minimization problem. This results in the Lagrangian function

$$T(\mathbf{s}, \lambda) = -\sum_{i=1}^{L} c_i s_i^2 + \frac{1}{2}\sum_{i=1}^{L} q_i s_i^4 + \lambda(\sum_{i=1}^{L} s_i^2 - L). \quad [4.4]$$

Taking the first derivative and setting it equal to zero yields three solutions, $s_i = 0$ and $s_i = \pm\sqrt{(c_i - \lambda)/q_i}$. If we examine the second derivative $\partial^2 T/\partial^2 s_i$, we find that the first solution results in a minimum if $\lambda \geq c_i$ and the second and third solutions result in a minimum if $\lambda < c_i$, as shown in the following derivation.

4.1.1.1. *Minima of Lagrangian [4.4]*

The first and second derivatives of $T(\mathbf{s}, \lambda)$ are given by:

$$\frac{\partial T}{\partial s_i} = 2s_i(-c_i + \lambda + q_i s_i^2)$$

$$\frac{\partial^2 T}{\partial s_i^2} = 2(-c_i + \lambda) + 6q_i s_i^2. \quad [4.5]$$

Setting the first derivative to zero and solving for s_i results in three solutions, $s_i = 0$ and $s_i = \pm\sqrt{(c_i - \lambda)/q_i}$. However, recalling the original definition $g_i = s_i^2$, the last two solutions give the same gain and have the same character with respect to the sign of the second derivative. Hence, we condense the last two solutions into $s_i = \sqrt{(c_i - \lambda)/q_i}$ from this point forward. Now, if we substitute these solutions into the second derivative, we have

$$\frac{\partial^2 T}{\partial s_i^2}|_{s_i=0} = 2(\lambda - c_i)$$

$$\frac{\partial^2 T}{\partial s_i^2}|_{s_i=\sqrt{\frac{c_i-\lambda}{q_i}}} = 4(c_i - \lambda). \qquad [4.6]$$

We notice that the second derivative will be greater than zero when using the first solution, $s_i = 0$, if $\lambda > c_i$. While the second derivative will be greater than zero when using the solution $s_i = \sqrt{(c_i - \lambda)/q_i}$, if $\lambda < c_i$. Recall that the sign of the second derivative determines whether the solution results in a maximum or a minimum. In our case, we require the solution to be a minimum. Note that if using the second solution and $\lambda > c_i$, there is no solution for g_i, since this would result in an imaginary value for s_i, which is not allowed.

It turns out that the solution to this problem is of the "water-filling" [PAL 05] variety. We find the constant λ according to the following procedure. First, we sort the entries of $\mathbf{c}$ in ascending order to form a new vector such that $c_{(1)} < c_{(2)} < \ldots < c_{(L)}$, where $c_{(j)}$ is the jth entry of the new vector. We subsequently rearrange the elements of $\mathbf{Q}$ to match the position of the original indices in the sorted $\mathbf{c}$ and to form a new matrix whose diagonal elements are $q_{(1)}, q_{(2)}, \ldots, q_{(L)}$. The optimal value of λ solves the following equation:

$$\sum_{j=1}^{L} \left(\frac{c_{(j)} - \lambda}{q_{(j)}} \right)_+ = L \qquad [4.7]$$

where we define the operator $(x)_+ = x$, if $x \geq 0$, and $(x)_+ = 0$, if $x < 0$.

In Figure 4.1(a), we depict how the optimal value λ can be chosen. On the abscissa of the figure is candidate values of λ, while the ordinate axis corresponds to various volumes of "water". The curve depicted is a function of the $\mathbf{c}$ and $\mathbf{q}$ vectors. If we trace down from the intersection of the volume L, we find the corresponding optimal value λ. We will refer to this algorithm as the water-filling PtNLMS algorithm.

We illustrate this water-filling problem in Figure 4.1(b). We have a pitcher containing a volume L of water. After pouring the contents of the pitcher into a vessel with the profile shown in Figure 4.1(b), we want to know the difference of the height the water reaches in the vessel and the zero-reference level of the vessel. This difference gives us the value of λ that we look for. The stairway sloped bottom of the vessel is defined by the treads of heights $c_{(i)}$ and with widths $1/q_{(i)}$.

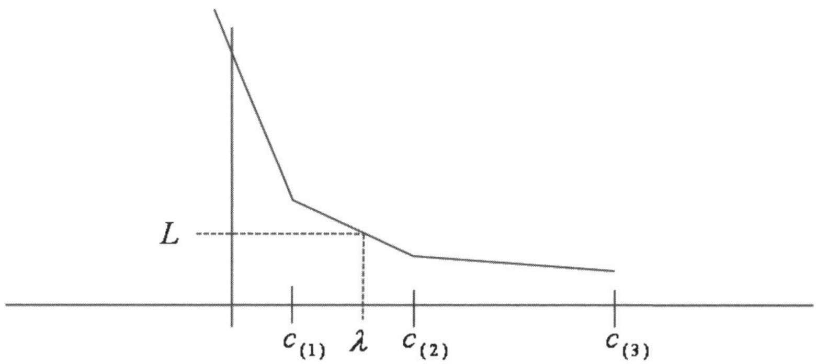

a) Interpretation of the solution for λ by plotting [4.7] as a function of λ

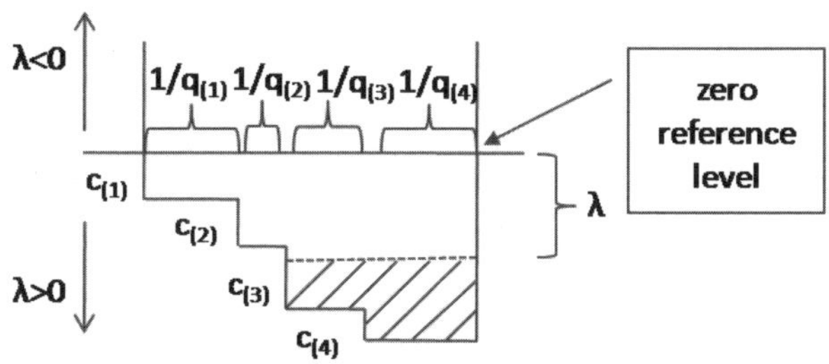

b) Interpretation of the solution for λ by water filling

Figure 4.1. *Interpretation of the solution for λ (a) by plotting [4.7] as a function of λ and (b) by water filling*

From [4.7] the candidate solutions are

$$\lambda_i = \frac{\sum_{j=i}^{L} \frac{c_{(j)}}{q_{(j)}} - L}{\sum_{j=i}^{L} \frac{1}{q_{(j)}}}. \qquad [4.8]$$

We choose $\lambda = \lambda_i$, if $c_{(i-1)} < \lambda_i < c_{(i)}$, where $c_{(0)} = -\infty$.

4.1.2. *Water-filling algorithm simplifications*

The water-filling algorithm can be simplified by approximating the term

$$
\begin{aligned}
q_i &= 2\beta_a^2\sigma_x^4\left(2E\left\{z_i^2\right\}+\sum_{j=1}^{L}E\left\{z_j^2\right\}+\frac{\sigma_v^2}{\sigma_x^2}\right)\\
&\approx 2\beta_a^2\sigma_x^4\left(\sum_{j=1}^{L}E\left\{z_j^2\right\}+\frac{\sigma_v^2}{\sigma_x^2}\right) && [4.9]\\
&\approx 2\beta_a^2\sigma_x^4\left(\sum_{j=1}^{L}E\left\{z_j^2\right\}\right). && [4.10]
\end{aligned}
$$

Approximation [4.9] assumes that the sum of all MSWDs is much larger than the ith MSWD (which is reasonable for long adaptive filters where the error in one coefficient is much less than the cumulative error in all other coefficients). Note this approximation makes q_i identical for all i. This eliminates the need to sort q_i. Approximation [4.10] assumes that the input signal power is much larger than the noise power, and that $\sigma_v^2/\sigma_x^2 \ll \sum_{j=1}^{L} E\left\{z_j^2\right\}$ (which is true at least at the beginning of adaptation).

As a final simplification, if we also assume that $\beta = 1$, then we can reduce the water-filling algorithm to the following form:

$$g_i = \frac{E\left\{z_i^2\right\}}{\frac{1}{L}\sum_{j=1}^{L}E\left\{z_j^2\right\}}. \qquad [4.11]$$

Here, we see that the gains are proportional to the MSWDs. We can estimate the MSWDs using the methods discussed in section 4.1.3. This approach resembles the gain given by the water-filling algorithm, with the benefit of less computational complexity. We refer to this algorithm as the z^2-proportionate algorithm. The derivation of this simplification is given in the following.

4.1.2.1. *Water-filling and z^2-proportionate algorithm relationship*

We will show that $\beta = 1$ implies $\lambda = 0$. Let us begin by applying simplifications [4.9] and [4.10]. After these simplifications, we note that q_i is independent of i, so we define $q_i = q$. Additionally, we make the approximation $\beta_a = \beta/(L\sigma_x^2 + \delta) \approx \beta/(L\sigma_x^2)$. If $\beta = 1$, we can rewrite [4.8] as:

$$\lambda_i = \frac{1}{L-i+1}\sum_{j=i}^{L} c_{(j)} - \frac{L}{L-i+1}q$$
$$= \frac{2}{L(L-i+1)}\left(\sum_{j=i}^{L} E\left\{z_{(j)}^2\right\} - \sum_{j=1}^{L} E\left\{z_j^2\right\}\right). \qquad [4.12]$$

Note that we substituted the values of c_j and q from [4.4] and [4.10], respectively. We see that $\lambda_i < 0$ for all $i \neq 1$ and $\lambda_1 = 0$. Since $c_{(i)} > 0$ for all i and we choose $\lambda = \lambda_i$ such that $c_{(i-1)} < \lambda_i < c_{(i)}$, λ must be in the first segment. In other words, $\lambda = \lambda_1 = 0$. Therefore, $\beta = 1$ implies $\lambda = 0$.

The water-filling algorithm has two solutions for the gain at any given time k, namely; $g_i = 0$ if $\lambda \geq c_i$ and $g_i = (c_i - \lambda)/q_i$ if $\lambda < c_i$. Since for $\beta = 1$, $\lambda = 0$, we can reduce the second solution to

$$g_i = \frac{c_i}{q_i} = \frac{E\left\{z_i^2\right\}}{\beta_a\sigma_x^2\sum_{j=1}^{L} E\left\{z_j^2\right\}} \approx \frac{E\left\{z_i^2\right\}}{\frac{1}{L}\sum_{j=1}^{L} E\left\{z_j^2\right\}}. \qquad [4.13]$$

Therefore, the water-filling algorithm reduces to z^2-proportionate algorithm.

4.1.3. *Implementation of algorithms*

The water-filling algorithm proposed as well as the z^2-proportionate are not feasible because we are required to know $E\left\{z_i^2\right\} = E\{[w_i - \hat{w}_i]^2\}$. We take the following approach to overcome this lack of knowledge.

4.1.3.1. *Biased estimation of MSWD*

In this approach, we make the following approximations $E\left\{z_i^2\right\} \approx (\widehat{E\{z_i\}})^2$ and $\sum_{j=1}^{L} E\left\{z_j^2\right\} \approx \sum_{j=1}^{L}(\widehat{E\{z_j\}})^2$ where we replace the MSWD with the square of the MWD. Note that an arbitrary random variable a, the notation $\hat{a}$ represents an estimate of a.

To find $\widehat{E\{z_i\}}$, we rewrite the error as $e = \sum_{j=1}^{L} x_j z_j + v$. Next, we multiply both sides of the equation by x_i and take the expectation (assuming x_i is a white signal).

This results in $E\{x_i e\} = \sigma_x^2 E\{z_i\}$. If we define $p_i = x_i e$, we can calculate $E\{p_i\}$ and then solve for $E\{z_i\}$. We update our estimate of $E\{p_i\}$ in the following fashion:

$$\widehat{E\{p_i\}} = \alpha(\widehat{E\{p_i\}})^- + (1-\alpha)p_i$$
$$\widehat{E\{z_i\}} = \widehat{E\{p_i\}}/\sigma_x^2,$$

where $0 \leq \alpha \leq 1$ and $(\widehat{E\{p_i\}})^- = E\{\widehat{p_i(k-1)}\}$. This approach has been called "biased" because we replace $E\{z_i^2\}$ with $(\widehat{E\{z_i\}})^2$. In doing so, the variance is assumed to be zero (only an approximation). This approach was used in [LI 08] and [SHI 04].

The major weakness of this approach is the sensitivity of the algorithm to the choice of α. If α is chosen too large (i.e. close to 1), the steady-state error approaches the noise floor but the transient performance can be unsatisfactory. Conversely, if α is set too small, the algorithm will reach steady-state rapidly; however, the steady-state error will have an additional misadjustment component that can be several decibels above the noise floor. Moreover, the approximation for $E\{z_i^2\}$ is poor in the steady-state where an estimate of the variance of z_i will be needed as well.

4.1.3.2. *Adaptive convex gain combination*

A potential solution to the above problems is presented here as an adaptive convex gain combination of the water-filling or z^2-proportionate gain with the NLMS gain. Let $\mathbf{g}^*$ represent the gain generated from the water-filling or z^2-proportionate algorithm and $\mathbf{1}$ be the $L \times 1$ vector of 1s. The gain used in the implementation of the proposed algorithms is the mixture of $\mathbf{g}^*$ and $\mathbf{1}$ given as $\mathbf{g} = (1-\zeta)\mathbf{g}^* + \zeta\mathbf{1}$. Here, ζ is a mixing parameter defined as:

$$\zeta = \min\left[1, \frac{\omega\sigma_v^2}{\sigma_x^2 \sum_{j=1}(\widehat{E\{z_j\}})^2 + \sigma_v^2}\right], \qquad [4.14]$$

where $\omega \geq 0$. The denominator term in [4.14] is an estimate of the MSE. Hence, as the estimated MSE approaches the noise floor, the algorithm acts more like the NLMS algorithm by equally distributing gain to all coefficients. This is reasonable since the estimate of $E\{z_i^2\}$ used is poor in steady-state and its usage in this regime should be avoided. Moreover, $E\{z_i^2\}$ should be evenly distributed in steady-state; therefore, equal gain for all weights should be applied. When the estimated MSE is large relative to the noise floor, then the algorithm inherits the characteristics of water-filling or z^2-proportionate algorithm. Now α can be chosen to ensure satisfactory transient performance. Some modification of [4.14] can be used as well. For example, the denominator term in [4.14] could be obtained directly by smoothing the square error e^2.

This gain selection methodology is a variant of the gain proposed in the sparseness-controlled PNLMS (SC-PNLMS). But instead of estimating sparsity, an estimate of the distance to the noise floor is used to set the gain.

4.1.4. *Simulation results*

4.1.4.1. *Algorithm comparison for white input*

In Figure 4.2(a) we compare the NLMS, PNLMS, water-filling, z^2-proportionate, recursive least squares (RLS) [HAY 02] and ideal water-filling algorithms for $\beta = 0.1$, $\rho = 0.01$, $\sigma_x^2 = 1$, $\sigma_v^2 = 10^{-4}$, $\delta = 10^{-4}$, $\delta_p = 0.01$ and $L = 512$. The RLS algorithm's forgetting factor and regularization parameter are both set to 1 [HAY 02]. The ideal water-filling algorithm uses the instantaneous value of the WD vector, $\mathbf{z}(k) = \mathbf{w} - \hat{\mathbf{w}}(k)$, as the input to the water-filling algorithm. The impulse response used in this simulation is given in Figure 4.2(b). The input signal consists of white noise. The z^2-proportionate and water-filling algorithms used the implementation described in section 4.1.3.2 with the values of $(\alpha,\omega) = (0.99, 5)$ and $(\alpha,\omega) = (0.999, 2)$, respectively. The different values of α and ω for the z^2-proportionate and water-filling algorithms result from tuning the algorithms for good transient and steady-state performance.

The NLMS algorithm has the slowest initial convergence but better overall convergence than the PNLMS algorithm. The water-filling and z^2-proportionate algorithms offer an improvement in the overall convergence rate relative to the PNLMS algorithm. The RLS algorithm has the fastest convergence at the expense of increased computational complexity.

The z^2-proportionate algorithm reaches steady-state faster than the water-filling algorithm. This result is due to the fact that the sorting operations used in the water-filling algorithm causes it to be more sensitive to errors in the estimation of $E\left\{z_i^2\right\}$.

4.1.4.2. *Algorithm comparison for non-sparse impulse responses*

In Figure 4.3(a), we present the performance of the NLMS, PNLMS, water-filling, z^2-proportionate and RLS algorithm for a dispersive impulse response. The impulse response used in these simulations is shown in Figure 4.3(b). Otherwise, the parameters used are the same as those given in section 4.1.4.1.

Under these conditions, the z^2-proportionate and water-filling algorithms have good convergence performance. These algorithms do not depend on sparsity during their derivation. The algorithms that assume sparsity such as the PNLMS struggle in this environment.

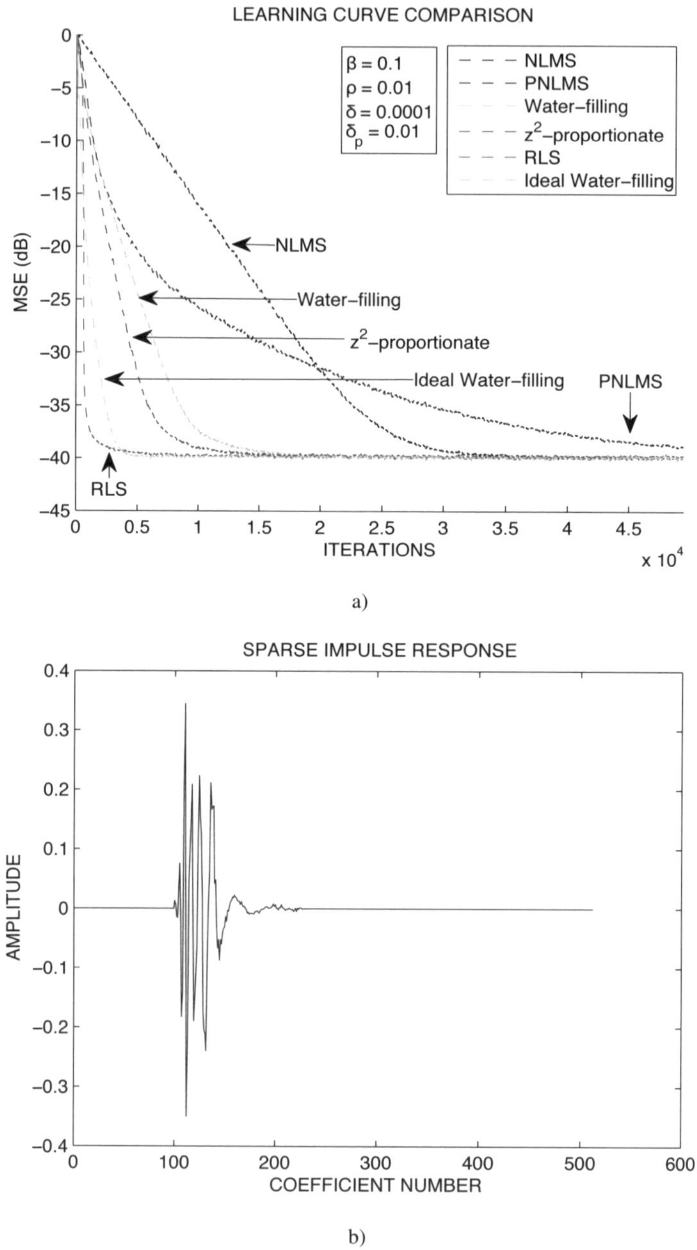

Figure 4.2. *White input: a) sparse impulse response algorithm comparison and b) sparse impulse response*

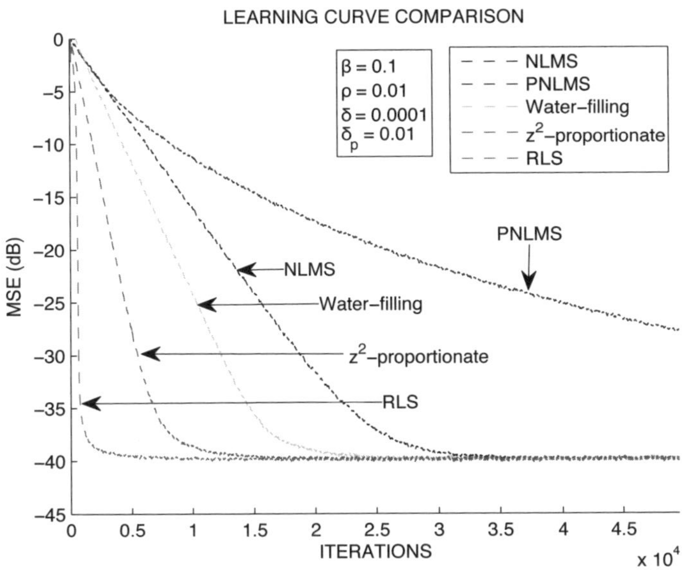

a)

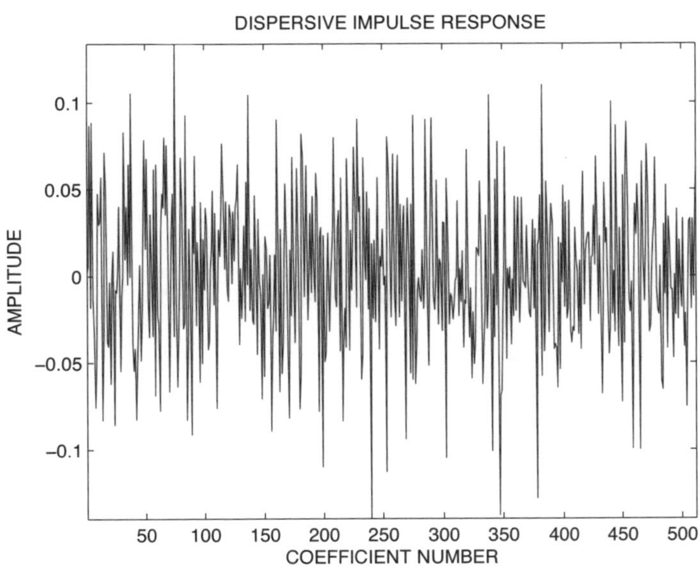

b)

Figure 4.3. *White input: a) dispersive impulse response algorithm comparison and b) dispersive impulse responses*

4.1.4.3. *Algorithm comparison for a time-varying impulse response*

The performance of the NLMS, PNLMS, water-filling, the z^2-proportionate and RLS algorithms are compared when the impulse response is time varying and the input signal is white as shown in Figure 4.4. The algorithm parameters are the same as those described in section 4.1.4.1. The impulse response is changed to the sparse impulse response in Figure 1.2(b) after 40,000 iterations. The algorithms maintain the same convergence properties with the exception of a few small changes due to the characteristics of the two different impulse responses. The RLS algorithm does not track the change in impulse response also. The RLS algorithm's forgetting factor and regularization parameter could potentially be tuned to improve its tracking performance.

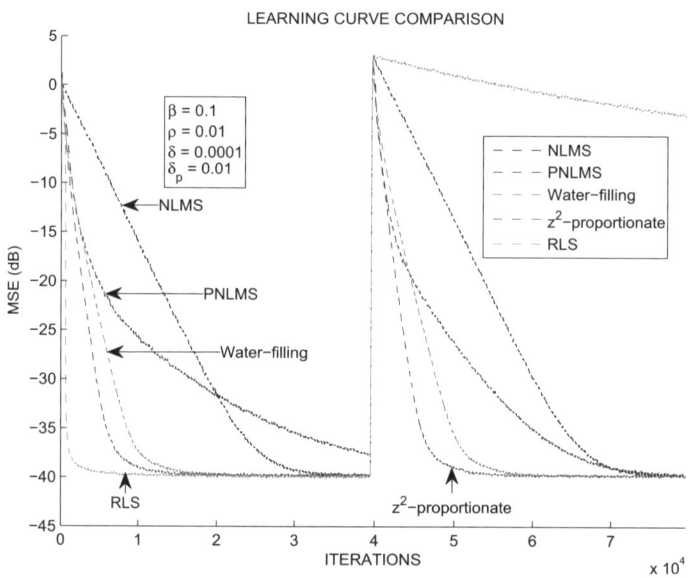

Figure 4.4. *Time-varying impulse response performance*

4.2. PtNLMS algorithm obtained by minimization of MSE modeled by exponential functions

In this section, using the proportionate-type steepest descent algorithm, we represent the current WDs in terms of initial WDs. Then, we attempt to minimize the MSE with respect to the time average of all gains applied up to a given instant. The corresponding optimal time averaged gains are found using a water-filling procedure. The stochastic counterpart is obtained in two steps. First, the true weights, which are unknown, are replaced by their current estimates in the expression for the optimal time averaged gains. Second, the current gains are calculated based on the difference between the estimated optimal cumulative gain and the actual given cumulative gain. Additionally, a simplified gain allocation method is proposed that avoids the sorting needed in the water-filling procedure. The resulting algorithm initially behaves like the PNLMS algorithm and as time proceeds the algorithm behaves like the NLMS algorithm. This type of behavior is typically desired and results in enhanced convergence performance. We present results for the new algorithms and compare them to other standard PtNLMS algorithms.

4.2.1. *WD for proportionate-type steepest descent algorithm*

Instead of minimizing J^+ given by [3.1] we are going to consider the minimization of the MSE of an associate proportionate-type steepest descent algorithm. From [DEN 05], we can express the deterministic ith WD at time $k+1$ (denoted as $\hat{z}_i^+$) recursively as:

$$\begin{aligned}\hat{z}_i^+ &= \left[1 - \beta_a \sigma_x^2 g_i(k)\right] \hat{z}_i(k) \\ &= \prod_{p=0}^{k} \left[1 - \beta_0 g_i(p)\right] \hat{z}_i(0).\end{aligned} \quad [4.15]$$

Additionally, if $\beta_0 g_i(p) << 1 \; \forall \, p = 0, 1, \ldots, k$, then we can approximate [4.15] by:

$$\hat{z}_i^+ \approx e^{-(k+1)\beta_0 \overline{g}_i(k)} w_i \quad [4.16]$$

where $\hat{z}_i(0) = w_i$ and

$$\overline{g}_i(k) = \frac{1}{k+1} \sum_{p=0}^{k} g_i(p).$$

The term $\overline{g}_i(k)$ is the time average of all gains applied.

4.2.2. *Water-filling gain allocation for minimization of the MSE modeled by exponential functions*

Let us consider minimization of the MSE of the steepest descent algorithm with respect to the average gains, that is

$$\begin{aligned}&\min_{\overline{\mathbf{g}}(k)} \hat{J}^+ = \sigma_v^2 + \sigma_x^2 \min_{\overline{\mathbf{g}}(k)} \left\{ \sum_{j=1}^{L} (\hat{z}_j^+)^2 \right\} \\ &\text{s.t. } \overline{g}_i(k) \geq 0 \\ &\sum_{i=1}^{L} \overline{g}_i(k) = L,\end{aligned} \quad [4.17]$$

where $(\hat{z}_j^+)^2$ is given by [4.16] and $\overline{\mathbf{g}}(k)$ is the vector representation of the average gains at time k, that is $\overline{\mathbf{g}}(k) = [\overline{g}_1(k), \overline{g}_2(k), \ldots, \overline{g}_L(k)]^T$.

To find the optimal gain, we define the Lagrangian as:

$$\begin{aligned} T(\mathbf{s}, \lambda) &= \hat{J}^+ + \lambda \left(\sum_{j=1}^{L} \overline{g}_j - L \right) \\ &= \sigma_v^2 + \sigma_x^2 \sum_{j=1}^{L} e^{-2(k+1)\beta_0 \overline{g}_j} w_j^2 + \lambda \left(\sum_{j=1}^{L} \overline{g}_j - L \right). \end{aligned} \quad [4.18]$$

For notational convenience, we suppress the time indexing on the average gain, that is $\overline{g}_i(k) = \overline{g}_i$. In the following, we substitute $s_j^2 = \overline{g}_j$ (s_j is real) into $T(\mathbf{s}, \lambda)$ and take the derivative with respect to s_i. This substitution ensures that our solutions for $\overline{g}_i \geq 0$. The result of this derivative is given by:

$$\frac{\partial T(\mathbf{s}, \lambda)}{\partial s_i} = 2 s_i \left[\lambda - 2(k+1) \sigma_x^2 \beta_0 e^{-2(k+1)\beta_0 s_i^2} w_i^2 \right]. \quad [4.19]$$

Setting the derivative to zero, there are two solutions for the gain:

$$\overline{g}_i = 0 \quad [4.20]$$

$$\overline{g}_i = \frac{1}{2(k+1)\beta_0} \ln \frac{2(k+1)\sigma_x^2 \beta_0 w_i^2}{\lambda}. \quad [4.21]$$

If we examine the second derivative $\partial^2 T / \partial s_i^2$, we see that the first solution [4.20] results in a minimum if $\lambda \geq 2(k+1)\sigma_x^2 \beta_0 w_i^2$ and the second solution [4.21] results in a minimum if $0 < \lambda < 2(k+1)\sigma_x^2 \beta_0 w_i^2$.

The solution to this problem is again of the "waterfilling" variety. We choose the constant λ according to the following rules. First, we sort the entries of $\mathbf{w} = [w_1, w_2, \ldots, w_L]^T$ into non-descending order to form a new vector such that $w_{(1)} \leq w_{(2)} \leq \ldots \leq w_{(L)}$. Next, we solve for λ_j such that

$$\sum_{i=j}^{L} \frac{1}{2(k+1)\beta_0} \ln \frac{2(k+1)\sigma_x^2 \beta_0 w_{(i)}^2}{\lambda_j} = L. \quad [4.22]$$

If λ_j satisfies the inequalities

$$2(k+1)\sigma_x^2\beta_0 w_{(j-1)}^2 \leq \lambda_j < 2(k+1)\sigma_x^2\beta_0 w_{(j)}^2, \qquad [4.23]$$

then we set $\lambda = \lambda_j$, where $w_{(0)}^2 = 0$. This value of λ is used to specify which coefficients receive zero gain and which do not.

4.2.2.1. *Calculation of Lagrange multipliers*

We seek to find λ_j that satisfies [4.22]. We can rearrange this expression such that

$$\sum_{i=j}^{L} \ln \frac{2(k+1)\sigma_x^2\beta_0}{\lambda_j} + \sum_{i=j}^{L} \ln w_{(i)}^2 = 2(k+1)L\beta_0. \qquad [4.24]$$

Rearranging terms further yields

$$\ln\left[2(k+1)\sigma_x^2\beta_0\right] - \ln\lambda_j + \frac{1}{L-j+1}\sum_{i=j}^{L} \ln w_{(i)}^2 = \frac{2(k+1)L\beta_0}{L-j+1} \qquad [4.25]$$

and finally solving for λ_j results in

$$\lambda_j = 2(k+1)\sigma_x^2\beta_0 \left[\prod_{i=j}^{L} w_{(i)}^2\right]^{\frac{1}{L-j+1}} e^{-\frac{2(k+1)\beta_0 L}{L-j+1}}. \qquad [4.26]$$

If we substitute λ_j into the second solution for the gain [4.21], we can write

$$\overline{g}_{(i)} = \frac{L}{L-j+1} + \frac{1}{(k+1)\beta_0}\left(\ln|w_{(i)}| - \frac{1}{L-j+1}\sum_{l=j}^{L} \ln|w_{(l)}|\right), \; i \geq j. \qquad [4.27]$$

Note that the optimality of the average gain is only for the instant $k+1$, not for instants before or after $k+1$. Hence, if $k+1$ is larger, the optimal average gain is distributed more evenly across all of the active coefficients, while the inactive coefficients receive zero gain.

4.2.2.2. *Usage of the proposed water-filling scheme in PtNLMS algorithm*

Up to this point, the implementation of the proposed water-filling algorithm has not been feasible because we require the knowledge of w_i. To avoid this problem, we substitute the estimated value of the impulse response $\hat{w}_i(k)$ for the true impulse response. Next, the estimated average gain is calculated using the water-filling procedure described in section 4.2.2 and the estimated impulse response $\hat{w}_i(k)$. The estimated optimal average gain can be represented as:

$$\hat{\bar{g}}_i = \begin{cases} 0, & \text{if } \lambda \geq 2(k+1)\sigma_x^2\beta_0\hat{w}_i^2 \\ \frac{L}{L-j+1} + \frac{1}{(k+1)\beta_0}\left(\ln|\hat{w}_i| - \frac{\sum_{l=j}^{L}\ln|\hat{w}_{(l)}|}{L-j+1}\right), & \text{if } \lambda < 2(k+1)\sigma_x^2\beta_0\hat{w}_i^2. \end{cases}$$

At this point, the instantaneous gain at time k is calculated. The instantaneous gain is defined as the gain that needs to be applied at the current time step in order to achieve the desired estimated optimal cumulative gain. The instantaneous gain is written as follows:

$$\Delta[|\hat{w}_i(k)|] = (k+1)\hat{\bar{g}}_i - \sum_{p=0}^{k-1} g_i(p), \quad [4.28]$$

where $g_i(p)$ are previously applied gains. Since the difference in [4.28] can be negative, we form

$$F[|\hat{w}_i(k)|] = \left(\Delta\ [\hat{w}_i(k)|]\right)_+ . \quad [4.29]$$

This ensures that none of the terms are negative. As a final step, minimum gain logic is implemented to ensure that all coefficients receive at least some small gain. This helps to avoid stalling. The remainder of the proposed algorithm is summarized in Table 1.1 using the function F defined in [4.29].

4.2.2.3. *Modified water-filling algorithm*

For long impulse responses, sorting and checking the inequality in [4.23] can be time intensive. Hence, as an alternative, we propose the following modification of the proposed algorithm. Instead of [4.27] we use

$$\hat{\bar{g}}_i = \left(1 + \frac{1}{(k+1)\beta_0}\left(\ln|\hat{w}_i(k)| - \frac{1}{L}\sum_{j=1}^{L}\ln|\hat{w}_j(k)|\right)\right)_+ . \quad [4.30]$$

Here, we have avoided sorting altogether. Then, we allow the algorithm to run as before. Again, we calculate the instantaneous gain and incorporate the minimum gain logic summarized in Table 1.1.

4.2.3. *Simulation results*

In this section, we present performance results for the two new proposed algorithms. The performance results are presented by estimating MSE as a function of time. For comparison purposes, the learning curves of the NLMS, PNLMS, MPNLMS, water-filling and RLS algorithms are also included. The RLS algorithm uses a value of 1 for the forgetting factor and regularization parameter.

The water-filling algorithm is implemented using the convex gain combination described in section 4.1.3.2 and the biased estimation of MSWDs described in section 4.1.3.1. The water-filling algorithm results presented in these simulations used the values $(\alpha,\omega) = (0.999, 2)$.

The learning curves were the result of averaging 10 Monte Carlo runs. Other relevant parameters used in these simulations are as follows: the input signal power was set to $\sigma_x^2 = 1$, $\sigma_v^2 = 10^{-4}$, $\beta = 0.1$, $\rho = 0.01$, $\delta_p = 0.01$, $\delta = 10^{-4}$ and $\mu = 3563$ (μ is a parameter used in the MPNLMS algorithm). The impulse response employed has a length of $L = 512$ and is shown in Figure 4.2(b).

In Figure 4.5, the MSE is plotted versus time for a white input signal and the sparse impulse response shown in Figure 4.2(b). Here, the reader can see that the proposed algorithms outperform the NLMS and PNLMS algorithms. The RLS algorithm has better performance at the price of significantly increased computational complexity.

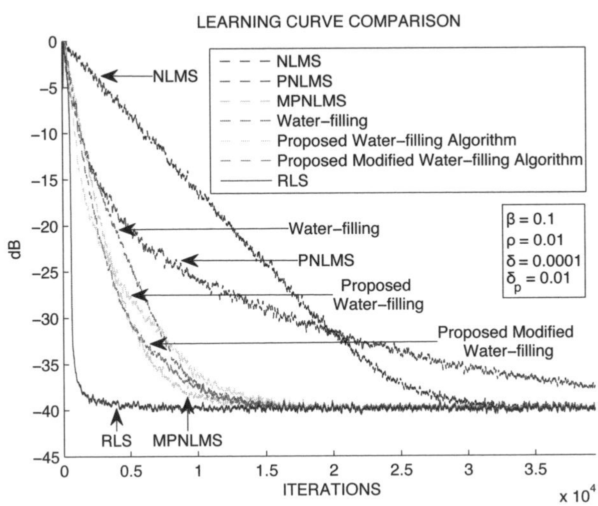

Figure 4.5. *Comparison of proposed water-filling algorithms for white input signal and sparse impulse response*

In Figure 4.6, the MSE is plotted for a white input signal and the non-sparse impulse response shown in Figure 4.3(b). The impulse response employed was generated by a zero-mean Gaussian process. The MPNLMS algorithm uses a value of $\mu = 7155$ with this impulse response. In this scenario, the two proposed algorithms have better convergence than the PNLMS algorithm and slower convergence than the NLMS.

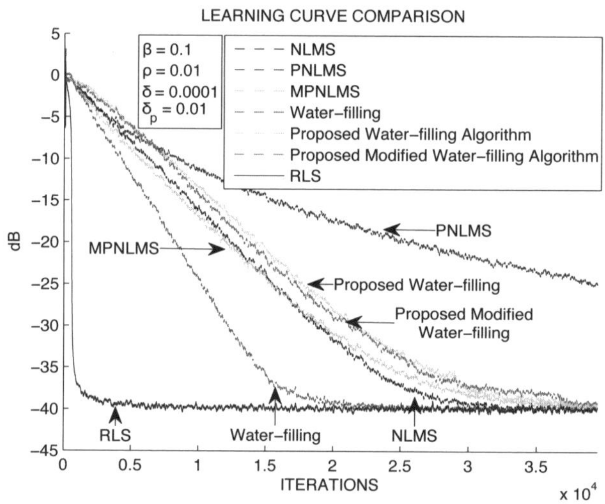

Figure 4.6. *Comparison of proposed water-filling algorithms for white input signal and dispersive impulse response*

The MSE performance for a time varying impulse response is shown in Figure 4.7. Here, at time 40,000, the impulse response is changed from the impulse response shown in Figure 4.2(b) to an alternate sparse impulse response that is shown in Figure 1.2(b). The proposed algorithms and RLS algorithm perform poorly after this change and would require additional reset logic to handle a time varying impulse response. This behavior was expected for the proposed algorithms due to the fact that the gain is based on all previous gains. After the change, the applied gain depends heavily on gains designed for the non-actual impulse response.

In Figures 4.8 and 4.9, the MSE performance is displayed for a colored input signal with moderate and strong coloration, respectively. The impulse response used in these simulations is given in Figure 4.2(b). The MPNLMS uses a value of $\mu = 4{,}115$ in Figure 4.8 and $\mu = 8{,}175$ in Figure 4.9. The input signal consists of colored noise generated by a single-pole system as follows:

$$x(k) = \gamma x(k-1) + n(k), \qquad [4.31]$$

where $x(0) = n(0)$, $n(k)$ is a white Gaussian random process with variance $\sigma_n^2 = 1$, and pole γ. In Figure 4.8, $\gamma = -0.5$ that implies $\sigma_x^2 = \sigma_n^2/(1-\gamma^2) = 1.333$. While in Figure 4.9, $\gamma = -0.9$ and $\sigma_x^2 = \sigma_n^2/(1-\gamma^2) = 5.263$. The water-filling algorithm is unstable in both of these figures. This is because the water-filling algorithm's derivation relies heavily on the assumption that the input signal is white. For moderate coloration, the proposed algorithms outperform the PNLMS and NLMS algorithms. For strong coloration, the proposed algorithms initially perform better than the NLMS and worse than the PNLMS algorithm.

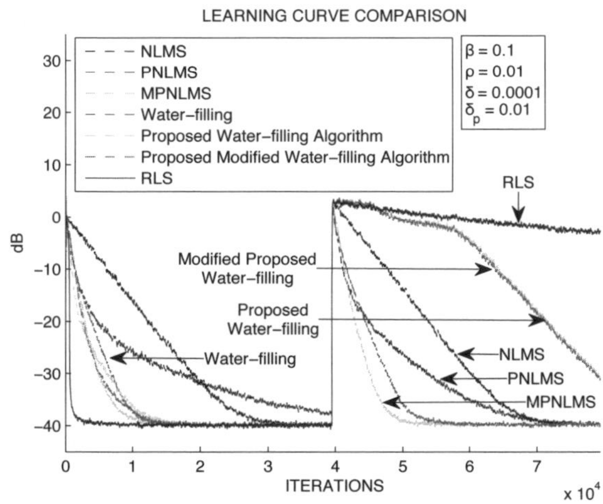

Figure 4.7. *Comparison of proposed water-filling algorithms for white input signal and a time varying sparse impulse response*

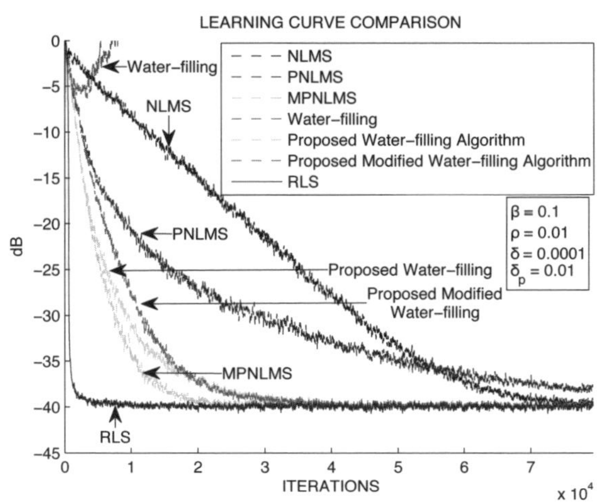

Figure 4.8. *Comparison of proposed water-filling algorithms for color input signal (pole = −0.5) and sparse impulse response*

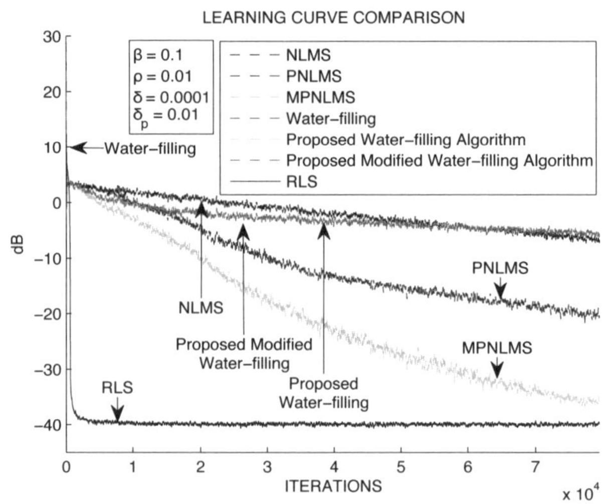

Figure 4.9. *Comparison of proposed water-filling algorithms for color input signal (pole = −0.9) and sparse impulse response*

4.3. PtNLMS algorithm obtained by minimization of the MSWD for colored input

The water-filling algorithm in section 4.1.1 was designed with the goal of minimizing the MSE by choosing optimal gains at each time step. This algorithm relied on the limiting assumption that the input signal was white. In this section, a colored water-filling (CWF) algorithm is derived and implemented that no longer requires that the input signal is white.

The algorithm results from minimizing the MSWD with respect to the gain. The implementation of this algorithm requires the estimation of the MWD and knowledge of the input signal covariance matrix. An estimation scheme for the MWD is given. One application of this algorithm is to perform system identification for echo cancellation.

4.3.1. *Optimal gain algorithm*

In this section, we seek the optimal gain at each time step k. Our approach to this problem is to minimize the MSWD with respect to the gain under the same two constraints given in section 4.1.1.

The recursion for the WD vector is defined by [3.2], that is

$$\mathbf{z}^+ = \mathbf{z} - \frac{\beta \mathbf{G}\mathbf{x}\mathbf{x}^T\mathbf{z}}{\mathbf{x}^T\mathbf{G}\mathbf{x} + \delta} - \frac{\beta \mathbf{G}\mathbf{x}v}{\mathbf{x}^T\mathbf{G}\mathbf{x} + \delta}. \quad [4.32]$$

Before proceeding further, let us state the assumptions that will be used in the following derivations. In addition to the independence assumptions 2.1 and 2.2, we have in place of the input, assumptions 2.3 or 3.1.

ASSUMPTION 4.2.– The input signal is a stationary Gaussian process with zero-mean and covariance matrix $\mathbf{R}$, where $[\mathbf{R}]_{ii} = \sigma_x^2$.

Hence, the input is no longer independent. Additionally, assumption 3.2 is still used. Now for

$$L >> \sqrt{2\mathbf{g}^T(\mathbf{R} \odot \mathbf{R})\mathbf{g}/\sigma_x^2}$$

the standard deviation of the term $\sum_{j=1}^{L} x_j^2 g_j + \delta$ becomes much smaller than the expected value, where $\odot$ represents the Hadamard product and $\mathbf{g} = \mathbf{diag}(\mathbf{G})$. A sufficient condition for this to assume is that

$$\mathcal{S} >> \frac{2\lambda_{\text{max}}(\mathbf{R})}{\sigma_x^2} \quad [4.33]$$

where $\mathcal{S}$ is the support size defined as

$$\mathcal{S} = \frac{[\sum_j g_j]^2}{\sum_j g_j^2} = \frac{L^2}{\sum_j g_j^2} \quad [4.34]$$

and $\lambda_{\text{max}}(\mathbf{R})$ is the largest eigenvalue of the covariance matrix $\mathbf{R}$. The condition in [4.33] is satisfied for large values of L, and $\mathbf{g}$ that is not extremely sparse. Hence, we can have it so that the denominator term is approximately constant.

As in section 4.1.1, we employ assumption 3.2 and use the definition $\beta_a = \beta/(L\sigma_x^2 + \delta)$. This allows us to rewrite the WD recursion as:

$$\mathbf{z}^+ = \mathbf{z} - \beta_a \mathbf{G}\mathbf{x}\mathbf{x}^T\mathbf{z} - \beta_a \mathbf{G}\mathbf{x}v. \quad [4.35]$$

Again, in this form the algorithm can be interpreted as a PtLMS algorithm.

4.3.1.1. *Optimal gain resulting from minimization of MSWD*

The criterion we try to minimize is the MSWD at time $k+1$. The square WD at time $k+1$ can be represented by:

$$\begin{aligned}\mathbf{z}^{+T}\mathbf{z}^{+} &= \mathbf{z}^T\mathbf{z} - \beta_a\mathbf{z}^T\mathbf{G}\mathbf{x}\mathbf{x}^T\mathbf{z} - \beta_a\mathbf{z}^T\mathbf{G}\mathbf{x}v\\ &-\beta_a\mathbf{z}^T\mathbf{x}\mathbf{x}^T\mathbf{G}\mathbf{z} + \beta_a^2\mathbf{z}^T\mathbf{x}\mathbf{x}^T\mathbf{G}^2\mathbf{x}\mathbf{x}^T\mathbf{z} + \beta_a^2\mathbf{z}^T\mathbf{x}\mathbf{x}^T\mathbf{G}^2\mathbf{x}v\\ &-\beta_a\mathbf{x}^T\mathbf{G}\mathbf{z}v + \beta_a^2\mathbf{x}^T\mathbf{G}^2\mathbf{x}\mathbf{x}^T\mathbf{z}v + \beta_a^2\mathbf{x}^T\mathbf{G}^2\mathbf{x}v^2.\end{aligned} \qquad [4.36]$$

Next, taking the expectation of [4.36] given the prior WD $\mathbf{z}$, and using assumption 4.3 yields:

$$\begin{aligned}E\left\{\mathbf{z}^{+T}\mathbf{z}^{+}|\mathbf{z}\right\} &= \mathbf{z}^T\mathbf{z} - 2\beta_a\mathbf{z}^T\mathbf{Diag}(\mathbf{R}\mathbf{z})\mathbf{g}\\ &+2\beta_a^2\mathbf{g}^T\mathbf{Diag}^2(\mathbf{R}\mathbf{z})\mathbf{g} + \beta_a^2\mathbf{z}^T\mathbf{R}\mathbf{z}\mathbf{g}^T\mathbf{Diag}\left[\mathbf{diag}(\mathbf{R})\right]\mathbf{g}\\ &+\beta_a^2\sigma_v^2\mathbf{g}^T\mathbf{Diag}\left[\mathbf{diag}(\mathbf{R})\right]\mathbf{g}.\end{aligned} \qquad [4.37]$$

ASSUMPTION 4.3.– The gain $\mathbf{g}$ depends only on the WD vector $\mathbf{z}$.

In [WAG 09] and earlier in assumption 4.1, we assumed that the gain was a deterministic function of time and took the expectation with respect to the input and prior WDs instead of assuming the prior WDs are given and $\mathbf{g}$ is only a function of $\mathbf{z}$. We could work in this way now, but the resulting feasible algorithm would be the same regardless of which set of the assumptions are used.

Next, we make the substitution $\mathbf{g} = \mathbf{s} \odot \mathbf{s}$ to ensure the solution $g_i \geq 0 \;\forall\, i$ ($\mathbf{s}$ is real) and construct the Lagrangian:

$$\begin{aligned}T(\mathbf{s},\lambda) &= \mathbf{z}^T\mathbf{z} - 2\beta_a\mathbf{z}^T\mathbf{Diag}(\mathbf{R}\mathbf{z})(\mathbf{s}\odot\mathbf{s}) + 2\beta_a^2\left(\mathbf{s}\odot\mathbf{s}\right)^T\mathbf{Diag}^2(\mathbf{R}\mathbf{z})(\mathbf{s}\odot\mathbf{s})\\ &+\beta_a^2\mathbf{z}^T\mathbf{R}\mathbf{z}\left(\mathbf{s}\odot\mathbf{s}\right)^T\mathbf{Diag}\left[\mathbf{diag}(\mathbf{R})\right](\mathbf{s}\odot\mathbf{s})\\ &+\beta_a^2\sigma_v^2\left(\mathbf{s}\odot\mathbf{s}\right)^T\mathbf{Diag}\left[\mathbf{diag}(\mathbf{R})\right](\mathbf{s}\odot\mathbf{s})\\ &+\lambda\left(\mathbf{1}^T(\mathbf{s}\odot\mathbf{s}) - L\right)\end{aligned} \qquad [4.38]$$

where $\mathbf{1}$ is again the $L \times 1$ vector of ones.

We can calculate the gradient and Hessian of the Lagrangian that are given by:

$$\begin{aligned}\frac{\partial T(\mathbf{s},\lambda)}{\partial \mathbf{s}} &= \{2\lambda - 4\beta_a\mathbf{Diag}\left[\mathbf{z}\odot\mathbf{R}\mathbf{z}\right] + 8\beta_a^2\mathbf{Diag}\left[\mathbf{R}\mathbf{z}\odot\mathbf{R}\mathbf{z}\odot(\mathbf{s}\odot\mathbf{s})\right]\\ &+ 4\beta_a^2\mathbf{z}^T\mathbf{R}\mathbf{z}\sigma_x^2\mathbf{Diag}\left(\mathbf{s}\odot\mathbf{s}\right) + 4\beta_a^2\sigma_x^2\sigma_v^2\mathbf{Diag}\left(\mathbf{s}\odot\mathbf{s}\right)\Big\}\,\mathbf{s}\end{aligned} \qquad [4.39]$$

and

$$\frac{\partial^2 T(\mathbf{s},\lambda)}{\partial \mathbf{s}^T \partial \mathbf{s}} = 2\lambda\mathbf{I} - 4\beta_a \mathbf{Diag}\left[\mathbf{z}\odot\mathbf{Rz}\right] + 8\beta_a^2 \mathbf{Diag}\left[\mathbf{Rz}\odot\mathbf{Rz}\odot(\mathbf{s}\odot\mathbf{s})\right]$$
$$+4\beta_a^2\mathbf{z}^T\mathbf{Rz}\sigma_x^2\mathbf{Diag}\left(\mathbf{s}\odot\mathbf{s}\right) + 4\beta_a^2\sigma_x^2\sigma_v^2\mathbf{Diag}\left(\mathbf{s}\odot\mathbf{s}\right)$$
$$+2\mathbf{diag}(\mathbf{s})\left\{8\beta_a^2\mathbf{Diag}\left[\mathbf{Rz}\odot\mathbf{Rz}\right] + 4\beta_a^2\mathbf{z}^T\mathbf{Rz}\sigma_x^2\mathbf{I} + 4\beta_a^2\sigma_x^2\sigma_v^2\mathbf{I}\right\}. \quad [4.40]$$

To aid in finding minimums of the Lagrangian, we rewrite equations [4.39] and [4.40] in component-wise form as follows:

$$\frac{\partial T(\mathbf{s},\lambda)}{\partial s_i} = \{2\lambda - 4\beta_a z_i\left[\mathbf{Rz}\right]_i$$
$$+8\beta_a^2\left[\mathbf{Rz}\right]_i^2 s_i^2 + 4\beta_a^2\mathbf{z}^T\mathbf{Rz}\sigma_x^2 s_i^2 + 4\beta_a^2\sigma_x^2\sigma_v^2 s_i^2\}\, s_i \quad [4.41]$$

and

$$\frac{\partial^2 T(\mathbf{s},\lambda)}{\partial s_i^2} = 2\lambda - 4\beta_a z_i\left[\mathbf{Rz}\right]_i + 8\beta_a^2\left[\mathbf{Rz}\right]_i^2 s_i^2$$
$$+ 4\beta_a^2\mathbf{z}^T\mathbf{Rz}\sigma_x^2 s_i^2 + 4\beta_a^2\sigma_x^2\sigma_v^2 s_i^2$$
$$+ 2\left\{8\beta_a^2\left[\mathbf{Rz}\right]_i^2 + 4\beta_a^2\mathbf{z}^T\mathbf{Rz}\sigma_x^2 + 4\beta_a^2\sigma_x^2\sigma_v^2\right\} s_i^2. \quad [4.42]$$

Examining the component-wise form of the gradient, there are two solutions

$$s_i^2 = 0$$
$$s_i^2 = \frac{4\beta_a z_i\left[\mathbf{Rz}\right]_i - 2\lambda}{8\beta_a^2\left[\mathbf{Rz}\right]_i^2 + 4\beta_a^2\mathbf{z}^T\mathbf{Rz}\sigma_x^2 + 4\beta_a^2\sigma_x^2\sigma_v^2}. \quad [4.43]$$

By substituting the first solution into the component-wise form of the Hessian, it turns out the first solution results in minimum when $\lambda - 2\beta_a z_i\left[\mathbf{Rz}\right]_i > 0$ and a maximum when $\lambda - 2\beta_a z_i\left[\mathbf{Rz}\right]_i < 0$. In contrast, when the second candidate solution is substituted into the component-wise form of the Hessian, a minimum occurs when $\lambda - 2\beta_a z_i\left[\mathbf{Rz}\right]_i < 0$ and no solution exists when $\lambda - 2\beta_a z_i\left[\mathbf{Rz}\right]_i > 0$. As a result, the gain that minimizes the MSWD at time $k+1$ can be written as:

$$g_i = \left(\frac{2\beta_a z_i\left[\mathbf{Rz}\right]_i - \lambda}{4\beta_a^2\left[\mathbf{Rz}\right]_i^2 + 2\beta_a^2\mathbf{z}^T\mathbf{Rz}\sigma_x^2 + 2\beta_a^2\sigma_x^2\sigma_v^2}\right)_+. \quad [4.44]$$

Now the solution can be obtained by a water-filling algorithm similar to the solution proposed for the white input case in section 4.1.1. First, make the following definitions:

$$c_i = 2\beta_a z_i \left[\mathbf{Rz}\right]_i$$
$$q_i = 4\beta_a^2 \left[\mathbf{Rz}\right]_i^2 + 2\beta_a^2 \mathbf{z}^T \mathbf{Rz} \sigma_x^2 + 2\beta_a^2 \sigma_x^2 \sigma_v^2. \qquad [4.45]$$

Next, find the constant λ according to the following procedure. First, we sort the entries of $\mathbf{c} = [c_1, c_2, \ldots c_L]^T$ in ascending order to form a new vector such that $c_{(1)} < c_{(2)} < \ldots < c_{(L)}$. We subsequently rearrange the elements of $\mathbf{q} = [q_1, q_2, \ldots q_L]^T$ to match the position of the original indices in the sorted $\mathbf{c}$ and to form a new vector whose elements are $q_{(1)}$, $q_{(2)}$, …, $q_{(L)}$. The optimal value of λ solves the following equation:

$$\sum_{j=1}^{L} \left(\frac{c_{(j)} - \lambda}{q_{(j)}} \right)_+ = L. \qquad [4.46]$$

From [4.46] the candidate solutions are

$$\lambda_i = \frac{\sum_{j=i}^{L} \frac{c_{(j)}}{q_{(j)}} - L}{\sum_{j=i}^{L} \frac{1}{q_{(j)}}}. \qquad [4.47]$$

We choose $\lambda = \lambda_i$ if $c_{(i-1)} < \lambda_i < c_{(i)}$, where $c_{(0)} = -\infty$.

4.3.1.2. *Implementation*

The algorithm presented so far is not feasible because it requires the knowledge of $z_i \left[\mathbf{Rz}\right]_i$, $\left[\mathbf{Rz}\right]_i^2$ and $\mathbf{z}^T\mathbf{Rz}$. We propose replacing these quantities with an estimate of their corresponding mean values.

We begin with

$$E\{\mathbf{p}\} = E\{\mathbf{x}e\} = E\{\mathbf{x}(\mathbf{x}^T\mathbf{z} + v)\} = \mathbf{R}E\left\{\mathbf{z}\right\} \qquad [4.48]$$

then $E\left\{\mathbf{z}\right\} = \mathbf{R}^{-1}E\left\{\mathbf{p}\right\}$. We update our estimate of $E\left\{\mathbf{p}\right\}$ in the following fashion:

$$\widehat{E\left\{\mathbf{p}\right\}} = \alpha \widehat{E\left\{\mathbf{p}^-\right\}} + (1-\alpha)\mathbf{p},$$

where $0 < \alpha < 1$. Then, we make the estimate $\widehat{E\left\{\mathbf{z}\right\}} = \mathbf{R}^{-1}\widehat{E\left\{\mathbf{p}\right\}}$.

Now, we make three approximations by replacing

$$z_i[\mathbf{Rz}]_i \approx \widehat{E\{z_i\}}\widehat{E\{p_i\}}$$
$$[\mathbf{Rz}]_i^2 \approx \left[\widehat{E\{p_i\}}\right]^2$$
$$\mathbf{z}^T\mathbf{Rz} \approx \widehat{E\{\mathbf{z}^T\}}\mathbf{R}\widehat{E\{\mathbf{z}\}}.$$

Note that these estimates are only approximate and good when the variance of z_i is small compared to the mean of z_i that is typically true in the transient regime.

If α is chosen too large (that is close to 1), the transient performance can be unsatisfactory. Conversely, if α is set too small, the steady-state error will be large. One solution to this problem is to use the adaptive convex gain combination presented in section 4.1.3.2.

4.3.2. *Relationship between minimization of MSE and MSWD*

Let the MSE at time $k+1$ be represented by $J(k+1) = J^+$. The MSE can be written as:

$$J^+ = \sigma_v^2 + E\{(\mathbf{x}^+)^T\mathbf{z}^+(\mathbf{z}^+)^T\mathbf{x}^+\}. \qquad [4.49]$$

Applying assumption 2.1, we can take the expectation with respect to the input signal first that yields

$$J^+ = \sigma_v^2 + E_{\mathbf{z}}\{(\mathbf{z}^+)^T\mathbf{Rz}^+\}. \qquad [4.50]$$

Next, applying the Cauchy–Schwarz inequality gives:

$$J^+ \leq \sigma_v^2 + \sqrt{E_{\mathbf{z}}\{(\mathbf{z}^+)^T\mathbf{z}^+\}}\sqrt{E_{\mathbf{z}}\{(\mathbf{z}^+)^T\mathbf{R}^2\mathbf{z}^+\}}. \qquad [4.51]$$

Let $\lambda_{\max}(\mathbf{R})$ represent the largest eigenvalue of the covariance matrix $\mathbf{R}$. Then, we can write

$$\begin{aligned} J^+ &\leq \sigma_v^2 + \sqrt{E_{\mathbf{z}}\{(\mathbf{z}^+)^T\mathbf{z}^+\}}\sqrt{E_{\mathbf{z}}\{\lambda_{max}^2(\mathbf{R})(\mathbf{z}^+)^T\mathbf{z}^+\}} \\ &= \sigma_v^2 + E_{\mathbf{z}}\{(\mathbf{z}^+)^T\mathbf{z}^+\}\lambda_{\max}(\mathbf{R}). \end{aligned} \qquad [4.52]$$

Hence, by minimizing the MSWD, we minimize an upper bound for J^+.

4.3.3. *Simulation results*

In Figures 4.10 and 4.11, we show the misalignment and MSE for the NLMS, PNLMS, MPNLMS, color water-filling and ideal color water-filling algorithms with $\beta = 0.02$, $\rho = 0.01$, $\sigma_v^2 = 10^{-4}$, $\delta = 10^{-4}$, $\delta_p = 0.01$ and $L = 50$, respectively. The misalignment at time k is defined by $M(k) = \mathbf{z}^T\mathbf{z}/\mathbf{w}^T\mathbf{w}$. The MPNLMS used the value 22,941 in the μ-law. The ideal color water-filling algorithm uses the instantaneous value of the WD, $\mathbf{z}(k) = \mathbf{w} - \hat{\mathbf{w}}(k)$, as the input to the water-filling algorithm. The color water-filling algorithm uses the implementation described in section 4.3.1.2 with $(\omega,\alpha) = (5, 0.999)$. The impulse response used in this simulation is given in Figure 4.12. The input signal consists of colored noise generated by the single-pole system given in [4.31] with $\gamma = -0.9$, $x(0) = n(0)$ and $n(k)$ is a white Gaussian random variable with variance $\sigma_n^2 = 1$. Therefore, $\sigma_x^2 = \sigma_n^2/(1-\gamma^2) = 5.263$.

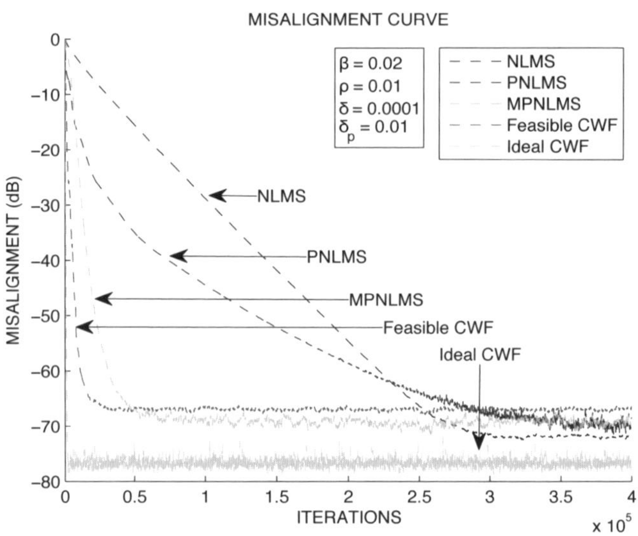

Figure 4.10. *Misalignment comparison*

The NLMS algorithm has the slowest convergence followed by the PNLMS algorithm and then the MPNLMS algorithm. The feasible and ideal CWF algorithms offer significant improvement in the convergence rate relative to the other algorithms.

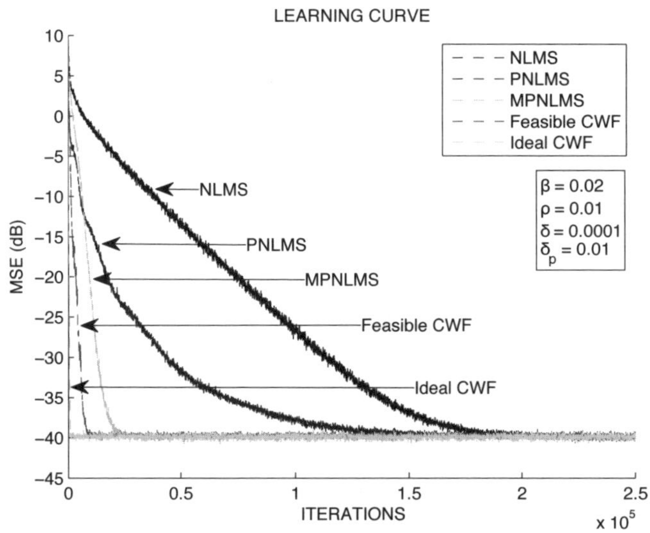

Figure 4.11. *MSE comparison*

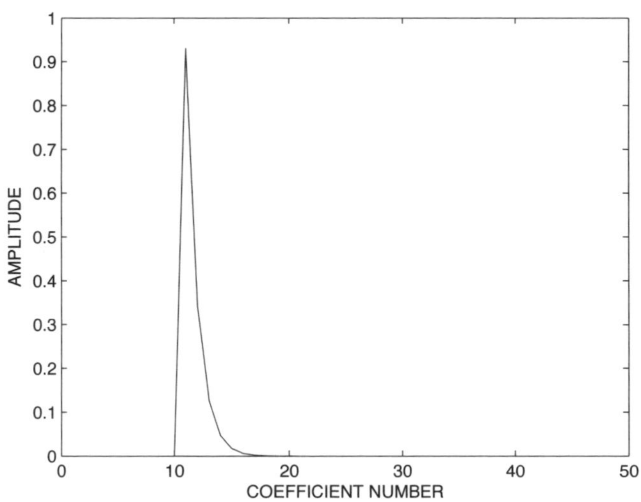

Figure 4.12. *Impulse response*

4.4. Reduced computational complexity suboptimal gain allocation for PtNLMS algorithm with colored input

The water-filling algorithm was designed with the goal of minimizing the MSE by choosing optimal gains at each time step. This algorithm relied on the limiting assumption that the input signal is white. A CWF algorithm was derived and implemented that no longer requires that the input signal be white. This algorithm resulted from minimizing the MSWD with respect to the gain. The implementation of this algorithm required the estimation of the MWD and knowledge of the input signal covariance matrix. In this section, two suboptimal algorithms are introduced for gain allocation in the colored input case. Each algorithm offers a reduction in computational complexity by removing the sorting function needed in the original algorithm.

4.4.1. *Suboptimal gain allocation algorithms*

The first suboptimal gain allocation uses the following gain

$$g_i = \frac{|\widehat{E\{z_i\}}\,\widehat{E\{p_i\}}|}{\frac{1}{L}\sum_{j=1}^{L}|\widehat{E\{z_j\}}\,\widehat{E\{p_j\}}|} \quad [4.53]$$

while the second suboptimal algorithm uses

$$g_i = \frac{\widehat{E\{p_i\}}^2}{\frac{1}{L}\sum_{j=1}^{L}\widehat{E\{p_j\}}^2}, \quad [4.54]$$

where $\widehat{E\{z_i\}}$ and $\widehat{E\{p_i\}}$ are defined in section 4.3.1. Both of these suboptimal algorithms avoid the sorting operation. The former algorithm will be referred to as the suboptimal gain allocation version 1 and the latter algorithm as the suboptimal gain allocation version 2. Suboptimal gain allocation version 2 is simpler than suboptimal gain allocation version 1 because it does not require multiplication with $\mathbf{R}^{-1}$ in order to form $\mathbf{g}$.

4.4.1.1. *Adaptive convex gain combination revisited*

In section 4.1.3.2, the mixing parameter was related to an estimate of the mean square deviation error that involves the calculation $\widehat{E\{\mathbf{z}\}} = \mathbf{R}^{-1}\widehat{E\{\mathbf{p}\}}$. This matrix multiplication is computationally complex. In an effort to make the algorithm implementation computationally less complex, we propose the following mixing parameter:

$$\zeta = \min\left[1, \frac{\omega\sigma_v^2}{\widehat{E\{e^2\}}}\right] \quad [4.55]$$

where $\omega \geq 0$,

$$\widehat{E\{e^2\}} = \psi \widehat{E\{(e^-)^2\}} + (1-\psi)e^2,$$

and $0 < \psi < 1$. The denominator term in [4.55] is related to an estimate of the MSE. Hence, as the estimated MSE approaches zero, the algorithm acts more like the NLMS by equally distributing gain to all coefficients. When the estimated MSE is large relative to σ_v^2, then the algorithm inherits the characteristics of CWF algorithm. Now, α can be chosen to ensure satisfactory transient performance. This implementation avoids the matrix multiplication required to calculate $\widehat{E\{\mathbf{z}\}}$.

4.4.2. *Simulation results*

In this section, we compare the learning curves for the NLMS, PNLMS, MPNLMS, CWF, ideal CWF, suboptimal gain allocation version 1 and suboptimal gain allocation version 2 algorithms with two different input signals. In the first example, colored noise generated by a single-pole system was the input signal. In the second example, speech was the input signal.

The following parameters were used in both Monte Carlo simulations, $\beta = 0.05$, $\rho = 0.01$, $\sigma_v^2 = 10^{-4}$, $\delta = 10^{-4}$ and $\delta_p = 0.01$, respectively. The ideal color water-filling algorithm uses the instantaneous value of the WD, $\mathbf{z}(k) = \mathbf{w} - \hat{\mathbf{w}}(k)$, as the input to the water-filling algorithm. The feasible color water-filling algorithms use the implementation described in sections 4.3.1.2 and 4.4.1.1 with $(\omega, \alpha, \psi) = (5, 0.99, 0.9)$.

4.4.2.1. *Single-pole input signal*

In this section, the input signal consists of colored noise generated by a single-pole system as [4.31], where $\gamma = -0.65$, $x(0) = n(0)$ and $n(k)$ is a white Gaussian random variable with variance $\sigma_n^2 = 1$. Therefore, $\sigma_x^2 = \sigma_n^2/(1-\gamma^2) = 1.7316$. The impulse response used in this simulation is shown in Figure 4.2(b). This impulse response has length $L = 512$ and corresponds to a real-world network echo path. For this example, the MPNLMS used the value 46,894 in the μ-law. The learning curves associated with the colored input signal are shown in Figure 4.13. A total of 10 Monte Carlo trials were used to generate these curves. The ideal CWF algorithm provides the best performance followed by the feasible implementation of the CWF algorithm. Both suboptimal algorithms offer improved convergence relative to the NLMS, PNLMS and MPNLMS algorithms for moderate input signal coloration.

4.4.2.2. *Speech input signal*

In this section, the learning curves are displayed when speech is the input signal. The CWF, ideal CWF and suboptimal gain allocation version 1 algorithms require knowledge of the input signal's covariance matrix. Because the input signal's covariance $\mathbf{R}$ is unknown when speech is the input signal, an estimate is generated in the following fashion:

$$\hat{\mathbf{R}}(k) = \varrho\hat{\mathbf{R}}(k-1) + (1-\varrho)\mathbf{x}\mathbf{x}^T, \quad [4.56]$$

where $0 < \varrho < 1$. For the simulation presented here, the value $\varrho = 0.98$ was used. Additionally, the CWF and suboptimal gain allocation version 1 both require the calculation of the inverse covariance matrix. Since the estimate $\hat{\mathbf{R}}(k)$ can be singular, we can find the pseudo-inverse of $\hat{\mathbf{R}}(k)$ and substitute this into the algorithms where necessary. The impulse used in this simulation is shown in Figure 4.12. For this example, the MPNLMS used the value 874 in the μ-law. The speech input signal and associated learning curve results are shown in Figures 4.14(a) and 4.14(b), respectively. Additionally, the learning curve results after averaging 100 uniform shifts of the input signal are shown in Figure 4.15.

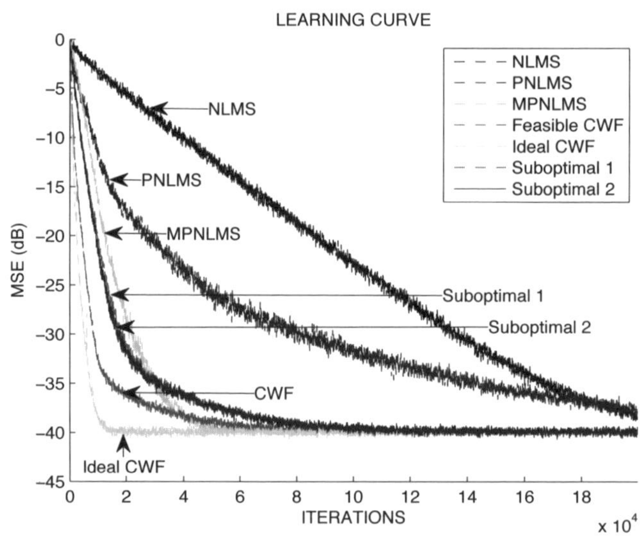

Figure 4.13. *MSE comparison*

Again the ideal CWF algorithm provides the best performance. Of the feasible algorithms, the CWF algorithm performs the best in the initial stages of convergence; however, the PNLMS algorithm eventually outperforms it. The two suboptimal algorithms have poor performance in the non-stationary input signal environment.

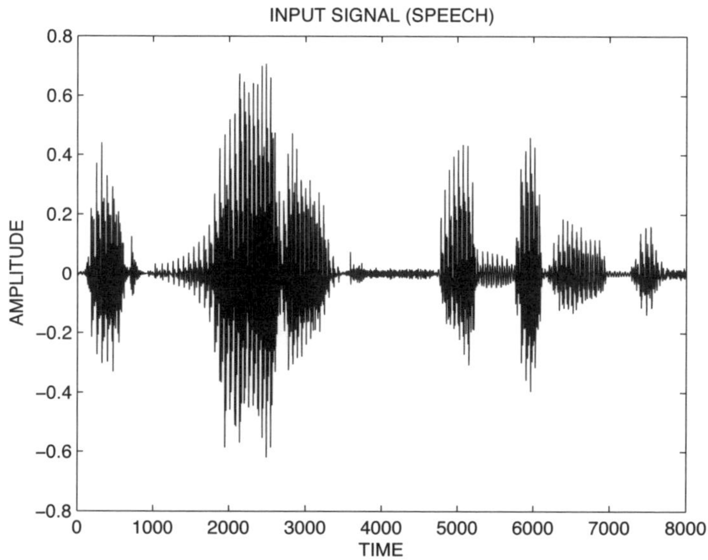

a)

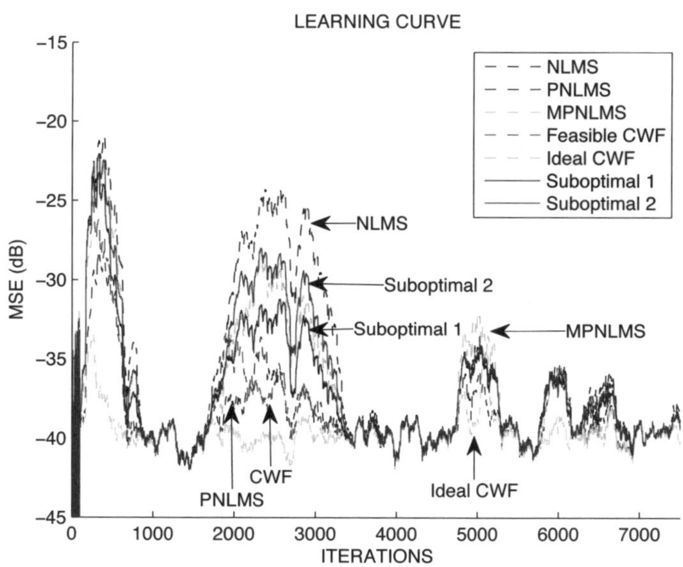

b)

Figure 4.14. *a) Input speech signal and b) MSE comparison for speech*

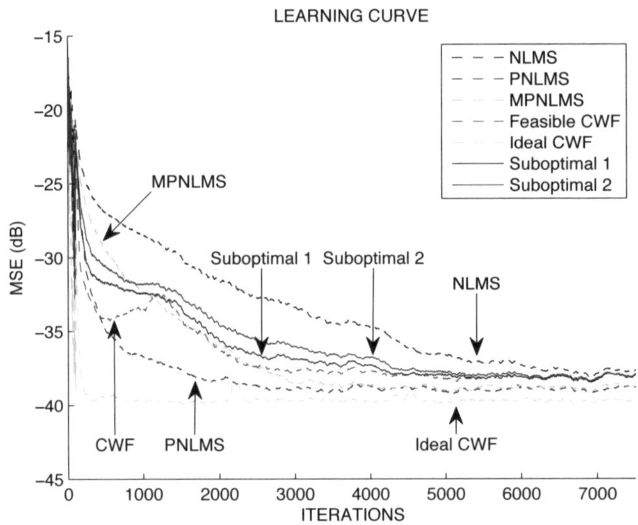

Figure 4.15. *MSE comparison for speech (averaged over 100 uniform shifts of the input signal)*

4.5. Summary

This chapter presented algorithms that attempt to find an optimal gain such that a user-defined criterion is minimized.

In section 4.1, the water-filling algorithm for white input signals was developed by choosing gains at each time step in a manner that minimized the MSE. Additionally, the z^2-proportionate algorithm was generated by simplifying the water-filling algorithm. Through simulation in white input scenarios, it was shown that the water-filling and z^2-proportionate algorithms have better learning curve convergence rates when compared to other standard algorithms such as the PNLMS and NLMS algorithms.

The focus of section 4.2 was on finding optimal gains that minimized the MSE of a proportionate steepest descent algorithm for white input signals. With increasing time, the optimal time averaged gains tend to be uniformly distributed along the coefficients. Two PtNLMS algorithms based on the estimate of the optimal time averaged gains are designed. The second algorithm developed is an approximation that is computationally less complex. Numerical examples showed that the new algorithms had faster convergence than the NLMS and PNLMS algorithms when the input is white, and the impulse response is sparse and time invariant.

In section 4.3, the CWF algorithm was introduced. This algorithm provides gains at each time step in a manner that tries to minimize the MSWD. Through simulation in colored input scenarios, it was shown that the feasible and ideal CWF algorithms have impressively better learning curve and misalignment convergence rates relative to other standard algorithms such as the MPNLMS, PNLMS and NLMS algorithms, when the steady-state errors are of the same level.

Finally, section 4.4 presented two suboptimal algorithms for gain allocation in the colored input case. Each algorithm offers a reduction in computational complexity by removing the sorting function needed in the original algorithm. For stationary colored input signals the suboptimal algorithms offer improved MSE convergence performance relative to other standard algorithms such the NLMS, PNLMS and MPNLMS. For non-stationary input signals, the suboptimal algorithms do not provide improved MSE convergence performance relative to standard algorithms. The suboptimal algorithms' parameters could potentially be tuned to provide better convergence performance.

5

Probability Density of WD for PtLMS Algorithms

Up to this point, we have been attempting to analyze both the transient and steady-state performance of a wide array of PtNLMS algorithms. These algorithms have been analyzed in Chapter 3 (also see [WAG 08]) by assuming the WD recursion that involves Gaussian quantities. Then, the recursions for the mean and second moment of the WD can be calculated and used to describe the evolution of the PtNLMS algorithm in time. However, the assumption of Gaussianity is not necessarily good for all types of PtNLMS algorithms. Therefore, a more accurate calculation of the PDF is needed. Ideally, algorithm designers would have knowledge of both the joint and conditional PDFs at any time allowing them to control algorithm properties. The conditional PDF is derived and presented here with the same goal of manipulating the convergence properties of the algorithm. Finally, the conditional PDF can be used to derive the steady-state joint PDF. The steady-state joint PDF has typically been assumed to be Gaussian in most literature; however, this is not necessarily a good assumption as shown in this chapter.

5.1. Proportionate-type least mean square algorithms

5.1.1. *Weight deviation recursion*

We begin by introducing the WD recursion for the PtLMS algorithm. The detail of the PtLMS algorithm is given in Table 5.1.

For notational simplicity, again we denote $\mathbf{z}(k+1)$, $\mathbf{z}(k)$, $\mathbf{x}(k)$, $g_l[\hat{\mathbf{w}}(k)]$, $v(k)$, $\sigma_v^2(k)$ by $\mathbf{z}^+$, $\mathbf{z}$, $\mathbf{x}$, g_l, v, σ_v^2, respectively.

We can express the recursion for the WD in component-wise form as expressed in equation [4.1]. Examining the PtLMS algorithm instead of the PtNLMS algorithm eases analysis and facilitates derivation of theoretical results.

Before proceeding, we use the following assumptions:

$\mathbf{x}(k)$	$=$	$[x(k), x(k-1), \ldots, x(k-L+1)]^T$
$\hat{y}(k)$	$=$	$\mathbf{x}^T(k)\hat{\mathbf{w}}(k)$
$e(k)$	$=$	$d(k) - \hat{y}(k)$
$g_l[\hat{\mathbf{w}}(k)]$	$\geq$	$0 \,\forall\, l \in \{1, 2, \ldots, L\}$. Specified by the user.
$\mathbf{G}(k)$	$=$	$\mathbf{Diag}\{g_1[\hat{\mathbf{w}}(k)], \ldots, g_L[\hat{\mathbf{w}}(k)]\}$
$\hat{\mathbf{w}}(k+1)$	$=$	$\hat{\mathbf{w}}(k) + \beta\mathbf{G}(k)\mathbf{x}(k)e(k)$

Table 5.1. *PtLMS algorithm with time-varying stepsize matrix*

ASSUMPTION 5.1.– The input signal is a Gaussian process with zero-mean and covariance matrix $\mathbf{R}(k)$.

In contrast to assumption 4.2, the input is not assumed stationary now. For notational convenience, $\mathbf{R}(k)$ is represented by $\mathbf{R}$.

ASSUMPTION 5.2.– The input $\mathbf{x}(k)$ at time k and weight deviation vectors at time k and all previous times, $\mathbf{z}(0)$, $\mathbf{z}(1)$, ..., $\mathbf{z}(k)$, are independent.

Note that this assumption is a strengthened version of assumption 2.1.

ASSUMPTION 5.3.– The measurement noise $v(k)$ is white Gaussian random process with zero-mean, variance $\sigma_v^2(k)$, and it is independent of the input.

Compared to assumption 2.2, here the stationarity is not assumed. On the other hand, $v(k)$ is now considered Gaussian, which was not the case before.

Next, an expression for the conditional PDF, $f(\mathbf{z}^+|\mathbf{z})$, is derived.

5.2. Derivation of the Conditional PDF of WD for the PtLMS algorithm

In this section, the conditional PDF of the current WDs given the preceding WDs is generated for a wide array of PtLMS algorithms. The conditional PDF is derived for colored input signals when noise is present as well as when noise is absent. In addition, the marginal conditional PDF for WDs is derived. Finally, potential applications of the derived conditional probability distributions are discussed and examples finding the steady-state probability distributions are presented.

5.2.1. *Conditional PDF derivation*

5.2.1.1. *Derivation of the joint conditional PDF*

Start by rearranging equation [4.1] as

$$z_i - z_i^+ = \beta_a g_i x_i (\sum_{j=1}^{L} x_j z_j + v). \qquad [5.1]$$

Defining $y_i = (z_i - z_i^+)/(\beta_a g_i)$ and $t = \sum_{j=1}^{L} x_j z_j + v$ yields $y_i = x_i t$. Note that $\mathbf{z}$ is assumed to be a known vector independent of $\mathbf{x}$ and v. We know that the distribution of t is Gaussian since it is the sum of Gaussian random variables, i.e. $t \sim \mathcal{N}(0, \sigma_t^2)$, where $\sigma_t^2 = \mathbf{z}^T\mathbf{R}\mathbf{z} + \sigma_v^2$.

Define the joint PDF of the random vector $\mathbf{y} = [y_1, y_2, \ldots y_L]^T$ as $f_{\mathbf{y}}(\boldsymbol{\nu})$ and the PDF of t as $f_t(\tau)$. Next, express the PDF of $\mathbf{y}$ in terms of the joint PDF of $(\mathbf{x}, t)$ as follows:

$$f_{\mathbf{y}}(\boldsymbol{\nu}) = \int_{-\infty}^{\infty} f_{\mathbf{y}}(\boldsymbol{\nu}|t = \tau) f_t(\tau) d\tau = \int_{-\infty}^{\infty} \frac{1}{|\tau|^L} f_{\mathbf{x},t}(\boldsymbol{\nu}/\tau, \tau) d\tau. \qquad [5.2]$$

$(\mathbf{x}, t)$ is jointly Gaussian with PDF given by:

$$f_{\mathbf{x},t}(\boldsymbol{\xi}, \tau) = \frac{1}{[(2\pi)^{L+1}\det(\mathbf{P})]^{\frac{1}{2}}} e^{-\frac{1}{2}[\boldsymbol{\xi}^T,\tau]\mathbf{P}^{-1}[\boldsymbol{\xi}^T,\tau]^T}$$

where $\mathbf{P}$ is the covariance matrix of $[\mathbf{x}, t]^T$ and $\det(\mathbf{P})$ is the determinant of the matrix $\mathbf{P}$. The covariance matrix $\mathbf{P}$ can be written as:

$$\mathbf{P} = \begin{bmatrix} \mathbf{R} & \mathbf{R}\mathbf{z} \\ \mathbf{z}^T\mathbf{R} & \mathbf{z}^T\mathbf{R}\mathbf{z} + \sigma_v^2 \end{bmatrix}.$$

To calculate the determinant and the inverse of $\mathbf{P}$, we rewrite $\mathbf{P}$ as:

$$\mathbf{P} = \begin{bmatrix} \mathbf{I} & \mathbf{0} \\ \mathbf{z}^T & 1 \end{bmatrix} \begin{bmatrix} \mathbf{R} & \mathbf{0} \\ \mathbf{0}^T & \sigma_v^2 \end{bmatrix} \begin{bmatrix} \mathbf{I} & \mathbf{z} \\ \mathbf{0}^T & 1 \end{bmatrix}.$$

The determinant can be found to be $\det(\mathbf{P}) = \sigma_v^2 \det(\mathbf{R})$.

Next, the inverse of the covariance matrix can be calculated as:

$$\mathbf{P}^{-1} = \begin{bmatrix} \mathbf{I} & \mathbf{0} \\ \mathbf{z}^T & 1 \end{bmatrix}^{-1} \begin{bmatrix} \mathbf{R}^{-1} & \mathbf{0} \\ \mathbf{0}^T & \frac{1}{\sigma_v^2} \end{bmatrix} \begin{bmatrix} \mathbf{I} & \mathbf{z} \\ \mathbf{0}^T & 1 \end{bmatrix}^{-1}.$$

It can be shown that

$$\begin{bmatrix} \mathbf{I} & \mathbf{0} \\ \mathbf{z}^T & 1 \end{bmatrix}^{-1} = \begin{bmatrix} \mathbf{I} & \mathbf{0} \\ -\mathbf{z}^T & 1 \end{bmatrix}$$

and

$$\begin{bmatrix} \mathbf{I} & \mathbf{z} \\ \mathbf{0}^T & 1 \end{bmatrix}^{-1} = \begin{bmatrix} \mathbf{I} & -\mathbf{z} \\ \mathbf{0}^T & 1 \end{bmatrix}.$$

Using these relationship yields:

$$\mathbf{P}^{-1} = \begin{bmatrix} \mathbf{R}^{-1} + \mathbf{z}\mathbf{z}^T & -\frac{\mathbf{z}}{\sigma_v^2} \\ -\frac{\mathbf{z}^T}{\sigma_v^2} & \frac{1}{\sigma_v^2} \end{bmatrix}. \qquad [5.3]$$

With this information, we can represent the joint PDF of $\mathbf{y}$ as:

$$f_{\mathbf{y}}(\boldsymbol{\nu}) = \frac{2e^{\frac{\mathbf{z}^T\boldsymbol{\nu}}{\sigma_v^2}}}{(2\pi)^{\frac{L+1}{2}}\sigma_v[\det(\mathbf{R})]^{\frac{1}{2}}} \int_0^{\infty} e^{-\frac{1}{2}\{[\boldsymbol{\nu}^T\mathbf{R}^{-1}\boldsymbol{\nu} + \frac{(\boldsymbol{\nu}^T\mathbf{z})^2}{\sigma_v^2}]\frac{1}{\tau^2} + \frac{1}{\sigma_v^2}\tau^2\}} \frac{d\tau}{\tau^L}. \qquad [5.4]$$

For notational convenience, let $\alpha = \boldsymbol{\nu}^T\mathbf{R}^{-1}\boldsymbol{\nu} + \frac{(\boldsymbol{\nu}^T\mathbf{z})^2}{\sigma_v^2}$ and $\gamma = 1/\sigma_v^2$.

5.2.1.1.1. Evaluation of integral [5.4]

To evaluate the integral in [5.4] substitute $\tau = e^u$, which yields:

$$I = \int_{-\infty}^{\infty} e^{-\frac{1}{2}\{\alpha e^{-2u} + \gamma e^{2u}\}} \frac{e^u du}{e^{Lu}}. \qquad [5.5]$$

Next, using the identity

$$\alpha e^{-2u} + \gamma e^{2u} = (\alpha + \gamma)\cosh(2u) - (\alpha - \gamma)\sinh(2u) \qquad [5.6]$$

results in

$$I = \int_{-\infty}^{\infty} e^{-\frac{\alpha+\gamma}{2}\cosh(2u) + \frac{\alpha-\gamma}{2}\sinh(2u) - (L-1)u} du. \qquad [5.7]$$

At this stage, let

$$\frac{\alpha + \gamma}{2} = \rho \cosh\theta$$

and

$$\frac{\alpha - \gamma}{2} = \rho \sinh\theta.$$

The goal here is to find (ρ,θ) in terms of (α,γ) and then substitute these values into [5.7]. Proceeding with this goal, we form

$$\rho^2[\cosh^2(\theta) - \sinh^2(\theta)] = \left(\frac{\alpha+\gamma}{2}\right)^2 - \left(\frac{\alpha-\gamma}{2}\right)^2 = \alpha\gamma. \qquad [5.8]$$

We note that $\cosh^2(\theta) - \sinh^2(\theta) = 1$, hence we have $\rho = \sqrt{\alpha\gamma}$.

Next, we solve for θ in terms of (α,γ), by starting with

$$\tanh(\theta) = \frac{e^\theta - e^{-\theta}}{e^\theta + e^{-\theta}} = \frac{\alpha - \gamma}{\alpha + \gamma}.$$

After some algebraic manipulation, it yields:

$$\theta = \frac{1}{2}\ln\frac{\alpha}{\gamma}.$$

Integral I may now be rewritten as:

$$I = \int_{-\infty}^{\infty} e^{-\sqrt{\alpha\gamma}\cosh(\frac{1}{2}\ln\frac{\alpha}{\gamma})\cosh(2u) + \sqrt{\alpha\gamma}\sinh(\frac{1}{2}\ln\frac{\alpha}{\gamma})\sinh(2u)} e^{-(L-1)u} du.$$

$$= \int_{-\infty}^{\infty} e^{-\sqrt{\alpha\gamma}\cosh\left[2(u - \frac{1}{4}\ln\frac{\alpha}{\gamma})\right] - (L-1)u} du. \qquad [5.9]$$

Substituting

$$v = u - \frac{1}{4}\ln\frac{\alpha}{\gamma}$$

into [5.9] gives

$$I = e^{-\frac{L-1}{4}\ln\frac{\alpha}{\gamma}} \int_{-\infty}^{\infty} e^{-\sqrt{\alpha\gamma}\cosh(2v)-(L-1)v} dv. \qquad [5.10]$$

Finally, substituting $\omega = 2v$, we have

$$I = \frac{1}{2}\left(\frac{\alpha}{\gamma}\right)^{-\frac{L-1}{4}} \int_{-\infty}^{\infty} e^{-\sqrt{\alpha\gamma}\cosh(\omega)-\frac{(L-1)}{2}\omega} d\omega. \qquad [5.11]$$

From [MEC 66], the modified Bessel function of the second kind is defined as:

$$\begin{aligned}
\mathbf{K}_n(r) &= \int_0^{\infty} e^{-r\cosh(\phi)}\cosh(n\phi)d\phi \\
&= \frac{1}{2}\int_0^{\infty} e^{-r\cosh(\phi)+n\phi}d\phi + \frac{1}{2}\int_0^{\infty} e^{-r\cosh(\phi)-n\phi}d\phi \\
&= \frac{1}{2}\int_{-\infty}^{0} e^{-r\cosh(\phi)-n\phi}d\phi + \frac{1}{2}\int_0^{\infty} e^{-r\cosh(\phi)-n\phi}d\phi \\
&= \frac{1}{2}\int_{-\infty}^{\infty} e^{-r\cosh(\phi)-n\phi}d\phi. \qquad [5.12]
\end{aligned}$$

The modified Bessel function of the second kind for $n = 0, 1, 2, 3$ and 4 is shown in Figure 5.1. There are also asymptotic forms of the modified Bessel function of the second kind [ABR 72], such as:

For $r >> |n^2 - 1/4| : K_n(r) \approx \sqrt{\frac{\pi}{2r}}e^{-r}$

For $0 < r < \sqrt{n+1} : K_n(r) \approx \frac{\Gamma(n)}{2}\left(\frac{2}{r}\right)^n$ if $n > 0$.

Applying the result of [5.12] into [5.11], we have

$$I = \frac{1}{2}\left(\frac{\alpha}{\gamma}\right)^{-\frac{L-1}{4}} \int_{-\infty}^{\infty} e^{-\sqrt{\alpha\gamma}\cosh(w)-\frac{(L-1)}{2}w} dw = \left(\frac{\alpha}{\gamma}\right)^{-\frac{L-1}{4}} \mathbf{K}_{\frac{L-1}{2}}(\sqrt{\alpha\gamma}). \qquad [5.13]$$

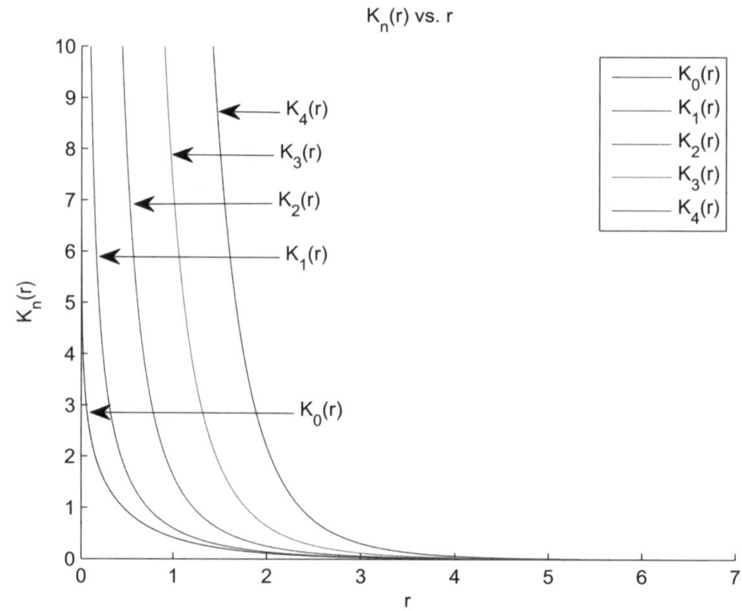

Figure 5.1. *Modified bessel function of the second kind*

Hence, [5.4] can be represented as:

$$f_{\mathbf{y}}(\boldsymbol{\nu}) = \frac{2e^{\frac{\mathbf{z}^T\boldsymbol{\nu}}{\sigma_v^2}} \left\{\sigma_v^2 \left[\boldsymbol{\nu}^T\mathbf{R}^{-1}\boldsymbol{\nu} + \frac{(\boldsymbol{\nu}^T\mathbf{z})^2}{\sigma_v^2}\right]\right\}^{-\frac{L-1}{4}}}{(2\pi)^{\frac{L+1}{2}}\sigma_v[\det(\mathbf{R})]^{\frac{1}{2}}} \times \mathbf{K}_{\frac{L-1}{2}}\left(\sqrt{\frac{1}{\sigma_v^2}[\boldsymbol{\nu}^T\mathbf{R}^{-1}\boldsymbol{\nu} + \frac{(\boldsymbol{\nu}^T\mathbf{z})^2}{\sigma_v^2}]}\right). \quad [5.14]$$

The final step involves substituting $\mathbf{y} = -\frac{1}{\beta_a}\mathbf{G}^{-1}(\mathbf{z}^+ - \mathbf{z})$, which gives after rearranging terms

$$f(\mathbf{z}^+|\mathbf{z}) = \frac{2e^{-\frac{1}{\beta_a\sigma_v^2}\mathbf{z}^T\mathbf{G}^{-1}(\mathbf{z}^+-\mathbf{z})}}{(2\pi\beta_a)^{\frac{L+1}{2}}\sigma_v[\det(\mathbf{R})]^{\frac{1}{2}}\det(\mathbf{G})} \times \frac{\mathbf{K}_{\frac{L-1}{2}}\left(\frac{\sqrt{(\mathbf{z}^+-\mathbf{z})^T\mathbf{G}^{-1}(\sigma_v^2\mathbf{R}^{-1}+\mathbf{z}\mathbf{z}^T)\mathbf{G}^{-1}(\mathbf{z}^+-\mathbf{z})}}{\beta_a\sigma_v^2}\right)}{[(\mathbf{z}^+-\mathbf{z})^T\mathbf{G}^{-1}(\sigma_v^2\mathbf{R}^{-1}+\mathbf{z}\mathbf{z}^T)\mathbf{G}^{-1}(\mathbf{z}^+-\mathbf{z})]^{\frac{L-1}{4}}}. \quad [5.15]$$

5.2.1.1.2. Special case–input is white stationary noise

Assume that the input noise is white, such that $\mathbf{R} = \sigma_x^2\mathbf{I}$, where $\mathbf{I}$ is the identity matrix. Note that $\det(\mathbf{R}) = \sigma_x^{2L}$. If this is the case, then [5.15] can be reduced to

$$f(\mathbf{z}^+|\mathbf{z}) = \frac{2e^{-\frac{1}{\beta_a\sigma_v^2}\sum_{i=1}^{L}\frac{z_i(z_i^+-z_i)}{g_i}}}{(2\pi\beta_a)^{\frac{L+1}{2}}\sigma_v\sigma_x^L\prod_{j=1}^{L}g_j}$$
$$\times\frac{\mathbf{K}_{\frac{L-1}{2}}\left(\frac{1}{\beta_a\sigma_v^2}\sqrt{\frac{\sigma_v^2}{\sigma_x^2}\sum_{i=1}^{L}\frac{(z_i^+-z_i)^2}{g_i^2}+\left[\sum_{i=1}^{L}\frac{(z_i^+-z_i)z_i}{g_i}\right]^2}\right)}{\left\{\frac{\sigma_v^2}{\sigma_x^2}\sum_{i=1}^{L}\frac{(z_i^+-z_i)^2}{g_i^2}+\left[\sum_{i=1}^{L}\frac{(z_i^+-z_i)z_i}{g_i}\right]^2\right\}^{\frac{L-1}{4}}}. \quad [5.16]$$

5.2.1.2. *Derivation of the joint conditional PDF with no measurement noise*

Now assume that there is no measurement noise so that $y_i = x_i t$ and $t = \sum_{i=1}^{L} x_i z_i$, that is $\mathbf{y} = t\mathbf{x}$. Using this information, the joint PDF of $(\mathbf{x}, t)$ can be written as:

$$f_{\mathbf{x},t}(\boldsymbol{\xi},\tau) = f_{t|\mathbf{x}}(\tau|\boldsymbol{\xi})f_{\mathbf{x}}(\boldsymbol{\xi}) = \delta(\tau - \sum_{j=1}^{L}\xi_j z_j)\frac{1}{(2\pi)^{\frac{L}{2}}(\det\mathbf{R})^{\frac{1}{2}}}e^{-\frac{1}{2}\boldsymbol{\xi}^T\mathbf{R}\boldsymbol{\xi}} \quad [5.17]$$

where $\delta(a)$ is the Dirac delta function evaluated for the argument a. Substituting [5.17] into [5.2] yields:

$$f_{\mathbf{y}}(\boldsymbol{\nu}) = \int_{-\infty}^{\infty} f_{\mathbf{x},t}(\boldsymbol{\nu}/\tau,\tau)\frac{d\tau}{|\tau|^L} = \int_{-\infty}^{\infty}\frac{\delta(\tau - \sum_{j=1}^{L}\frac{\nu_j}{\tau}z_j)}{(2\pi)^{\frac{L}{2}}(\det\mathbf{R})^{\frac{1}{2}}}e^{-\frac{1}{2\tau^2}\boldsymbol{\nu}^T\mathbf{R}\boldsymbol{\nu}}\frac{d\tau}{|\tau|^L}. \quad [5.18]$$

Next, we note that the argument of the Dirac delta function becomes zero when $\tau = \pm\sqrt{\boldsymbol{\nu}^T\mathbf{z}}$. In addition $f_{\mathbf{y}}(\boldsymbol{\nu}) = 0$ for $\boldsymbol{\nu}^T\mathbf{z} < 0$. Using this fact, we can rewrite [5.18] as:

$$f_{\mathbf{y}}(\boldsymbol{\nu}) = \int_{-\infty}^{\infty}\frac{\frac{1}{2}\delta(\tau+\sqrt{\boldsymbol{\nu}^T\mathbf{z}})+\frac{1}{2}\delta(\tau-\sqrt{\boldsymbol{\nu}^T\mathbf{z}})}{(2\pi)^{\frac{L}{2}}(\det\mathbf{R})^{\frac{1}{2}}}e^{-\frac{1}{2\tau^2}\boldsymbol{\nu}^T\mathbf{R}\boldsymbol{\nu}}\frac{d\tau}{|\tau|^L}$$
$$= \frac{1}{(2\pi)^{\frac{L}{2}}(\det\mathbf{R})^{\frac{1}{2}}}\frac{e^{-\frac{1}{2}\boldsymbol{\nu}^T\mathbf{R}^{-1}\boldsymbol{\nu}/\boldsymbol{\nu}^T\mathbf{z}}}{(\boldsymbol{\nu}\mathbf{z})^{\frac{L}{2}}}. \quad [5.19]$$

Next, we make the substitution $\mathbf{y} = -\frac{1}{\beta_a}\mathbf{G}^{-1}(\mathbf{z}^+ - \mathbf{z})$ that yields:

$$f(\mathbf{z}^+|\mathbf{z}) = \frac{e^{\frac{1}{2}\frac{(\mathbf{z}^+-\mathbf{z})^T\mathbf{G}^{-1}\mathbf{R}^{-1}\mathbf{G}^{-1}(\mathbf{z}^+-\mathbf{z})}{\beta_a\mathbf{z}^T\mathbf{G}^{-1}(\mathbf{z}^+-\mathbf{z})}}}{(2\pi\beta_a)^{\frac{L}{2}}(\det\mathbf{R})^{\frac{1}{2}}\det\mathbf{G}\left[-\mathbf{z}^T\mathbf{G}^{-1}(\mathbf{z}^+ - \mathbf{z})\right]^{\frac{L}{2}}} \qquad [5.20]$$

if $\mathbf{z}^T\mathbf{G}^{-1}(\mathbf{z}^+ - \mathbf{z}) < 0$, otherwise $f(\mathbf{z}^+|\mathbf{z}) = 0$. Hence, the term $\mathbf{z}^T\mathbf{G}^{-1}(\mathbf{z}^+ - \mathbf{z})$ defines a boundary that divides the conditional PDF into two regions. This condition also shows that the weighted update $\mathbf{G}^{-1}(\mathbf{z}^+ - \mathbf{z})$ needs to be in a direction opposite of $\mathbf{z}$, otherwise $f(\mathbf{z}^+|\mathbf{z}) = 0$.

5.2.1.3. *Derivation of marginal conditional PDF*

In this section, the derivation of the marginal conditional PDF is described. We begin by expressing the $f_{y_i}(\nu_i)$ in terms of the PDF of (x_i, t) as follows:

$$f_{y_i}(\nu_i) = \int_{-\infty}^{\infty} f_{y_i}(\nu_i|t = \tau)f_t(\tau)d\tau = \int_{-\infty}^{\infty}\frac{1}{|\tau|}f_{x_i,t}(\nu_i/\tau,\tau)d\tau. \qquad [5.21]$$

Again (x, t) is jointly Gaussian with PDF given by:

$$f_{x_i,t}(\xi_i, \tau) = \frac{1}{[(2\pi)^2\det(\hat{\mathbf{P}})]^{\frac{1}{2}}}e^{-\frac{1}{2}[\xi_i,\tau]\hat{\mathbf{P}}^{-1}[\xi_i,\tau]^T}$$

where $\hat{\mathbf{P}}$ is the covariance matrix of $[x_i, t]^T$ and $\det(\hat{\mathbf{P}})$ is the determinant of the matrix $\hat{\mathbf{P}}$. The covariance matrix $\hat{\mathbf{P}}$ is given by:

$$\hat{\mathbf{P}} = \begin{bmatrix} r_{ii} & p_i \\ p_i & \mathbf{z}^T\mathbf{R}\mathbf{z} + \sigma_v^2 \end{bmatrix}.$$

where p_i is the ith component of the vector $\mathbf{p} = \mathbf{R}\mathbf{z}$ and $r_{ii} = [\mathbf{R}]_{ii}$. The covariance matrix $\hat{\mathbf{P}}$ is positive definite if $\mathbf{R}$ is positive definite and $\sigma_v^2 > 0$.

With this information, we can represent the PDF of y_i as:

$$f_{y_i}(\nu_i) = \frac{e^{\frac{\nu_i p_i}{r_{ii}[\mathbf{z}^T\mathbf{R}\mathbf{z}+\sigma_v^2]-p_i^2}}}{\pi\sqrt{r_{ii}[\mathbf{z}^T\mathbf{R}\mathbf{z} + \sigma_v^2] - p_i^2}}\int_0^{\infty} e^{-\frac{1}{2}\{\frac{\hat{\alpha}}{\tau^2}+\hat{\gamma}\tau^2\}}\frac{d\tau}{\tau} \qquad [5.22]$$

where

$$\hat{\alpha} = \frac{\nu_i^2(\mathbf{z}^T\mathbf{R}\mathbf{z} + \sigma_v^2)}{r_{ii}(\mathbf{z}^T\mathbf{R}\mathbf{z} + \sigma_v^2) - p_i^2}$$

and

$$\hat{\gamma} = \frac{r_{ii}}{r_{ii}(\mathbf{z}^T\mathbf{R}\mathbf{z} + \sigma_v^2) - p_i^2}.$$

This integral can be evaluated using the techniques presented in section 5.2.1.1.1. After evaluating the integral in [5.22] and substituting $y_i = -\frac{(z_i^+ - z_i)}{\beta_a g_i}$, the marginal PDF is given by:

$$f(z_i^+|\mathbf{z}) = \frac{e^{-\frac{1}{\beta_a g_i}\frac{p_i(z_i^+ - z_i)}{r_{ii}(\mathbf{z}^T\mathbf{R}\mathbf{z}+\sigma_v^2)-p_i^2}}}{\beta_a g_i \pi\sqrt{r_{ii}(\mathbf{z}^T\mathbf{R}\mathbf{z} + \sigma_v^2) - p_i^2}} \times \mathbf{K}_0\left[\frac{\sqrt{r_{ii}(\mathbf{z}^T\mathbf{R}\mathbf{z} + \sigma_v^2)}}{r_{ii}(\mathbf{z}^T\mathbf{R}\mathbf{z} + \sigma_v^2) - p_i^2}\frac{|z_i^+ - z_i|}{\beta_a g_i}\right]. \quad [5.23]$$

The same result given in [5.23] can be obtained using [OMU 65] where the distribution of the product of dependent Gaussian variables is calculated.

5.2.1.4. *Derivation of the marginal conditional PDF with no measurement noise*

Assume that there is no measurement noise. In this case, the covariance matrix becomes:

$$\hat{\mathbf{P}}|_{\sigma_v^2=0} = \begin{bmatrix} r_{ii} & p_i \\ p_i & \mathbf{z}^T\mathbf{R}\mathbf{z}\end{bmatrix} = \begin{bmatrix} \mathbf{e}_i^T\mathbf{R}\mathbf{e}_i & \mathbf{e}_i^T\mathbf{R}\mathbf{z} \\ \mathbf{z}^T\mathbf{R}\mathbf{e}_i^T & \mathbf{z}^T\mathbf{R}\mathbf{z}\end{bmatrix}$$

where $\mathbf{e}_i$ denotes a vector with 1 at the ith component and 0 everywhere else. It can be shown that $\hat{\mathbf{P}}|_{\sigma_v^2=0}$ is positive definite if $\mathbf{z} \neq z_i\mathbf{e}_i$. The proof starts by writing the determinant and then applying Schwarz's inequality:

$$\det \hat{\mathbf{P}}|_{\sigma_v^2=0} = \mathbf{e}_i^T\mathbf{R}\mathbf{e}_i\mathbf{z}^T\mathbf{R}\mathbf{z} - (\mathbf{e}_i^T\mathbf{R}\mathbf{z})^2 \geq \mathbf{e}_i^T\mathbf{R}\mathbf{e}_i\mathbf{z}^T\mathbf{R}\mathbf{z} - \mathbf{e}_i^T\mathbf{R}\mathbf{e}_i\mathbf{z}^T\mathbf{R}\mathbf{z} = 0. \quad [5.24]$$

The only case when the equality holds is if $\mathbf{z} = z_i\mathbf{e}_i$. The marginal PDF with no measurement noise has three different forms.

5.2.1.4.1. Form 1

For $\mathbf{z} \neq z_i\mathbf{e}_i$, the marginal PDF is [5.23] with σ_v^2 set to zero.

5.2.1.4.2. Form 2

When $\mathbf{z} = \mathbf{0}$, the marginal PDF becomes $f(z_i^+|\mathbf{z} = \mathbf{0}) = \delta(z_i^+)$.

5.2.1.4.3. Form 3

When $\mathbf{z} = z_i\mathbf{e}_i$ and $z_i \neq 0$, we can write

$$f_{\mathbf{x},t}(\boldsymbol{\xi}, \tau) = f_{t|\mathbf{x}}(\tau|\boldsymbol{\xi}) f_{\mathbf{x}}(\boldsymbol{\xi}) = \delta(\tau - \sum_{j=1}^{L} \xi_j z_j) f_{\mathbf{x}}(\boldsymbol{\xi}) = \delta(\tau - \xi_i z_i) f_{\mathbf{x}}(\boldsymbol{\xi}). \qquad [5.25]$$

Next, $f_{x_i,t}(\xi_i, \tau)$ can be found by integrating [5.25] over all x_j where $j \neq i$. This operation yields:

$$f_{x_i,t}(\xi_i, \tau) = \delta(\tau - \xi_i z_i) \frac{1}{\sqrt{2\pi r_{ii}}} e^{-\frac{\xi_i^2}{2r_{ii}}}. \qquad [5.26]$$

Since $y_i = x_i t$, we can write

$$f_{y_i}(\nu_i) = \int_{-\infty}^{\infty} f_{x_i,t}\left(\frac{\nu_i}{\tau}, \tau\right) \frac{d\tau}{|\tau|} = \int_{-\infty}^{\infty} \delta\left(\tau - \frac{\nu_i}{\tau} z_i\right) \frac{1}{\sqrt{2\pi r_{ii}}} e^{-\frac{\nu_i^2}{2r_{ii}\tau^2}} \frac{d\tau}{\tau}. \qquad [5.27]$$

The argument of the Dirac delta function in [5.27] becomes zero when $\tau = \pm\sqrt{\nu_i z_i}$. Also, $f_{y_i}(\nu_i) = 0$ for $\nu_i z_i < 0$. After evaluating the integral in [5.27] and performing the transformation of variables $y_i = -\frac{z_i^+ - z_i}{\beta_a g_i}$ yields:

$$f(z_i^+|\mathbf{z} = \mathbf{e_i} z_i) = \frac{e^{-\frac{|z_i^+ - z_i|}{2\beta_a g_i r_{ii} |z_i|}}}{\sqrt{2\beta_a g_i \pi r_{ii} z_i (z_i - z_i^+)}} \qquad [5.28]$$

if $z_i(z_i^+ - z_i) < 0$, otherwise $f(z_i^+|\mathbf{z}) = 0$ if $z_i(z_i^+ - z_i) \geq 0$.

5.3. Applications using the conditional PDF

The conditional PDFs derived in this chapter can be used in several applications. For instance, the evolution of $f\left[\mathbf{z}(k)\right]$ may be calculated analytically or numerically. In addition, the steady-state properties of $f\left[\mathbf{z}(k)\right]$ can be examined. Another application is to use the knowledge of the conditional PDF to design an algorithm that attempts to maximize the conditional PDF for the true weights at every time instance. In this section, we will present several of these applications.

5.3.1. *Methodology for finding the steady-state joint PDF using the conditional PDF*

In general, in order to find the steady-state PDF $f(\mathbf{z})$, we need to solve the integral equation given by:

$$f\left(\mathbf{z}^{+}\right) = \int_{-\infty}^{\infty} \cdots \int_{-\infty}^{\infty} f\left(\mathbf{z}^{+}|\mathbf{z}\right) f\left(\mathbf{z}\right) d\mathbf{z} \tag{5.29}$$

where for an arbitrary vector $\mathbf{a}$ of length L the notation $d\mathbf{a}$ represents $da_1 da_2 \ldots da_L$. This is a problem of finding the eigenfunction corresponding to the eigenvalue 1, which can be solved numerically. Note that the conditional PDF $f\left(\mathbf{z}^{+} | \, \mathbf{z}\right)$ is stationary and defines a Markov chain that is assumed to converge to a stationary Markov chain whose state-space PDF $f\left(\mathbf{z}^{+}\right)$ is the same as $f(\mathbf{z})$ [DOO 53]. The derivation showing that $\mathbf{z}(0), \mathbf{z}(1), \ldots, \mathbf{z}(k)$, form a Markov chain follows next for the interested reader.

5.3.1.1. *Markov chain proof*

The goal is to show that

$$f\left[\mathbf{z}(k+1)|\mathbf{z}(k), \mathbf{z}(k-1), \ldots, \mathbf{z}(0)\right] = f\left[\mathbf{z}(k+1)|\mathbf{z}(k)\right], \tag{5.30}$$

that is $\mathbf{z}(0), \mathbf{z}(1), \ldots, \mathbf{z}(k)$ form a Markov chain.

We begin by writing equation [4.1] in vector form as

$$\mathbf{z}(k+1) = \left[\mathbf{I} - \beta_a \mathbf{G}(k)\mathbf{x}(k)\mathbf{x}^T(k)\right]\mathbf{z}(k) - \beta_a \mathbf{G}(k)\mathbf{x}(k)v(k). \tag{5.31}$$

Next, we express

$$\begin{aligned} & f\left[\mathbf{z}(k+1)|\mathbf{z}(k), \mathbf{z}(k-1), \ldots, \mathbf{z}(0)\right] \\ & \quad = \int_{-\infty}^{\infty} \cdots \int_{-\infty}^{\infty} f\left[\mathbf{z}(k+1)|\mathbf{z}(k), \mathbf{z}(k-1), \ldots, \mathbf{z}(0), \mathbf{x}(k), v(k)\right] \\ & \quad \times f\left[\mathbf{x}(k), v(k)|\mathbf{z}(k), \mathbf{z}(k-1), \ldots, \mathbf{z}(0)\right] d\mathbf{x}(k) dv(k). \end{aligned} \tag{5.32}$$

Next, since we assumed $\mathbf{x}(k)$, $v(k)$ and $\mathbf{z}(k), \ldots, \mathbf{z}(0)$ are jointly independent in assumptions 5.2 and 5.3, we can write

$$f\left[\mathbf{x}(k), v(k)|\mathbf{z}(k), \mathbf{z}(k-1), \ldots, \mathbf{z}(0)\right] = f\left[\mathbf{x}(k), v(k)\right]. \tag{5.33}$$

In addition from [5.31] it is straightforward to show that

$$\begin{aligned} & f\left[\mathbf{z}(k+1)|\mathbf{z}(k), \mathbf{z}(k-1), \ldots, \mathbf{z}(0), \mathbf{x}(k), v(k)\right] \\ & \quad = f\left[\mathbf{z}(k+1)|\mathbf{z}(k), \mathbf{x}(k), v(k)\right]. \end{aligned} \tag{5.34}$$

Finally, substituting [5.33] and [5.34] into [5.32] yields:

$$\begin{aligned} & f\left[\mathbf{z}(k+1)|\mathbf{z}(k), \mathbf{z}(k-1), \ldots, \mathbf{z}(0)\right] \\ &= \int_{-\infty}^{\infty} \cdots \int_{-\infty}^{\infty} f\left[\mathbf{z}(k+1)|\mathbf{z}(k), \mathbf{x}(k), v(k)\right] f\left[\mathbf{x}(k), v(k)\right] d\mathbf{x}(k) dv(k) \\ &= \int_{-\infty}^{\infty} \cdots \int_{-\infty}^{\infty} f\left[\mathbf{z}(k+1), \mathbf{x}(k), v(k)|\mathbf{z}(k)\right] d\mathbf{x}(k) dv(k) \\ &= f\left[\mathbf{z}(k+1)|\mathbf{z}(k)\right] \quad \text{Q.E.D.} \end{aligned} \qquad [5.35]$$

5.3.1.2. *Steady-state PDF for a one-dimensional example*

As an example, the steady-state PDF $f\left[\mathbf{z}(k)\right]$ based on the theory presented in this section will be compared to a simulated steady-state PDF with the same parameters. In this example, $L = 1$, $\sigma_x^2 = 1$, $\sigma_v^2 = 0.1$, $\beta_a = 0.1$, $w_1 = 0.1$, and the number of Monte Carlo runs used was 10^7. The gain at any time k was given by $g_1[\hat{w}_1(k)] = 1 + \ln(1 + \mu|\hat{w}_1(k)|)$, where $\mu = 10$. Time-varying gain was chosen to accentuate the shape of the steady-state PDF and because it is related to the gain in the MPNLMS algorithm.

To find the steady-state PDF $f(z_1)$, we need to solve the integral equation given by:

$$f\left(z_1^+\right) = \int_{-\infty}^{\infty} f\left(z_1^+|z_1\right) f\left(z_1\right) dz_1, \qquad [5.36]$$

which will be solved numerically.

In Figure 5.2, three curves are shown. The first curve was generated by numerically solving the eigenfunction problem associated with [5.36], the second curve was generated through Monte Carlo simulations using the algorithm in Table 5.1, and the third curve was generated by estimating the mean and variance of the data obtained by the simulations and fitting a Gaussian curve to the data using these estimates. The function $f(z_1)$ versus z_1 was plotted for each curve. As it is seen from the figure, the theoretical steady-state PDF and the steady-state PDF obtained by simulation are very close to each other, while the steady-state PDF obtained by Gaussian approximation has lighter tails and is not as peaked.

5.3.1.3. *Steady-state PDF for a two-dimensional example*

In this section, a two-dimensional (2D) example is presented. The input signal was white with variance $\sigma_x^2 = 1$. The parameters used in this simulation were $L = 2$, $\sigma_x^2 = 1$, $\sigma_v^2 = 0.1$, $\beta_a = 5$, $\mathbf{w} = [0, 0.01]^T$, $\rho = 0.01$, $\delta_p = 10^{-4}$ and the number of Monte Carlo runs used was 10^7. The gain applied to the estimation of the ith component of the impulse response at any time k was calculated using the MPNLMS gain logic with $\mu = 0.01$. The MPNLMS gain logic is described in section 1.4.7 and Table 1.1 or alternatively [DEN 05]. In Figures 5.3, 5.4 and 5.5, the steady-state PDFs of the 2D problem are shown using the histogram of simulated data, Gaussian distribution fitted to the simulated data and solution of [5.36] corresponding to an eigenvalue of 1, respectively. It is easily seen that the theoretical solution and the histogram of simulated data both share similar forms while the Gaussian fitted to the simulated data differs significantly.

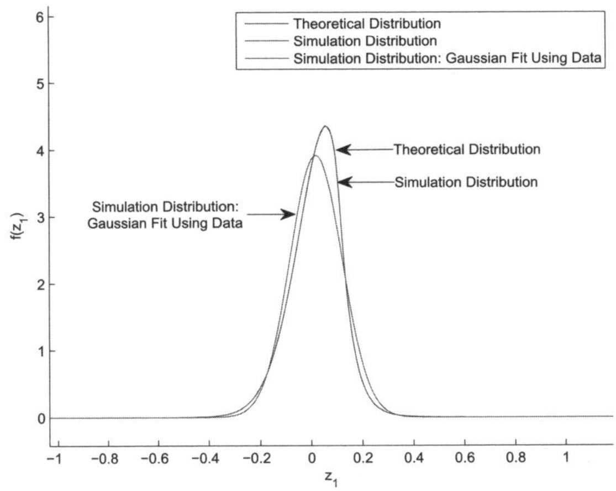

Figure 5.2. *Steady-state PDF example for L = 1*

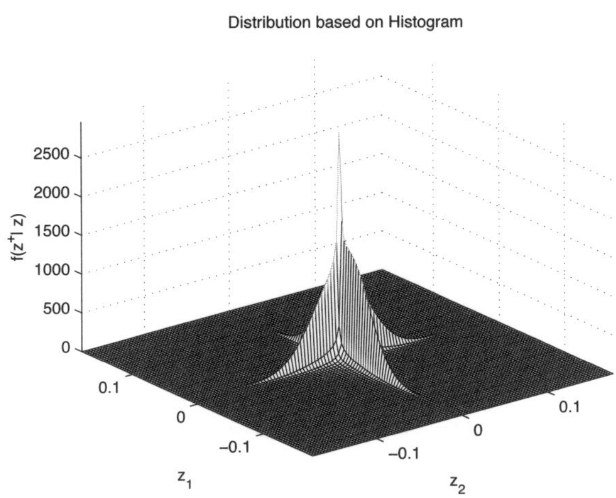

Figure 5.3. *Steady-state PDF resulting from the histogram of simulated data for $L = 2$*

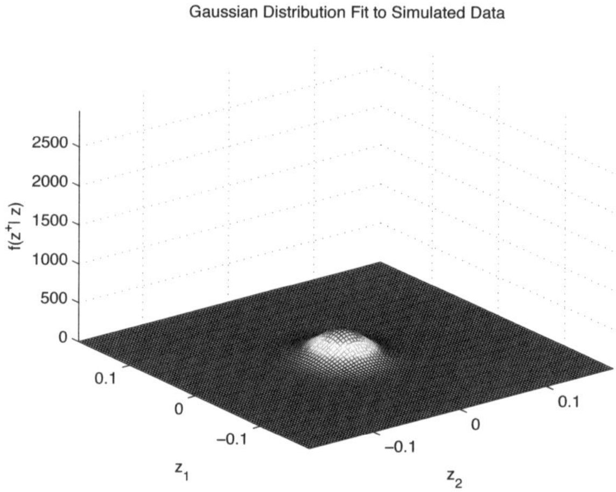

Figure 5.4. *Steady-state PDF resulting from gaussian fit to simulated data for $L = 2$*

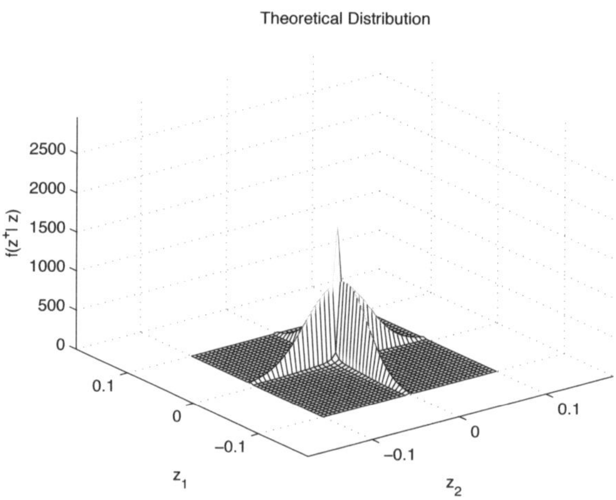

Figure 5.5. *Theoretical steady-state PDF for $L = 2$*

5.3.2. *Algorithm based on constrained maximization of the conditional PDF*

In this section, we apply a constrained optimization approach to the maximization of the weight conditional PDF at any time step. The input signal is stationary, white and has the properties as described in assumption 5.1, that is $\mathbf{R}(k) = \sigma_x^2 \mathbf{I}$. For this application, we assume that

$$f(\mathbf{z}^+|\mathbf{z}) \approx \prod_{i=1}^{L} f(z_i^+|\mathbf{z}),$$

where $f(z_i^+|\mathbf{z})$ is given by [5.23]. The same approach was taken using $f(\mathbf{z}^+|\mathbf{z})$ directly; however, no solution has been found to date.

Our goal is to find the gains $\mathbf{g}$ that maximize $f(\mathbf{0}|\mathbf{z})$ under the constraint that $g_i \geq 0\ \forall i$ and $\sum_{i=1}^{L} g_i = L$. To facilitate the solution of this problem, we introduce:

1) $g_i = s_i^2$ and maximize with respect to s_i (real) to ensure $g_i \geq 0$;

2) the Lagrange multiplier λ to incorporate the constraint $\sum_{i=1}^{L} g_i = L$;

3) usage of the natural logarithm, $\ln(\cdot)$, to aid in finding the solution.

We begin by defining the Lagrangian as:

$$\begin{aligned}\Lambda(\mathbf{s}, \lambda) &= \sum_{i=1}^{L} \ln f(z_i^+|\mathbf{z})|_{z_i^+=0} + \lambda \left(\sum_{i=1}^{L} s_i^2 - L \right) \\ &= \sum_{i=1}^{L} h_i + \lambda \left(\sum_{i=1}^{L} s_i^2 - L \right)\end{aligned} \qquad [5.37]$$

where

$$h_i = \frac{a_i}{s_i^2} - \ln b_i - 2\ln s_i + \ln K_0(\frac{c_i}{s_i^2})$$

and K_0 is the modified Bessel function of the second kind and of the order zero. We have made the following definitions:

$$\begin{aligned} a_i &= \frac{z_i^2}{\beta_a\left[\sigma_x^2(||\mathbf{z}||_2^2 - z_i^2) + \sigma_v^2\right]} \\ b_i &= \pi\sigma_x\beta_a\sqrt{\sigma_x^2(||\mathbf{z}||_2^2 - z_i^2) + \sigma_v^2} \\ c_i &= \frac{\sqrt{||\mathbf{z}||_2^2 + \frac{\sigma_v^2}{\sigma_x^2}}}{\beta_a\left(\sigma_x^2(||\mathbf{z}||_2^2 - z_i^2) + \sigma_v^2\right)}|z_i|. \end{aligned} \qquad [5.38]$$

Using the Lagrangian results in the following optimization problem:

$$\max_{\mathbf{s}, \sum_{i=1}^{L} s_i^2 = L} \quad \ln f(\mathbf{0}|\mathbf{z}) = \Lambda\,(\mathbf{s}, \lambda)|_{(\mathbf{s},\lambda)\in\{\text{stationary points of } \Lambda\}}. \qquad [5.39]$$

To solve this problem, we take the derivative of $\ln f(\mathbf{0}|\mathbf{z})$ with respect to s and set it to zero. This derivative is

$$\frac{\partial h_i}{\partial s_j} = \begin{cases} 0, & i \neq j \\ -2\frac{a_i}{s_i^3} - \frac{2}{s_i} + 2\frac{c_i}{s_i^3}\frac{K_1(\frac{c_i}{s_i^2})}{K_0(\frac{c_i}{s_i^2})}, & i = j \end{cases} \qquad [5.40]$$

where K_1 is the modified Bessel function of the second kind of first order and $\frac{\partial K_0(x)}{\partial x} = -K_1(x)$ [ABR 72].

At this point, we simplify this derivative by assuming c_i/s_i^2 is large enough such that we can make the approximation

$$\frac{K_1(\frac{c_i}{s_i^2})}{K_0(\frac{c_i}{s_i^2})} \approx 1$$

and then we have

$$\frac{\partial \Lambda(\mathbf{s}, \lambda)}{\partial s_i} = -2\frac{a_i}{s_i^3} - \frac{2}{s_i} + 2\frac{c_i}{s_i^3} + 2\lambda s_i.$$

Setting $\frac{\partial \Lambda(\mathbf{s},\lambda)}{\partial s_i} = 0$, we obtain two possible solutions for s_i^2,

$$\begin{aligned} s_{i,1}^2 &= \frac{1 + \sqrt{1 - 4\lambda(c_i - a_i)}}{2\lambda} \\ s_{i,2}^2 &= \frac{1 - \sqrt{1 - 4\lambda(c_i - a_i)}}{2\lambda}. \end{aligned} \qquad [5.41]$$

Note that $c_i - a_i$ is always non-negative. It is seen that the second solution $s_{i,2}^2$ provides maximum for $\lambda \leq 1/[4(c_i - a_i)]$. For $\lambda > 1/[4(c_i - a_i)]$, there is no solution. To have a solution $\forall i$, $\lambda \leq 1/[4\max_i(c_i - a_i)]$. To find λ, we solve numerically $\sum_{i=1}^{L} s_{i,2}^2 = L$. Then, we can calculate the gains using $s_{i,2}^2$.

5.3.2.1. *Arguments for solution existence*

At this point, we still need to prove that a λ always exists such that $\sum_{i=1}^{L} s_{i,2}^2 = L$. We start by defining $S = \sum_{i=1}^{L} s_{i,2}^2$. If we reorganize the terms of S, we find that

$$\begin{aligned} S &= \sum_{i=1}^{L} \frac{1 - \sqrt{1 - 4\lambda(c_i - a_i)}}{2\lambda} \frac{1 + \sqrt{1 - 4\lambda(c_i - a_i)}}{1 + \sqrt{1 - 4\lambda(c_i - a_i)}} \\ &= 2\sum_{i=1}^{L} \frac{c_i - a_i}{1 + \sqrt{1 - 4\lambda(c_i - a_i)}}. \end{aligned} \qquad [5.42]$$

Examining S, we note that the following limits exist:

$$\lim_{\lambda \to -\infty} S = 0$$

$$\lim_{\lambda \to 0} S = \sum_{i=1}^{L} (c_i - a_i)$$

$$\lim_{\lambda \to \frac{1}{4 \max_i (c_i - a_i)}} S \geq \sum_{i=1}^{L} (c_i - a_i). \quad [5.43]$$

In Figure 5.6, we show $S(\lambda)$ for $\mathbf{c} - \mathbf{a} = [1, 1, 1, 1, 2]^T$. From this figure, we see that $\lim_{\lambda \to 0} S = \sum_{i=1}^{L} (c_i - a_i)$.

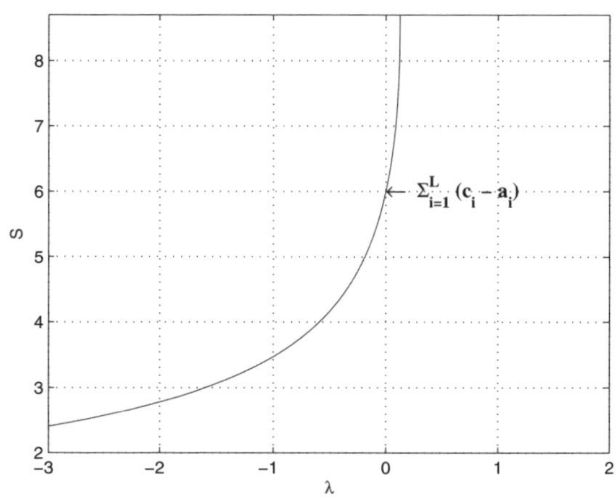

Figure 5.6. *$S(\lambda)$ versus λ*

To prove that a solution always exists, we set out to prove that $\sum_{i=1}^{L} (c_i - a_i) \geq L$. To begin, we write

$$\sum_{i=1}^{L} (c_i - a_i) = \sum_{i=1}^{L} \frac{|z_i|(\sqrt{||\mathbf{z}||_2^2 + \frac{\sigma_v^2}{\sigma_x^2}} - |z_i|)}{\beta_a \sigma_x^2 (||\mathbf{z}||_2^2 - z_i^2 + \frac{\sigma_v^2}{\sigma_x^2})} = \sum_{i=1}^{L} \frac{|z_i|}{\beta_a \sigma_x^2 (\sqrt{||\mathbf{z}||_2^2 + \frac{\sigma_v^2}{\sigma_x^2}} + |z_i|)}$$

$$= \sum_{i=1}^{L} \frac{|z_i|}{\beta_a \sigma_x^2 \sqrt{||\mathbf{z}||_2^2 + \frac{\sigma_v^2}{\sigma_x^2}} (1 + \frac{|z_i|}{\sqrt{||\mathbf{z}||_2^2 + \frac{\sigma_v^2}{\sigma_x^2}}})}. \quad [5.44]$$

At this point, we recognize that

$$1+\frac{|z_i|}{\sqrt{||\mathbf{z}||_2^2+\frac{\sigma_v^2}{\sigma_x^2}}}\leq 2.$$

In addition we approximate

$$\beta_a=\frac{\beta}{\sigma_x^2 L+\delta}\approx\frac{\beta}{\sigma_x^2 L},$$

where $0<\beta<2$. Note that in this chapter, we are dealing with the PtLMS algorithm. However, we can relate the PtLMS algorithm to the PtNLMS algorithm via the relation $\beta_a=\beta/(\sigma_x^2 L+\delta)$ as was done in section 3.2 when using assumption 3.2. Applying these approximations yields:

$$\sum_{i=1}^{L}(c_i-a_i)\geq\frac{\sum_{i=1}^{L}|z_i|}{2\beta_a\sigma_x^2\sqrt{||\mathbf{z}||_2^2+\frac{\sigma_v^2}{\sigma_x^2}}}$$

$$=\frac{L}{2\beta}\frac{||\mathbf{z}||_1}{\sqrt{||\mathbf{z}||_2^2+\frac{\sigma_v^2}{\sigma_x^2}}}. \qquad [5.45]$$

Before examining the general case, we describe what happens when $\sigma_v^2/\sigma_x^2=0$. If this is the case, then we have

$$\sum_{i=1}^{L}(c_i-a_i)\geq\frac{L}{2\beta}\frac{||\mathbf{z}||_1}{||\mathbf{z}||_2}. \qquad [5.46]$$

We know that $||\mathbf{z}||_1/||\mathbf{z}||_2\geq 1$, therefore we can guarantee a solution when there is no noise if $0\leq\beta\leq 1/2$. Typically, $||\mathbf{z}||_1/||\mathbf{z}||_2>>1$ and hence the LHS of [5.46] remains larger than L for all values of interest for β (i.e. $0<\beta<2$).

When $\sigma_v^2/\sigma_x^2>0$, the condition for a solution can also be derived. The worst-case scenario occurs when $||\mathbf{z}||_2^2$ becomes very small. This happens when we approach steady-state and allows us to use the approximation $||\mathbf{z}||_2^2\approx\beta\sigma_v^2/(2\sigma_x^2)$. It is obtained after equating [2.42], where now the adaptation stepsize is denoted by β_a, and [3.1] that gives:

$$E\{||\mathbf{z}||_2^2\}\approx\frac{\beta_a\sigma_v^2 L}{2}$$

that is

$$E\{||\mathbf{z}||_2^2\}\approx\frac{\beta\sigma_v^2 L}{2\sigma_x^2}.$$

Next, we assumed $||\mathbf{z}||_2^2 \approx E\{||\mathbf{z}||_2^2\}$. The argument for solution existence further goes as follows:

$$\sum_{i=1}^{L}(c_i - a_i) \geq \frac{L}{2\beta}\frac{||\mathbf{z}||_1}{\sqrt{||\mathbf{z}||_2^2 + \frac{2}{\beta}||\mathbf{z}||_2^2}}$$

$$= \frac{L}{2\beta}\frac{||\mathbf{z}||_1}{||\mathbf{z}||_2}\frac{1}{\sqrt{1+\frac{2}{\beta}}}. \quad [5.47]$$

We again use the fact that $||\mathbf{z}||_1/||\mathbf{z}||_2 \geq 1$. Then, our condition for the existence of a solution becomes $0 < \beta < \sqrt{5}/2 - 1$. But typically, $||\mathbf{z}||_1/||\mathbf{z}||_2 >> 1$ and therefore a solution can exist for all values of interest for β (i.e. $0 < \beta < 2$).

5.3.2.2. *Feasible conditional PDF constrained maximization algorithms*

The algorithm proposed in the previous sections is not feasible. Specifically, we need to know $z_i(k) = w_i - \hat{w}_i(k)$ that requires the knowledge of the optimal impulse response. The feasible version of the algorithm replaces $z_i(k)$ with the estimate $\widehat{E\{z_i(k)\}}$. The estimate of $\widehat{E\{z_i(k)\}}$ is performed using the implementation discussed in section 4.1.3. To calculate a_i, b_i and c_i in [5.38], we need to estimate $z_i^2(k)$ as well. We make this estimate using $\widehat{E\{z_i(k)\}}^2$. Also, the estimate of $|z_i(k)|$ in [5.38] is done using $|\widehat{E\{z_i(k)\}}|$.

In addition, other algorithms could be generated by improving the current estimate of $K_1(\frac{c_i}{s_i^2})/K_0(\frac{c_i}{s_i^2}) \approx 1$. For instance, we examined approximating this ratio through the parametric equation

$$\frac{K_1(\frac{c_i}{s_i^2})}{K_0(\frac{c_i}{s_i^2})} \approx 1 + \varrho(\frac{c_i}{s_i^2})^{\varsigma},$$

where $0 < \varrho < 1$ and $\varsigma < 0$. We were able to generate an alternate algorithm using $\varsigma = -1$ for any value of ϱ. However, the performance of this algorithm was equivalent to using $K_1(\frac{c_i}{s_i^2})/K_0(\frac{c_i}{s_i^2}) \approx 1$, hence these results will not be presented here.

5.3.2.3. *Results*

We calculate the performance of several algorithms by computing the following metric:

$$L(k) = \sum_{i=1}^{L} \ln f(z_i(k+1) = 0|\mathbf{z}(k)).$$

In Figure 5.7, we compute and compare $L(k)$ of four algorithms, namely the NLMS, PNLMS, feasible conditional PDF maximizing algorithm and the non-feasible conditional PDF maximizing algorithm. Note that the non-feasible conditional PDF maximizing algorithm uses the true value of $\mathbf{w}$. The parameters used in these simulations were as follows: $\sigma_x^2 = 1$, $\sigma_v^2 = 10^{-4}$, $\beta_a = 10^{-4}$, $\rho = 0.1$, $\delta = 0.01L$ and $\delta_p = 0.01$. In addition, we chose $\alpha = 0.99$, $\omega = 2$ and used a real-world impulse response with length $L = 512$, as shown in Figure 4.2(b). Next, we compared the MSE of each algorithm in Figure 5.8.

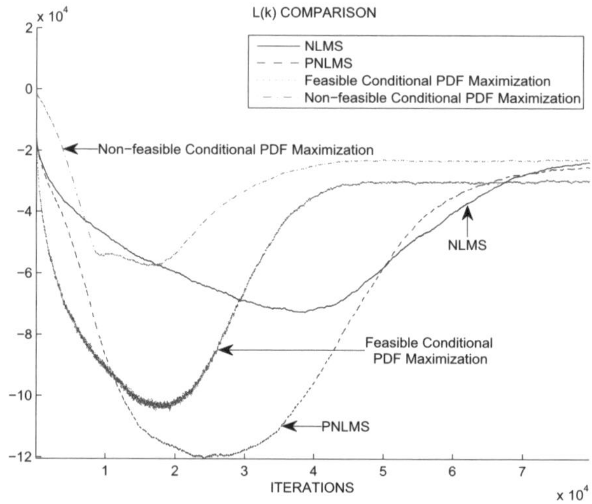

Figure 5.7. *$L(k)$ for non-feasible conditional PDF maximizing, feasible conditional PDF maximizing, NLMS and PNLMS algorithms*

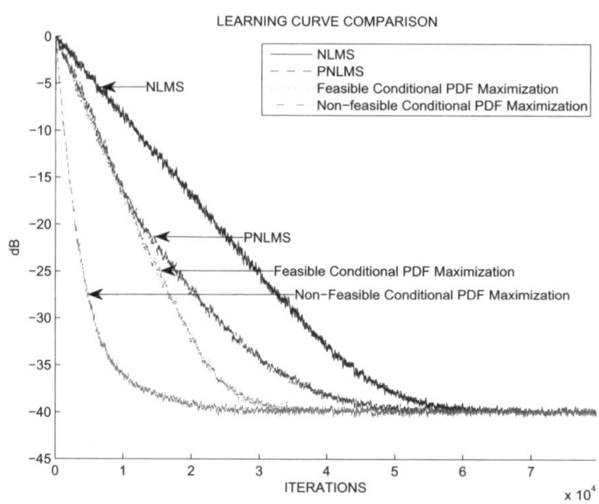

Figure 5.8. *MSE for non-feasible Conditional PDF maximizing, feasible conditional PDF maximizing, NLMS and PNLMS algorithms*

We see that the metric $L(k)$ is maximized for the non-feasible conditional PDF maximizing algorithm. The feasible conditional PDF algorithm achieves its maximum faster than the PNLMS and NLMS algorithms. However, the steady-state value of $L(k)$ achieved by the NLMS and PNLMS algorithms is greater than that of the feasible conditional PDF algorithm. In addition, the feasible conditional PDF maximizing algorithm improves the MSE performance. On the basis of these preliminary results, it appears that the conditional PDF maximizing algorithm may offer some performance benefits.

Initially, the metric $L(k)$ also shows a precipitous drop for all of the algorithms before recovering and reaching its steady-state value. To explain this phenomenon, we first recall that our impulse response is sparse and most of the coefficients have true values of zero. Hence, we initially have $z_i(k) = 0$ for most coefficients. Therefore, the probability of the WD being zero in the next step is high. Once we apply the gain, the WD of these coefficients naturally drifts from the value of zero causing the decrease in $L(k)$. As time proceeds, the coefficients reach steady-state and the WD has less variation about zero, increasing the value of $L(k)$.

5.4. Summary

In this chapter, we described a closed-form solution for the joint conditional PDF of the PtLMS algorithm. It was shown that the joint conditional PDF for the current WDs given the prior WDs is not Gaussian and therefore the first and second moments calculated by assuming Gaussianity are of dubious value for describing the evolution of the WD in time. Two applications were subsequently proposed using the joint conditional PDF of the PtLMS algorithm. The first application showed that it is possible to find the steady-state PDF for WDs using the conditional PDF. Again the steady-state PDF of the PtLMS algorithm was not Gaussian, which is often assumed during the analysis. The second application proposed uses the constrained maximization of the conditional PDF as the basis of a PtNLMS algorithm. Simulation results were presented showing the strengths and weaknesses of the proposed algorithm.

6

Adaptive Step-Size PtNLMS Algorithms

In the previous chapters, we have proposed several schemes for gain allocation in PtNLMS algorithms for fast decay at any time instant. For instance, the proposed gain allocation schemes are based on (1) maximization of one-step decay of the mean square output error, (2) maximization of one-step conditional probability density for true weight values, (3) maximization of one-step decay of the MSWD. In this chapter, an adaptation of the μ-law for compression of weight estimates using the output square error is presented. Additionally, we will propose a simplification of the adaptive μ-law algorithm, which approximates the logarithmic function with a piecewise linear function. It will be shown that there is no significant loss in performance. Comparisons between the algorithms presented in earlier chapters with the μ-law compression algorithm will be presented for sparse echo-cancellation scenarios as well as for white input, color input and voice inputs.

6.1. Adaptation of μ-law for compression of weight estimates using the output square error

The adaptive MPNLMS (AMPNLMS) algorithm is a modification of the MPNLMS algorithm in section 1.4.7. In the MPNLMS algorithm, the parameter μ of the μ-law compression is constant whereas in the AMPNLMS algorithm the parameter μ is allowed to vary with time. This modification provides the algorithm with more flexibility when attempting to minimize the MSE. We summarize the calculation of the gain defining F-function done by the AMPNLMS algorithm in Table 6.1, where the F-function is defined by (M). The algorithm begins by forming an estimate of the MSE. The estimate of the MSE is given by $\zeta(k+1)$ and is obtained by time averaging, where $0 < \xi < 1$ is a constant. The estimated MSE is then scaled by the factor ν to form $\tilde{\epsilon}_L(k)$. The term "$\tilde{\epsilon}_L(k)$" is the distance to the steady-state MSE (noise floor) that is considered to be the achievement of convergence when reached by the MSE. Next, the term "$\epsilon_c(k)$" is calculated. The term "$\epsilon_c(k)$" is the distance each WD must be from zero to achieve convergence. Finally, the μ-law compression constant $\mu(k)$ is related to $1/\epsilon_c(k)$.

$$
\begin{array}{lll}
\zeta(k+1) & = \xi\zeta(k) + (1-\xi)e^2(k) & \\
\tilde{\epsilon}_L(k) & = \frac{\zeta(k+1)}{\nu} & \\
\epsilon_c(k) & = \sqrt{\frac{\tilde{\epsilon}_L(k)}{L\sigma_x^2}} & \\
\mu(k) & = \frac{1}{\epsilon_c(k)} & \\
F[|\hat{w}_l(k)|] & = \ln[1 + \mu(k)|\hat{w}_l(k)|] & \text{(M)} \\
F[|\hat{w}_l(k)|] & = \begin{cases} \ln[\mu(k)|\hat{w}_l(k)|] \text{ if } |\hat{w}_l(k)| > \epsilon_c(k) \\ 0 \text{ if } |\hat{w}_l(k)| < \epsilon_c(k) \end{cases} & \text{(E)}
\end{array}
$$

Table 6.1. *AMPNLMS/AEPNLMS algorithm*

The strategy employed by the AMPNLMS is to start out with a large value for $\epsilon_c(k)$ and slowly decrease the required ϵ-neighborhood to be reached by the converged algorithm. In doing so, the AMPNLMS algorithm initially behaves like the PNLMS algorithm and then transitions to perform like the NLMS algorithm as time progresses. This transition reflects our knowledge of the impulse response. Initially, we know that the impulse response is sparse and therefore we direct our resources in a manner to most efficiently estimate the impulse response. As the time passes, our *a priori* knowledge [which is $\hat{\mathbf{w}}(k)$] becomes close to the true value of the impulse response and the coefficient estimate errors are uniformly distributed along all coefficients, in contrast to the initial situation. Therefore, it is advantageous to employ an NLMS-like adaptation scheme.

Just as we modified the MPNLMS algorithm to create the AMPNLMS algorithm, we can perform the same operation to create the adaptive EPNLMS (AEPNLMS) algorithm from the EPNLMS algorithm in section 1.4.8. Once again we relate current choice of $\epsilon_c(k)$ to the MSE. The calculation of the gain defining F-function for the AEPNLMS algorithm is summarized in Table 6.1, where the F-function is defined by (E).

The AEPNLMS algorithm is more sensitive to the choice of algorithm parameters in comparison to the AMPNLMS algorithm.

6.2. AMPNLMS and AEPNLMS simplification

The segmented PNLMS (SPNLMS) algorithm was proposed in [DEN 06] as a means to avoid the calculation of the logarithm function in the MPNLMS and EPNLMS algorithms. The gain defining F-function is calculated based on

$$
F[|\hat{w}_l(k)|, k] = \begin{cases} \frac{|\hat{w}_l(k)|}{\kappa} & \text{if } |\hat{w}_l(k)| < \kappa \\ 1 & \text{if } |\hat{w}_l(k)| \geq \kappa. \end{cases}
$$

The SPNLMS algorithm is a two-segment linear approximation of the logarithm function. In this case, the first linear segment has slope $1/\kappa$ over the range $0 < |\hat{w}_l(k)| < \kappa$, while the second linear segment has slope zero for all $|\hat{w}_l(k)| > \kappa$. In Figure 6.1, we show an example of the F-function for $\kappa = 1/200 = 0.005$. Note that tuning the parameter κ can potentially improve algorithm performance. For the impulse response chosen in [DEN 06], the parameter κ was set to 0.005, which resulted in adequate learning curve performance.

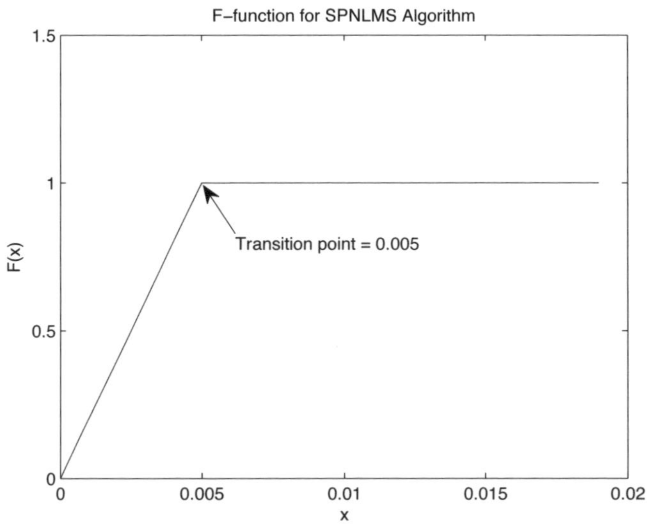

Figure 6.1. *SPNLMS F-function with* $\kappa = 0.005$.

On the basis of this concept, we introduce the adaptive SPNLMS (ASPNLMS) algorithm. The ASPNLMS algorithm attempts to avoid the computation of the logarithm term in the AMPNLMS and AEPNLMS algorithms. The ASPNLMS algorithm is given in Table 6.2 where we introduce the scaling factor Υ to adjust the algorithm's performance.

$$
\begin{aligned}
\zeta(k+1) &= \xi\zeta(k) + (1-\xi)e^2(k) \\
\tilde{\epsilon}_L(k) &= \frac{\zeta(k+1)}{\nu} \\
\epsilon_c(k) &= \sqrt{\frac{\tilde{\epsilon}_L(k)}{L\sigma_x^2}} \\
F[|\hat{w}_l(k)|] &= \begin{cases} \frac{|\hat{w}_l(k)|}{\Upsilon\epsilon_c(k)} \text{ if } |\hat{w}_l(k)| < \Upsilon\epsilon_c(k) \\ 1 \text{ if } |\hat{w}_l(k)| \geq \Upsilon\epsilon_c(k) \end{cases}
\end{aligned}
$$

Table 6.2. *ASPNLMS algorithm*

6.3. Algorithm performance results

In this section, we present the MSE versus iteration of the ASPNLMS, AMPNLMS and AEPNLMS algorithms. The following input parameters are used in these simulations, unless otherwise specified, $\beta = 0.1$, $\rho = 0.01$, $\sigma_x^2 = 1$, $\sigma_v^2 = 10^{-4}$, $\delta = 10^{-4}$, $\delta_p = 0.01, L = 512$, $\nu = 1{,}000$ and $\xi = 0.99$. In all simulations, the parameter $\kappa = 0.005$ is chosen for the SPNLMS algorithm. The impulse response used in these simulations is given in Figure 4.2(b). We will examine the performance of these algorithms for white, colored and speech input signals. The effects of varying parameters ξ and ν on the ASPNLMS, AMPNLMS and AEPNLMS algorithms will be examined. Also, it will be shown that the ASPNLMS algorithm is very sensitive to Υ, while the AEPNLMS is very sensitive to ρ.

6.3.1. *Learning curve performance of the ASPNLMS, AMPNLMS and AEPNLMS algorithms for a white input signal*

We begin by comparing the learning curve performance of the ASPNLMS, AMPNLMS and AEPNLMS algorithms for a white input signal. For reference, we also include the learning curves of the NLMS, PNLMS, MPNLMS, EPNLMS and SPNLMS. The results of this simulation can be seen in Figure 6.2. We let $\Upsilon = 10$ in the ASPNLMS algorithm. The SPNLMS algorithm requires less computations and outperforms both the MPNLMS and EPNLMS algorithm in this case. Similarly, the ASPNLMS outperforms both the AMPNLMS and AEPNLMS algorithms as well as requiring less computations. The SPNLMS and ASPNLMS do not always outperform their counterpart algorithms but can with some tuning of the input parameters. Specifically for the ASPNLMS algorithm, the Υ parameter can greatly affect the algorithm performance.

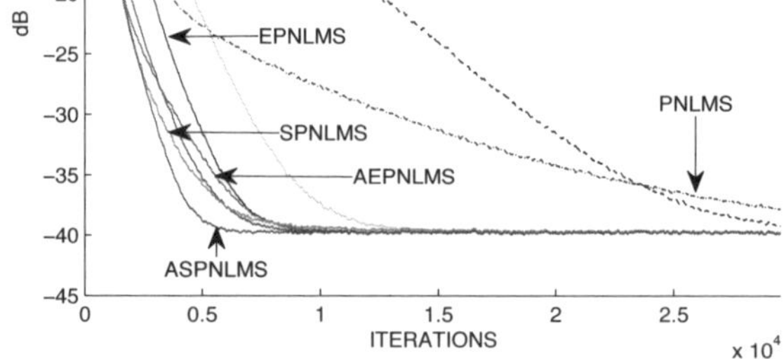

Figure 6.2. *White input algorithm comparison*

6.3.2. *Learning curve performance of the ASPNLMS, AMPNLMS and AEPNLMS algorithms for a color input signal*

Next, we compare all of the algorithms when operating in a colored input scenario. The input process is given by:

$$x(k) = -\gamma x(k-1) + \psi(k),$$

where $\psi(k)$ is a white noise process with variance $\sigma_\psi^2 = 1$ and $\gamma \in (-1, 1)$.

In Figure 6.3, we plot all of the algorithms for $\gamma = 0.9$. The ASPNLMS algorithm has the best performance followed by the AMPNLMS and AEPNLMS algorithms. The adaptation of the $\mu(k)$ allows the AMPNLMS and AEPNLMS algorithms to overcome the different input signal environment.

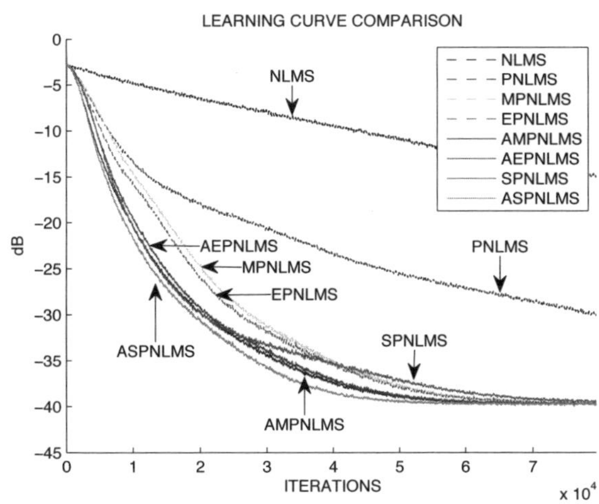

Figure 6.3. *Color input algorithm comparison*

6.3.3. *Learning curve performance of the ASPNLMS, AMPNLMS and AEPNLMS algorithms for a voice input signal*

Next, we compare the learning curve performance with a voice input signal. The impulse used in this simulation is shown in Figure 4.12. The input speech signal is shown in Figure 6.4(a) and the learning curve performance of the algorithms of interest is shown in Figure 6.4(b), where algorithm results have been averaged using 100 uniform shifts of the input signal. The noise power was reduced to $\sigma_v^2 = 10^{-8}$ in this simulation. The algorithms used the proportionate affine projection method introduced in [LIU 09] with $P = 5$.

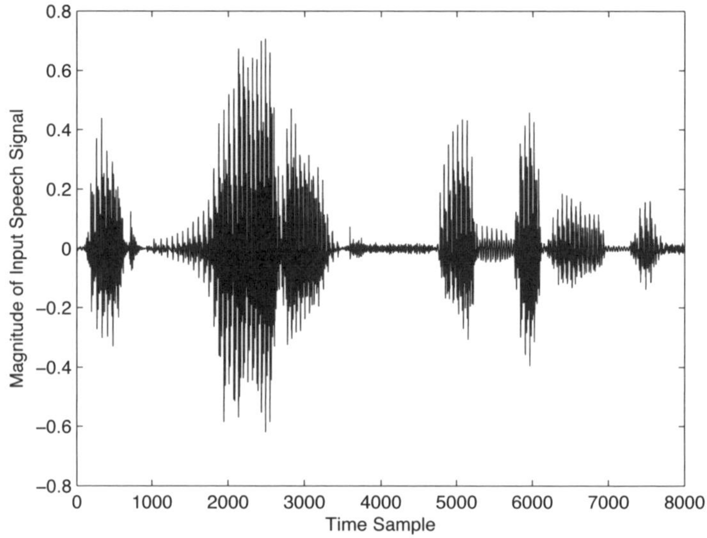

a) Speech signal

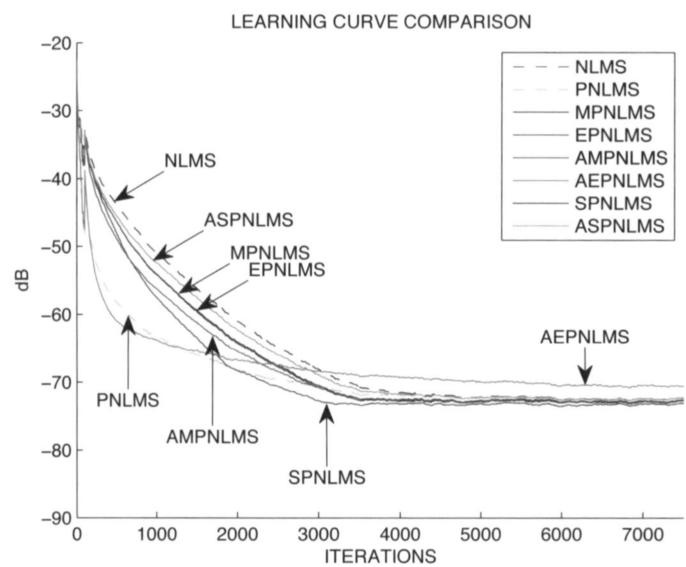

b) Learning curve performance

Figure 6.4. *Voice input algorithm comparison (averaged over 100 uniform shifts of input signal)*

The learning curve comparison will be performed over two intervals. The first interval is the initial convergence period, which is dominated by impulse response learning errors. The second interval is the post-initial, which is dominated by fluctuations around the true impulse response values. During the initial interval, the algorithms have the following convergence performance ranked from best to worst performance: AEPNLMS, PNLMS, SPNLMS, AMPNLMS, MPNLMS, EPNLMS, ASPNLMS and finally NLMS. The convergence performance of the MPNLMS and EPNLMS algorithms is nearly the same. During the post-initial interval the algorithms have the following convergence ranked from best to worst again: SPNLMS, AMPNLMS, MPNLMS, EPNLMS, PNLMS, ASPNLMS, NLMS and finally AEPNLMS. The AMPNLMS, MPNLMS and EPNLMS algorithms have nearly identical convergence performance in the post-initial interval. The post-initial learning curve performance is more relevant when the impulse response does not change.

6.3.4. *Parameter effects on algorithms*

In this section, we examine the effects of varying parameters used in the AMPNLMS, AEPNLMS and ASPNLMS algorithms on their respective learning curves. The impulse response used in simulations corresponds to a real-world network echo path given in Figure 6.5. The input is zero-mean, stationary and white.

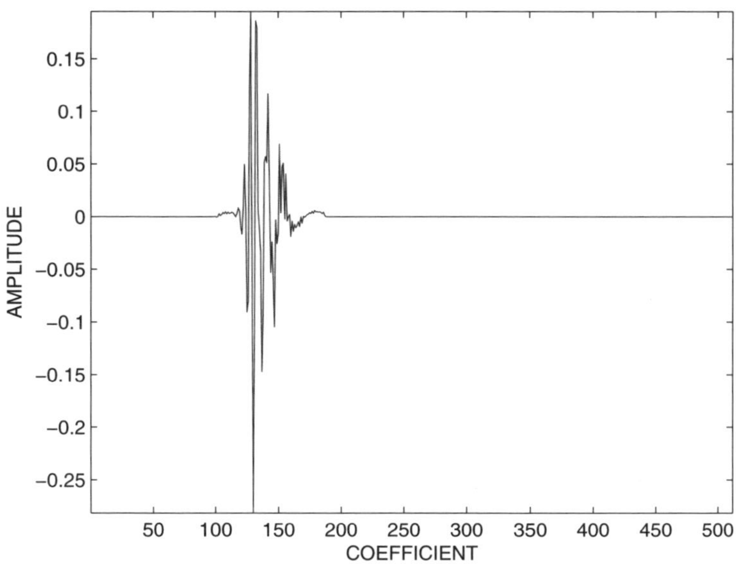

Figure 6.5. *Impulse response*

6.3.4.1. *ν parameter effects*

We compare the estimated MSE performance of the AMPNLMS, AEPNLMS and ASPNLMS using different values of ν in Figures 6.6(a)–6.6(c). Specifically, we have chosen $\nu = 1, 10, 100$and $1, 000$. The values $\xi = 0.99$ and $\Upsilon = 10$ are fixed in these simulations. Of the four considered values for ν, the value $\nu = 1{,}000$ provides all three algorithms with the best performance.

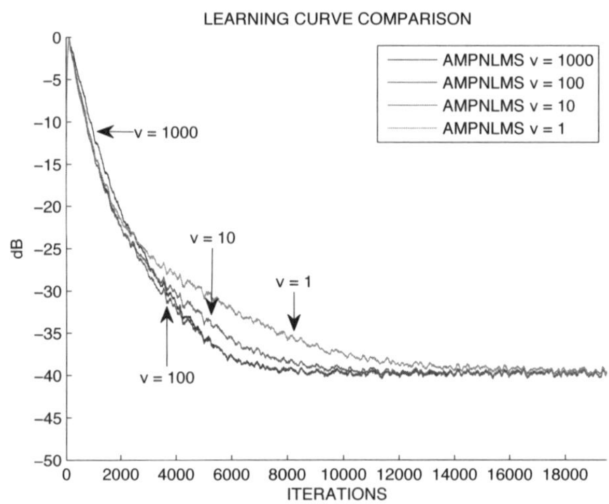

a) AMPNLMS ν comparison

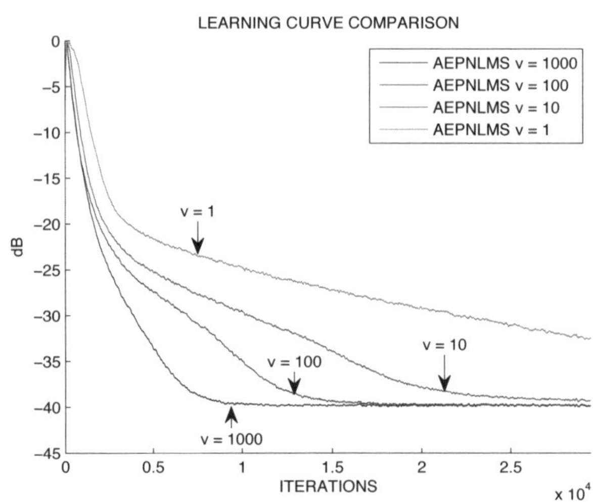

b) AEPNLMS ν comparison

Figure 6.6. *ν comparison*

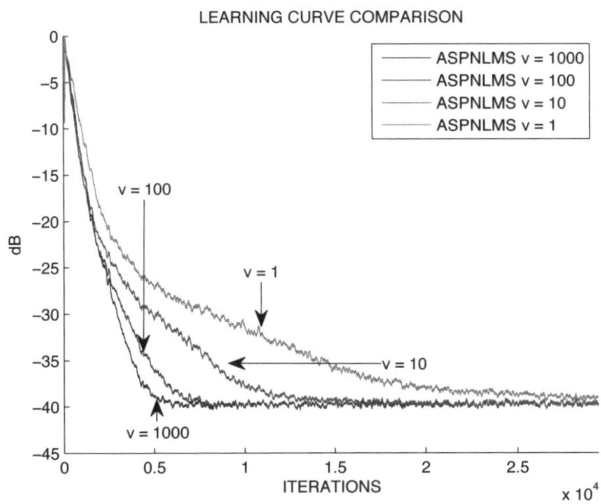

c) ASPNLMS ν comparison

Figure 6.6. *(Continued) ν comparison*

6.3.4.2. *ξ parameter effects*

Next, the sensitivity of the AMPNLMS, AEPNLMS and ASPNLMS algorithms to the parameter ξ is examined. In Figures 6.7(a)–6.7(c), we compare the estimated MSE performance of the AMPNLMS, AEPNLMS and ASPNLMS algorithms for a fixed value of $\nu = 1,000$, and varying $\xi = 0.5, 0.9, 0.99$ and 0.999. Varying the value of ξ does not have as great an effect on the MSE performance as the ν parameter does have.

6.3.4.3. *Effects of Υ on ASPNLMS algorithm*

In Figure 6.8, we examine the effects of changing Υ on the learning curve of the ASPNLMS algorithm. The MSE is plotted for Υ = 1, 10, 100 and 1,000 and the parameters $\xi = 0.99$, $\nu = 1,000$ are fixed. The ASPNLMS algorithm convergence is very sensitive to the choice of Υ. The optimal choice of Υ will be related to the impulse response. This limitation is a potential shortcoming of the ASPNLMS algorithm.

6.3.4.4. *Effects of ρ on AEPNLMS algorithm*

In this section, the MSE performance of the AEPNLMS algorithm is plotted for $\rho = 0.1$, 0.01, 0.001 and 0.0001 in Figure 6.9. In these simulations, the parameters $\xi = 0.99$ and $\nu = 1,000$ are fixed. The AEPNLMS is very sensitive to the choice of the ρ parameter.

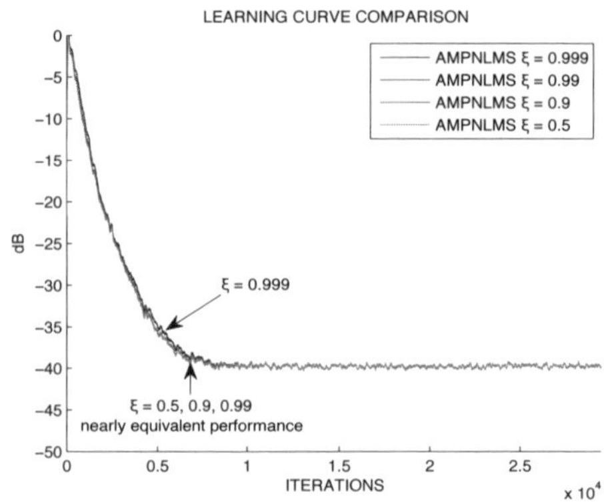

a) AMPNLMS ξ comparison

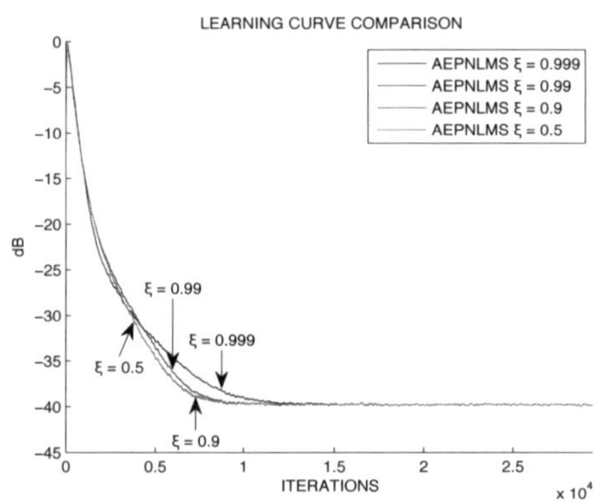

b) AEPNLMS ξ comparison

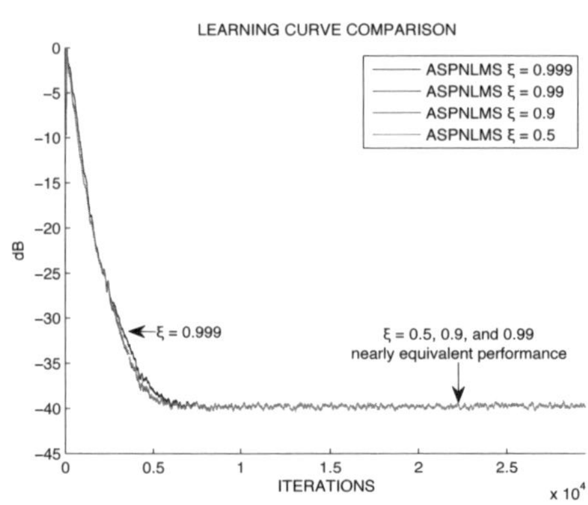

c) ASPNLMS ξ comparison

Figure 6.7. ξ *comparison*

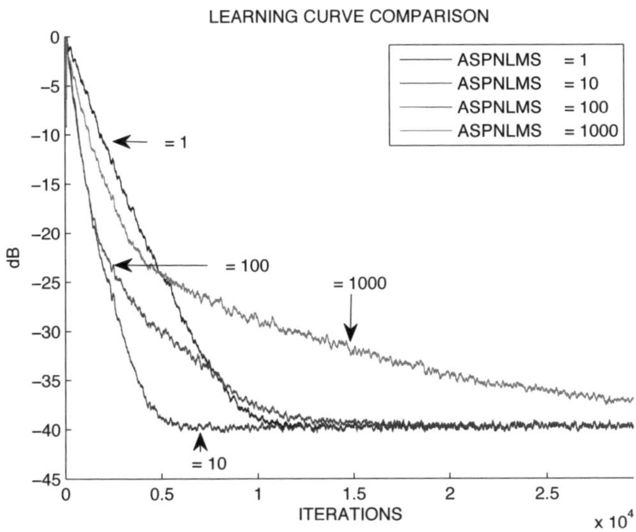

Figure 6.8. *ASPNLMS Υ comparison*

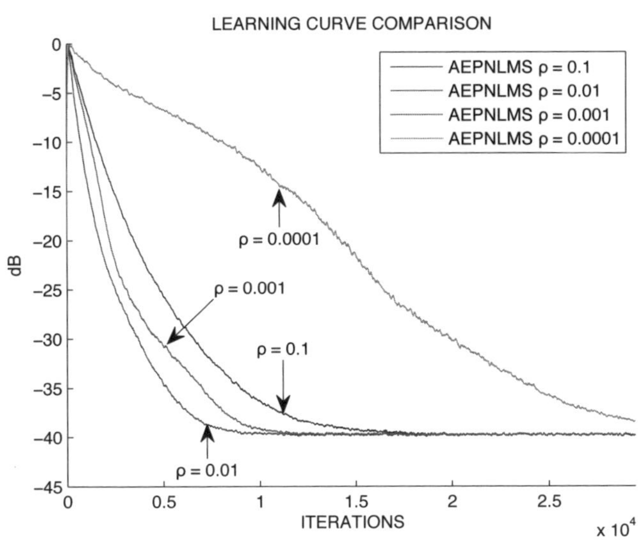

Figure 6.9. *AEPNLMS ρ comparison*

6.4. Summary

In this chapter, three new PtNLMS algorithms have been discussed. The AMPNLMS algorithm is a modification of the MPNLMS where the parameter μ is allowed to vary with time. The adaptive μ parameter is related to the MSE. In doing so, the ϵ-neighborhood of the unknown impulse response, which the algorithm is required to converge to, is slowly tightened as time passes. The tightening is controlled by the evolving MSE. This modification results in superior MSE convergence. Similarly, the AEPNLMS algorithm is a modification of the EPNLMS algorithm with an adaptive μ parameter. This algorithm shows improvement with respect to the EPNLMS algorithm; however, like the EPNLMS algorithm, the AEPNLMS algorithm displays sensitivity to the choice of algorithm parameter ρ. This limitation implies that more parameter tuning is required to achieve acceptable learning curve performance. The final algorithm introduced in this chapter, ASPNLMS, is a simplification of the AMPNLMS and AEPNLMS algorithms. The ASPNLMS algorithm avoids the usage of the logarithm function by approximating the logarithm with a two-segment linear function. This algorithm reduces the computational complexity and can offer superior convergence performance to the AMPNLMS and AEPNLMS algorithms. The drawback of the ASPNLMS algorithm is its sensitivity to the choice of parameter Υ.

7

Complex PtNLMS Algorithms

The complex least mean square (cLMS) adaptive filter [WID 75] was originally proposed to extend the LMS algorithm from real-valued signals to complex-valued signals. In this chapter, the PtNLMS algorithm is extended from real-valued signals to complex-valued signals. The resulting algorithm is named the complex PtNLMS (cPtNLMS) [WAG 12b] algorithm. The cPtNLMS algorithm updates the real and imaginary parts of the unknown impulse response by applying separate real-valued gains.

The cPtNLMS algorithm is derived as a special case of the complex proportionate-type affine projection (cPtAP) algorithm. The cPtAP algorithm is of practical importance in communication systems, for example, when working with microwave radio channels [SPI 96b] or cable modem channels [SPI 96a]. There, the ability to estimate an unknown complex impulse response is required and the input signal is complex, colored, and has an unknown covariance matrix. The cPtAP algorithm can also be used when the input signal has non-stationary statistics, such as speech. Motivated by the derivation of the affine projection adaptive filter (APAF) [HAY 02], the cPtAP algorithm is derived by minimizing the weighted squared Euclidean norm of the change in the weight vector subject to the constraints that multiple *a posteriori* output errors are equal to zero.

Several simplifications of the cPtNLMS and cPtAP algorithms will be proposed. In addition, the complex water-filling (cWF) gain allocation algorithm for white input signals is proposed and derived, followed by the cWF gain allocation algorithm for colored input signals.

The final section of this chapter deals with the topic of self-orthogonalizing adaptive filters [HAY 02]. The concept behind the self-orthogonalizing adaptive filter involves, first, whitening the input signal and then applying the cLMS filter to the whitened signal. This approach will be extended from the cLMS algorithm to cPtNLMS algorithms. The resulting algorithm is named the transform domain cPtNLMS (TD-cPtNLMS) algorithm.

7.1. Complex adaptive filter framework

All signals are complex throughout this chapter. Let us assume there is some complex input signal denoted as $\mathbf{x}(k)$ for time k that excites an unknown system with complex impulse response $\mathbf{w}$. Let the output of the system be $y(k) = \mathbf{x}^H(k)\mathbf{w}(k)$, where $\mathbf{x}(k) = [x(k), x(k-1), \ldots, x(k-L+1)]^T$ and L is the length of the filter. The measured output of the system $d(k)$ contains complex-valued measurement noise $v(k)$ and is equal to the sum of $y(k)$ and $v(k)$. The impulse response of the system is estimated with the adaptive filter coefficient vector $\hat{\mathbf{w}}(k)$, which also has length L. The output of the adaptive filter is given by $\hat{y}(k) = \mathbf{x}^H(k)\hat{\mathbf{w}}(k)$. The error signal $e(k)$ is equal to the difference of the measured output, $d(k)$ and the output of the adaptive filter $\hat{y}(k)$. Finally, we define $j = \sqrt{-1}$.

7.2. cPtNLMS and cPtAP algorithm derivation

Because the cPtAP algorithm is an extension of the cPtNLMS algorithm from a single constraint to multiple constraints, the derivations of both algorithms are very similar. Therefore, only the derivation of the cPtAP algorithm will be presented in this section. When it is appropriate, differences between the derivations of the cPtNLMS and cPtAP algorithms will be pointed out and explained.

The estimated weight vector can be written in terms of real and imaginary parts $\hat{\mathbf{w}} = \hat{\mathbf{w}}_R + j\hat{\mathbf{w}}_I$, where $\hat{\mathbf{w}}_R$ and $\hat{\mathbf{w}}_I$ are vectors of length L consisting of the real and imaginary components of $\hat{\mathbf{w}}$, respectively. Motivated by the derivation of the APAF and NLMS algorithms, let us consider the following minimization problem:

$$\min_{\hat{\mathbf{w}}^+} (\hat{\mathbf{w}}_R^+ - \hat{\mathbf{w}}_R)^T \mathbf{M}_R^{-1} (\hat{\mathbf{w}}_R^+ - \hat{\mathbf{w}}_R) + (\hat{\mathbf{w}}_I^+ - \hat{\mathbf{w}}_I)^T \mathbf{M}_I^{-1} (\hat{\mathbf{w}}_I^+ - \hat{\mathbf{w}}_I) \quad [7.1]$$

such that

$$\mathbf{d} = \begin{bmatrix} d(n) \\ d(n-1) \\ \vdots \\ d(n-P+1) \end{bmatrix} = \begin{bmatrix} \mathbf{x}^H(n) \\ \mathbf{x}^H(n-1) \\ \vdots \\ \mathbf{x}^H(n-P+1) \end{bmatrix} \hat{\mathbf{w}}^+ = \mathbf{X}^H \hat{\mathbf{w}}^+, \quad [7.2]$$

where $\mathbf{M}_R$ and $\mathbf{M}_I$ are real-valued, non-negative and diagonal matrices, which have the property that $\mathrm{Tr}[\mathbf{M}_R] = \mathrm{Tr}[\mathbf{M}_I] = L$ and P is a positive integer. For $P = 1$ the constraint is reduced to:

$$d = \mathbf{x}^H(n)\hat{\mathbf{w}}^+$$

and the solution to this problem results in the cPtNLMS algorithm.

The method of Lagrange multipliers will be used to replace this constrained minimization problem with one of unconstrained minimizations. Prior to performing this step the following definitions are introduced to aid in the derivation. Let

$$\hat{\omega} = \begin{bmatrix} \hat{\mathbf{w}}_R \\ \hat{\mathbf{w}}_I \end{bmatrix} \quad \mathbf{M} = \begin{bmatrix} \mathbf{M}_R & \mathbf{0} \\ \mathbf{0} & \mathbf{M}_I \end{bmatrix}. \qquad [7.3]$$

The following form of $\mathbf{X}^H\hat{\mathbf{w}}$ will also be employed:

$$\begin{aligned}
\mathbf{X}^H\hat{\mathbf{w}} &= (\mathbf{X}_R^T - j\mathbf{X}_I^T)(\hat{\mathbf{w}}_R + j\hat{\mathbf{w}}_I) \\
&= \mathbf{X}_R^T\hat{\mathbf{w}}_R + \mathbf{X}_I^T\hat{\mathbf{w}}_I + j\mathbf{X}_R^T\hat{\mathbf{w}}_I - j\mathbf{X}_I^T\hat{\mathbf{w}}_R \\
&= [\mathbf{X}_R^T,\, \mathbf{X}_I^T]\begin{bmatrix} \hat{\mathbf{w}}_R \\ \hat{\mathbf{w}}_I \end{bmatrix} + j[-\mathbf{X}_I^T,\, \mathbf{X}_R^T]\begin{bmatrix} \hat{\mathbf{w}}_R \\ \hat{\mathbf{w}}_I \end{bmatrix} \\
&= [\mathbf{X}^H,\, j\mathbf{X}^H]\begin{bmatrix} \hat{\mathbf{w}}_R \\ \hat{\mathbf{w}}_I \end{bmatrix} = [\mathbf{X}^H,\, j\mathbf{X}^H]\hat{\omega}.
\end{aligned} \qquad [7.4]$$

Using these definitions the minimization problem can be rewritten as:

$$\min_{\hat{\omega}^+} J(\hat{\omega}^+) = (\hat{\omega}^+ - \hat{\omega})^T\mathbf{M}^{-1}(\hat{\omega}^+ - \hat{\omega})$$

$$+\boldsymbol{\lambda}^T\left(\mathbf{d} - [\mathbf{X}^H, j\mathbf{X}^H]\hat{\omega}^+\right) + \boldsymbol{\lambda}^H\left(\mathbf{d}^* - [\mathbf{X}^T, -j\mathbf{X}^T]\hat{\omega}^+\right), \qquad [7.5]$$

where $\boldsymbol{\lambda}$ is the Lagrangian multiplier vector of length L. Next taking the derivative of $J(\hat{\omega}^+)$ with respect to $\hat{\omega}^+$ and setting the result to zero yields:

$$\frac{\partial J(\hat{\omega}^+)}{\partial\hat{\omega}^+} = 2\mathbf{M}^{-1}(\hat{\omega}^+ - \hat{\omega}) - \begin{bmatrix} \mathbf{X}^* \\ j\mathbf{X}^* \end{bmatrix}\boldsymbol{\lambda} - \begin{bmatrix} \mathbf{X} \\ -j\mathbf{X} \end{bmatrix}\boldsymbol{\lambda}^* = 0. \qquad [7.6]$$

Multiplying [7.6] from the left by $\mathbf{M}$ and rearranging terms allows us to write:

$$2(\hat{\omega}^+ - \hat{\omega}) = \mathbf{M}\begin{bmatrix} \mathbf{X}^* \\ j\mathbf{X}^* \end{bmatrix}\boldsymbol{\lambda} + \mathbf{M}\begin{bmatrix} \mathbf{X} \\ -j\mathbf{X} \end{bmatrix}\boldsymbol{\lambda}^*. \qquad [7.7]$$

Next defining the error vector as:

$$\mathbf{e} = \begin{bmatrix} d(n) - \mathbf{x}^H(n)\hat{\mathbf{w}}(n) \\ d(n-1) - \mathbf{x}^H(n-1)\hat{\mathbf{w}}(n) \\ \vdots \\ d(n-P+1) - \mathbf{x}^H(n-P+1)\hat{\mathbf{w}}(n) \end{bmatrix} = \mathbf{d} - \mathbf{X}^H\hat{\mathbf{w}} \qquad [7.8]$$

and combining with [7.4] results in:

$$\begin{aligned} \left[\mathbf{X}^H, j\mathbf{X}^H\right](\hat{\boldsymbol{\omega}}^+ - \hat{\boldsymbol{\omega}}) &= \mathbf{e} \\ \left[\mathbf{X}^T, -j\mathbf{X}^T\right](\hat{\boldsymbol{\omega}}^+ - \hat{\boldsymbol{\omega}}) &= \mathbf{e}^*. \end{aligned}$$

In addition, the following definitions are employed:

$$\begin{aligned} \mathbf{A} &= \mathbf{X}^T(\mathbf{M}_R + \mathbf{M}_I)\mathbf{X}^* \\ \mathbf{B} &= \mathbf{X}^T(\mathbf{M}_R - \mathbf{M}_I)\mathbf{X} \end{aligned}$$

to form the following linear system of equations:

$$2\begin{bmatrix} \mathbf{e}^* \\ \mathbf{e} \end{bmatrix} = \begin{bmatrix} \mathbf{A} & \mathbf{B} \\ \mathbf{B}^* & \mathbf{A}^* \end{bmatrix} \begin{bmatrix} \boldsymbol{\lambda} \\ \boldsymbol{\lambda}^* \end{bmatrix}. \qquad [7.9]$$

Matrix multiplying equation [7.9] from the left with:

$$\begin{bmatrix} \mathbf{I} & -\mathbf{B}\left[\mathbf{A}^*\right]^{-1} \\ \mathbf{0} & \mathbf{I} \end{bmatrix} \qquad [7.10]$$

yields:

$$2\begin{bmatrix} \mathbf{I} & -\mathbf{B}\left[\mathbf{A}^*\right]^{-1} \\ \mathbf{0} & \mathbf{I} \end{bmatrix} \begin{bmatrix} \mathbf{e}^* \\ \mathbf{e} \end{bmatrix} = \begin{bmatrix} \mathbf{A} - \mathbf{B}\left[\mathbf{A}^*\right]^{-1}\mathbf{B}^* & \mathbf{0} \\ \mathbf{B}^* & \mathbf{A}^* \end{bmatrix} \begin{bmatrix} \boldsymbol{\lambda} \\ \boldsymbol{\lambda}^* \end{bmatrix}. \qquad [7.11]$$

By inspection of [7.11] the solution for $\boldsymbol{\lambda}$ is given by:

$$\boldsymbol{\lambda} = 2\left\{\mathbf{A} - \mathbf{B}\left[\mathbf{A}^*\right]^{-1}\mathbf{B}^*\right\}^{-1}\left\{\mathbf{e}^* - \mathbf{B}\left[\mathbf{A}^*\right]^{-1}\mathbf{e}\right\}. \qquad [7.12]$$

Note that for $P = 1$, equation [7.12] is reduced to:

$$\lambda = 2\frac{\mathbf{x}^H(\mathbf{M}_R + \mathbf{M}_I)\mathbf{x}e^* - \mathbf{x}^T(\mathbf{M}_R - \mathbf{M}_I)\mathbf{x}e}{\left[\mathbf{x}^H(\mathbf{M}_R + \mathbf{M}_I)\mathbf{x}\right]^2 - |\mathbf{x}^T(\mathbf{M}_R - \mathbf{M}_I)\mathbf{x}|^2}. \qquad [7.13]$$

Returning our attention to [7.7], this equation can be rewritten as:

$$2(\hat{\boldsymbol{\omega}}^+ - \hat{\boldsymbol{\omega}}) = \begin{bmatrix} \mathbf{M}_R\mathbf{X}^* \\ j\mathbf{M}_I\mathbf{X}^* \end{bmatrix} \boldsymbol{\lambda} + \begin{bmatrix} \mathbf{M}_R\mathbf{X} \\ -j\mathbf{M}_I\mathbf{X} \end{bmatrix} \boldsymbol{\lambda}^*. \qquad [7.14]$$

Using the definition in [7.3] allows us to write:

$$\begin{aligned} 2(\hat{\mathbf{w}}_R^+ - \hat{\mathbf{w}}_R) &= \mathbf{M}_R\mathbf{X}^*\boldsymbol{\lambda} + \mathbf{M}_R\mathbf{X}\boldsymbol{\lambda}^* \\ 2(\hat{\mathbf{w}}_I^+ - \hat{\mathbf{w}}_I) &= j\mathbf{M}_I\mathbf{X}^*\boldsymbol{\lambda} - j\mathbf{M}_I\mathbf{X}\boldsymbol{\lambda}^*. \end{aligned} \qquad [7.15]$$

Next using [7.15] we form:

$$\begin{aligned} \hat{\mathbf{w}}^+ - \hat{\mathbf{w}} &= (\hat{\mathbf{w}}_R^+ - \hat{\mathbf{w}}_R) + j(\hat{\mathbf{w}}_I^+ - \hat{\mathbf{w}}_I) \\ &= \frac{1}{2}\mathbf{M}_R\mathbf{X}^*\boldsymbol{\lambda} + \frac{1}{2}\mathbf{M}_R\mathbf{X}\boldsymbol{\lambda}^* - \frac{1}{2}\mathbf{M}_I\mathbf{X}^*\boldsymbol{\lambda} + \frac{1}{2}\mathbf{M}_I\mathbf{X}\boldsymbol{\lambda}^* \\ &= \frac{1}{2}(\mathbf{M}_R - \mathbf{M}_I)\mathbf{X}^*\boldsymbol{\lambda} + \frac{1}{2}(\mathbf{M}_R + \mathbf{M}_I)\mathbf{X}\boldsymbol{\lambda}^*. \end{aligned} \qquad [7.16]$$

Next the step-size parameter β is introduced to allow control over the update. The resulting cPtAP algorithm with separate gains for real and imaginary coefficients is given by:

$$\hat{\mathbf{w}}^+ = \hat{\mathbf{w}} + \frac{\beta}{2}(\mathbf{M}_R - \mathbf{M}_I)\mathbf{X}^*\boldsymbol{\lambda} + \frac{\beta}{2}(\mathbf{M}_R + \mathbf{M}_I)\mathbf{X}\boldsymbol{\lambda}^*. \qquad [7.17]$$

The cPtNLMS is obtained by setting $P = 1$ and substituting [7.13] into [7.16] yields:

$$\begin{aligned} \hat{\mathbf{w}}^+ &= \hat{\mathbf{w}} \qquad [7.18] \\ &+\beta\frac{[\mathbf{x}^H(\mathbf{M}_R + \mathbf{M}_I)\mathbf{x}e^* - \mathbf{x}^T(\mathbf{M}_R - \mathbf{M}_I)\mathbf{x}e]}{[\mathbf{x}^H(\mathbf{M}_R + \mathbf{M}_I)\mathbf{x}]^2 - |\mathbf{x}^T(\mathbf{M}_R - \mathbf{M}_I)\mathbf{x}|^2}(\mathbf{M}_R - \mathbf{M}_I)\mathbf{x}^* \\ &+\beta\frac{[\mathbf{x}^H(\mathbf{M}_R + \mathbf{M}_I)\mathbf{x}e - \mathbf{x}^H(\mathbf{M}_R - \mathbf{M}_I)\mathbf{x}^*e^*]}{[\mathbf{x}^H(\mathbf{M}_R + \mathbf{M}_I)\mathbf{x}]^2 - |\mathbf{x}^T(\mathbf{M}_R - \mathbf{M}_I)\mathbf{x}|^2}(\mathbf{M}_R + \mathbf{M}_I)\mathbf{x}. \end{aligned}$$

7.2.1. *Algorithm simplifications*

The cPtAP algorithm given in [7.17] can be simplified under certain conditions. For instance, it is straightforward to show that by setting $\mathbf{M}_R = \mathbf{M}_I = \mathbf{G}$ in [7.12], $\boldsymbol{\lambda}$ is reduced to:

$$\boldsymbol{\lambda} = \left[\mathbf{X}^T\mathbf{G}\mathbf{X}^*\right]^{-1}\mathbf{e}^* \qquad [7.19]$$

and hence [7.17] can be rewritten as:

$$\hat{\mathbf{w}}^+ = \hat{\mathbf{w}} + \beta \mathbf{G}\mathbf{X}\left[\mathbf{X}^H \mathbf{G}\mathbf{X}\right]^{-1} \mathbf{e}. \qquad [7.20]$$

As it turns out [7.20], with $\beta = 1$, is the solution to the following minimization:

$$\min_{\hat{\mathbf{w}}^+} (\hat{\mathbf{w}}^+ - \hat{\mathbf{w}})^H \mathbf{G}^{-1}(\hat{\mathbf{w}}^+ - \hat{\mathbf{w}}), \text{ such that } \mathbf{d} = \mathbf{X}^H \hat{\mathbf{w}}^+, \qquad [7.21]$$

where $\mathbf{G}$ is the step-size control matrix. This version of the cPtAP algorithm uses one real-valued gain to simultaneously update both the real and imaginary parts of the estimated coefficient. Similarly, the cPtNLMS algorithm given in [7.18] can be simplified by setting $\mathbf{M}_R = \mathbf{M}_I = \mathbf{G}$ and results in:

$$\hat{\mathbf{w}}^+ = \hat{\mathbf{w}} + \beta \frac{\mathbf{G}\mathbf{x}e}{\mathbf{x}^H \mathbf{G}\mathbf{x}}. \qquad [7.22]$$

Equation [7.22] is the solution to the following minimization:

$$\min_{\hat{\mathbf{w}}^+} (\hat{\mathbf{w}}^+ - \hat{\mathbf{w}})^H \mathbf{G}^{-1}(\hat{\mathbf{w}}^+ - \hat{\mathbf{w}}), \text{ such that } d = \mathbf{x}^H \hat{\mathbf{w}}^+. \qquad [7.23]$$

A separate simplification to [7.17] can be made if it is assumed that:

$$\mathbf{X}^T(\mathbf{M}_R - \mathbf{M}_I)\mathbf{X} \approx 0. \qquad [7.24]$$

Using this approximation [7.12] is reduced to:

$$\boldsymbol{\lambda} = 2\left[\mathbf{X}^T(\mathbf{M}_R + \mathbf{M}_I)\mathbf{X}^*\right]^{-1} \mathbf{e}^*. \qquad [7.25]$$

Combining [7.17] and [7.25] results in:

$$\begin{aligned}\hat{\mathbf{w}}^+ = \hat{\mathbf{w}} &+ \beta \mathbf{M}_R \left[\mathbf{X}^* \mathbf{A}^{-1}\mathbf{e}^* + \mathbf{X}(\mathbf{A}^*)^{-1}\mathbf{e}\right] \\ &+ \beta \mathbf{M}_I \left[\mathbf{X}(\mathbf{A}^*)^{-1}\mathbf{e} - \mathbf{X}^* \mathbf{A}^{-1}\mathbf{e}^*\right]. \end{aligned} \qquad [7.26]$$

This version of the cPtAP algorithm reduces the computational complexity of [7.17] and will be referred to as the simplified cPtAP algorithm. Similarly, the cPtNLMS algorithm in [7.18] can be simplified if it is assumed that:

$$\mathbf{x}^T(\mathbf{M}_R - \mathbf{M}_I)\mathbf{x} \approx 0. \qquad [7.27]$$

Using this approximation [7.18] is reduced to:

$$\hat{\mathbf{w}}^+ = \hat{\mathbf{w}} + \beta \frac{\mathbf{M}_R(\mathbf{x}e + \mathbf{x}^* e^*) + \mathbf{M}_I(\mathbf{x}e - \mathbf{x}^* e^*)}{\mathbf{x}^H(\mathbf{M}_R + \mathbf{M}_I)\mathbf{x}}. \qquad [7.28]$$

This version of the cPtNLMS algorithm will be referred to as the simplified cPtNLMS algorithm.

7.2.2. *Alternative representations*

There are alternative ways to represent [7.16]. For instance, we could rearrange terms such that:

$$\begin{aligned}\hat{\mathbf{w}}^+ - \hat{\mathbf{w}} &= (\hat{\mathbf{w}}_R^+ - \hat{\mathbf{w}}_R) + j(\hat{\mathbf{w}}_I^+ - \hat{\mathbf{w}}_I)\\ &= \mathbf{M}_R \frac{\mathbf{X}\boldsymbol{\lambda}^* + \mathbf{X}^*\boldsymbol{\lambda}}{2} + \mathbf{M}_I \frac{\mathbf{X}\boldsymbol{\lambda}^* - \mathbf{X}^*\boldsymbol{\lambda}}{2}\\ &= \mathbf{M}_R \mathrm{Re}(\mathbf{X}\boldsymbol{\lambda}^*) + j\mathbf{M}_I \mathrm{Im}(\mathbf{X}\boldsymbol{\lambda}^*).\end{aligned} \quad [7.29]$$

Using [7.29] and introducing the step-size parameter β will result in an alternate form of the cPtAP algorithm. In this version of the cPtAP algorithm, the estimated impulse response coefficients are updated by one purely real term multiplying $\mathbf{M}_R$ and another purely imaginary term multiplying $\mathbf{M}_I$. Equivalent results can be obtained for the cPtNLMS algorithm by setting $P = 1$.

7.2.3. *Stability considerations of the cPtNLMS algorithm*

We will now prove that the denominator term in [7.18] is always non-negative. The denominator can be written as:

$$\begin{aligned}&\left[\mathbf{x}^H(\mathbf{M}_R + \mathbf{M}_I)\mathbf{x}\right]^2 - |\mathbf{x}^T(\mathbf{M}_R - \mathbf{M}_I)\mathbf{x}|^2\\ &= \mathbf{x}^H\mathbf{M}_R\mathbf{x}\mathbf{x}^H\mathbf{M}_R\mathbf{x} - \mathbf{x}^T\mathbf{M}_R\mathbf{x}\mathbf{x}^H\mathbf{M}_R\mathbf{x}^*\\ &\quad + \mathbf{x}^H\mathbf{M}_I\mathbf{x}\mathbf{x}^H\mathbf{M}_R\mathbf{x} + \mathbf{x}^T\mathbf{M}_I\mathbf{x}\mathbf{x}^H\mathbf{M}_R\mathbf{x}^*\\ &\quad + \mathbf{x}^H\mathbf{M}_R\mathbf{x}\mathbf{x}^H\mathbf{M}_I\mathbf{x} + \mathbf{x}^T\mathbf{M}_R\mathbf{x}\mathbf{x}^H\mathbf{M}_I\mathbf{x}^*\\ &\quad + \mathbf{x}^H\mathbf{M}_I\mathbf{x}\mathbf{x}^H\mathbf{M}_I\mathbf{x} - \mathbf{x}^T\mathbf{M}_I\mathbf{x}\mathbf{x}^H\mathbf{M}_I\mathbf{x}^*.\end{aligned}$$

This can be subsequently written as:

$$\begin{aligned}&\left[\mathbf{x}^H(\mathbf{M}_R + \mathbf{M}_I)\mathbf{x}\right]^2 - |\mathbf{x}^T(\mathbf{M}_R - \mathbf{M}_I)\mathbf{x}|^2\\ &= \mathbf{x}^H\mathbf{M}_R\mathbf{x}\mathbf{x}^H\mathbf{M}_R\mathbf{x} - |\mathbf{x}^T\mathbf{M}_R\mathbf{x}|^2\\ &\quad + \mathbf{x}^H\mathbf{M}_I\mathbf{x}\mathbf{x}^H\mathbf{M}_R\mathbf{x} + 2\mathrm{Re}\left[\mathbf{x}^T\mathbf{M}_I\mathbf{x}\mathbf{x}^H\mathbf{M}_R\mathbf{x}^*\right]\\ &\quad + \mathbf{x}^H\mathbf{M}_R\mathbf{x}\mathbf{x}^H\mathbf{M}_I\mathbf{x} - |\mathbf{x}^T\mathbf{M}_I\mathbf{x}|^2\\ &\quad + \mathbf{x}^H\mathbf{M}_I\mathbf{x}\mathbf{x}^H\mathbf{M}_I\mathbf{x}.\end{aligned}$$

In the following, we used the inequalities:

$$|\mathbf{x}^T\mathbf{M}_R\mathbf{x}| = |\sum_{i=1}^{L} [\mathbf{M}_R]_{ii}\, x_i^2| \leq \sum_{i=1}^{L} [\mathbf{M}_R]_{ii}\, |x_i|^2 = \mathbf{x}^H\mathbf{M}_R\mathbf{x} \qquad [7.30]$$

$$|\mathbf{x}^T\mathbf{M}_I\mathbf{x}| = |\sum_{i=1}^{L} [\mathbf{M}_I]_{ii}\, x_i^2| \leq \sum_{i=1}^{L} [\mathbf{M}_I]_{ii}\, |x_i|^2 = \mathbf{x}^H\mathbf{M}_I\mathbf{x} \qquad [7.31]$$

$$\text{Re}\left[\mathbf{x}^T\mathbf{M}_I\mathbf{x}\mathbf{x}^H\mathbf{M}_R\mathbf{x}^*\right] \geq -|\mathbf{x}^T\mathbf{M}_I\mathbf{x}||\mathbf{x}^H\mathbf{M}_R\mathbf{x}^*| \qquad [7.32]$$

to show that:

$$\begin{aligned}&\left[\mathbf{x}^H(\mathbf{M}_R+\mathbf{M}_I)\mathbf{x}\right]^2 - |\mathbf{x}^T(\mathbf{M}_R-\mathbf{M}_I)\mathbf{x}|^2\\ &\geq 2\mathbf{x}^H\mathbf{M}_R\mathbf{x}\mathbf{x}^H\mathbf{M}_I\mathbf{x} - 2\mathbf{x}^H\mathbf{M}_R\mathbf{x}\mathbf{x}^H\mathbf{M}_I\mathbf{x} = 0.\end{aligned} \qquad [7.33]$$

7.2.4. *Calculation of stepsize control matrix*

In this section, several examples of cPtNLMS algorithms are shown. The results presented here can be readily extended to the cPtAP algorithm as well. The calculation of the step-size control matrix for the cPtNLMS algorithm using one real-valued gain per coefficient is the same as shown for the PtNLMS algorithm in Table 1.1.

$F_R[\|\hat{w}_{R,l}(k)\|, k]$	= Specified by the user
$F_I[\|\hat{w}_{I,l}(k)\|, k]$	= Specified by the user
$\gamma_{min,R}(k)$	$= \rho \max\{\delta_p, F_R[\|\hat{w}_{R,1}(k)\|, k], \ldots, F_R[\|\hat{w}_{R,L}(k)\|, k]\}$
$\gamma_{min,I}(k)$	$= \rho \max\{\delta_p, F_I[\|\hat{w}_{I,1}(k)\|, k], \ldots, F_I[\|\hat{w}_{I,L}(k)\|, k]\}$
$\gamma_{R,l}(k)$	$= \max\{\gamma_{min,R}(k), F_R[\|\hat{w}_{R,l}(k)\|, k]\}$
$\gamma_{I,l}(k)$	$= \max\{\gamma_{min,I}(k), F_I[\|\hat{w}_{I,l}(k)\|, k]\}$
$m_{R,l}(k)$	$= \frac{\gamma_{R,l}(k)}{\frac{1}{L}\sum_{i=1}^{L}\gamma_{R,i}(k)}$
$m_{I,l}(k)$	$= \frac{\gamma_{I,l}(k)}{\frac{1}{L}\sum_{i=1}^{L}\gamma_{I,i}(k)}$
$\mathbf{M}_R(k)$	$= \mathbf{Diag}\{m_{R,1}(k), \ldots, m_{R,L}(k)\}$
$\mathbf{M}_I(k)$	$= \mathbf{Diag}\{m_{I,1}(k), \ldots, m_{I,L}(k)\}$

Table 7.1. *Step-size control matrix for cPtNLMS algorithm using separate real-valued gains for coefficients' real and imaginary parts*

The calculation of the step-size control matrices for the cPtNLMS algorithm using separate real-valued gains for coefficients real and imaginary parts is shown in Table 7.1. In this case, the user specifies two functions $F_R[|\hat{w}_{R,l}(k)|, k]$ and $F_I[|\hat{w}_{I,l}(k)|, k]$, which govern how the real and imaginary parts of a coefficient are updated. Next a minimum gain for the real and imaginary parts is calculated,

$\gamma_{min,R}(k)$ and $\gamma_{min,I}(k)$, respectively. Finally, the step-size control matrix for the real $\mathbf{M}_R(k)$ and imaginary $\mathbf{M}_I(k)$ parts are obtained. Some examples of the terms $F_R[|\hat{w}_{R,l}(k)|, k]$ and $F_I[|\hat{w}_{I,l}(k)|, k]$ include $F_R[|\hat{w}_{R,l}(k)|, k] = |\hat{w}_{R,l}(k)|$ and $F_I[|\hat{w}_{I,l}(k)|, k] = |\hat{w}_{I,l}(k)|$. This yields the complex PNLMS algorithm using separate gains for coefficient real and imaginary parts. In a similar manner, the complex MPNLMS algorithm can be created by setting $F_R[|\hat{w}_{R,l}(k)|, k] = \ln(1 + \mu|\hat{w}_{R,l}(k)|)$ and $F_I[|\hat{w}_{I,l}(k)|, k] = \ln(1 + \mu|\hat{w}_{I,l}(k)|)$.

The cPtAP algorithms presented in the subsequent section's simulations are listed next. The complex affine projection (cIAP) algorithm uses $\mathbf{G} = \mathbf{I}$, where $\mathbf{I}$ is the identity matrix. The complex proportionate affine projection (cPAP) algorithm using one gain to simultaneously update the real and imaginary coefficients (cPAP one-gain) employs the gain control logic function $F[|\hat{w}_l(k)|, k] = |\hat{w}_l(k)|$ for $l = 1, 2, \ldots, L$. The cPAP algorithm using separate gains to update the real and imaginary coefficients (cPAP two-gain) employs the gain control logic functions $F_R[|\hat{w}_{R,l}(k)|, k] = |\hat{w}_{R,l}(k)|$ and $F_I[|\hat{w}_{I,l}(k)|, k] = |\hat{w}_{I,l}(k)|$ for $l = 1, 2, \ldots, L$. Finally, the simplified cPAP algorithm using separate gains to update the real and imaginary coefficients (simplified cPAP) employs the same gain control logic functions as the cPAP two-gain algorithm.

In non-stationary environments, the inversion of the term:

$$\mathbf{A} - \mathbf{B}\left[\mathbf{A}^*\right]^{-1}\mathbf{B}^* \qquad [7.34]$$

in [7.12] may cause numerical difficulties. To guard against such a possibility, we add a small term $\delta\mathbf{I}$ prior to performing the inversion, where $\delta > 0$. This modification is referred to as regularization [HAY 02]. Regularization is performed on cPtAP algorithms for which simulation results are presented. Note that the size of the term in [7.34] is $P \times P$. In practice, P is typically less than 10, hence the inversion of [7.34] is not computationally burdensome.

7.3. Complex water-filling gain allocation algorithm for white input signals: one gain per coefficient case

In this section, the (cWF) gain allocation algorithm with one gain per coefficient, under the assumption of white input signals, is derived. The cWF gain allocation algorithm for white input signals is derived by minimizing the MSE at each time step. After the derivation of the cWF gain allocation algorithm, the implementation of the proposed algorithm is discussed.

7.3.1. *Derivation*

The cWF gain allocation algorithm is derived under the assumptions 2.1, 4.1, and the following two assumptions that are complex signal counterparts of assumptions 2.2 and 3.1.

ASSUMPTION 7.1.– The measurement noise $v(k)$ is a white complex circular stationary process with zero-mean, variance σ_v^2, and it is independent of the input.

ASSUMPTION 7.2.– The input signal is a white complex circular Gaussian stationary random process with zero-mean and variance σ_x^2.

Next we define the weight deviation as $\mathbf{z} = \mathbf{w} - \hat{\mathbf{w}}$. Using this definition the error can be written as:

$$e = \mathbf{x}^H\mathbf{w} - \mathbf{x}^H\hat{\mathbf{w}} + v = \mathbf{x}^H\mathbf{z} + v. \quad [7.35]$$

This implies that:

$$\begin{aligned} |e|^2 = e^*e &= (\mathbf{x}^H\mathbf{z} + v)^*(\mathbf{x}^H\mathbf{z} + v) \\ &= \mathbf{z}^H\mathbf{x}\mathbf{x}^H\mathbf{z} + v^*\mathbf{x}^H\mathbf{z} + v\mathbf{x}^T\mathbf{z}^* + v^*v. \end{aligned} \quad [7.36]$$

Next, taking the expectation of [7.36] and using assumptions 2.1, 7.1, and 7.2 yield:

$$J = E\{|e|^2\} = \sigma_x^2 E\{\mathbf{z}^T\mathbf{z}^*\} + \sigma_v^2 = \sigma_x^2 \sum_{i=1}^{L} E\{|z_i|^2\} + \sigma_v^2. \quad [7.37]$$

The goal then becomes to minimize J at each time step by choosing the step-size control matrix $\mathbf{G}$ appropriately. Next we will express the MSWD in terms of $\mathbf{G}$. Before doing this, note that recursion in [7.22] can be simplified by introducing the approximation:

$$\mathbf{x}^H\mathbf{G}\mathbf{x} = \sum_{i=1}^{L} |x_i|^2 g_i \approx \sigma_x^2 \sum_{i=1}^{L} g_i = \sigma_x^2 L. \quad [7.38]$$

Here the value $|x_i|^2$ has been replaced by its expected value $E\{|x_i|^2\} = \sigma_x^2$ and then the property that the sum of the gains equals L has been employed. The last approximation is an extension of assumption 3.2 to complex-valued signals. Using this approximation and the definition, $\beta_a = \beta/(\sigma_x^2 L)$, it is possible to write:

$$\mathbf{z}^+ = \mathbf{z} - \beta_a \mathbf{G}\mathbf{x}\mathbf{x}^H\mathbf{z} - \beta_a \mathbf{G}\mathbf{x}v. \quad [7.39]$$

In this form, the algorithm can be interpreted as a cPtLMS algorithm. Writing this recursion in component-wise form and taking the expectation yield:

$$z_l^+ = z_l - \beta_a g_l x_l \sum_{i=1}^{L} x_i^* z_i - \beta_a g_l x_l v \quad [7.40]$$

$$E\left\{z_l^+\right\} = E\left\{z_l\right\} - \beta_a \sigma_x^2 g_l E\left\{z_l\right\}. \quad [7.41]$$

Next we form the component-wise square weight deviation:

$$|z_l^+|^2 = |z_l|^2 - \beta_a g_l x_l \sum_{i=1}^{L} x_i^* z_i z_l^* - \beta_a g_l x_l^* \sum_{i=1}^{L} x_i z_i^* z_l$$
$$-\beta_a g_l x_l v z_l^* - \beta_a g_l x_l^* v^* z_l$$
$$+\beta_a^2 g_l^2 |x_l|^2 \sum_{i=1}^{L} x_i z_i^* v + \beta_a^2 g_l^2 |x_l|^2 \sum_{i=1}^{L} x_i^* z_i v^*$$
$$+\beta_a^2 g_l^2 |x_l|^2 \sum_{r=1}^{L} \sum_{s=1}^{L} x_r z_r^* x_s^* z_s + \beta_a^2 g_l^2 |x_l|^2 |v|^2. \qquad [7.42]$$

Taking the expectation results in:

$$E\left\{|z_l^+|^2\right\} = E\left\{|z_l|^2\right\} - 2\beta_a g_l \sigma_x^2 E\left\{|z_l|^2\right\} + \beta_a^2 g_l^2 \sigma_x^2 \sigma_v^2$$
$$+\beta_a^2 g_l^2 \sum_{r=1}^{L} \sum_{s=1}^{L} z_r^* z_s E\{x_l x_l^* x_r x_s^*\}. \qquad [7.43]$$

The expectation in the last term is given by [SAY 03]:

$$E\{x_l x_l^* x_r x_s^*\} = \begin{cases} \sigma_x^4, & r = s \neq l \\ 2\sigma_x^4, & r = s = l \\ 0, & \text{otherwise} \end{cases}. \qquad [7.44]$$

Therefore, [7.43] becomes:

$$E\left\{|z_l^+|^2\right\} = E\left\{|z_l|^2\right\} - 2\beta_a g_l \sigma_x^2 E\left\{|z_i|^2\right\} + \beta_a^2 g_l^2 \sigma_x^2 \sigma_v^2$$
$$+\beta_a^2 g_l^2 \sigma_x^4 \left(E\left\{|z_l|^2\right\} + \sum_{i=1}^{L} E\left\{|z_i|^2\right\} \right). \qquad [7.45]$$

At this point we define:

$$c_l \equiv 2\beta_a \sigma_x^2 E\left\{|z_l|^2\right\}$$
$$q_l \equiv 2\beta_a^2 \sigma_x^4 \left(E\left\{|z_l|^2\right\} + \sum_{i=1}^{L} E\left\{|z_i|^2\right\} + \frac{\sigma_v^2}{\sigma_x^2} \right)$$
$$\mathbf{Q} = \mathbf{Diag}(\mathbf{q}).$$

Then, we can recast the minimization problem as:

$$\min_{\substack{\mathbf{g} \\ \mathbf{1}^T\mathbf{g}=L \\ g_i \geq 0 \ \forall \ i}} \frac{J^+ - \sigma_v^2}{\sigma_x^2} - \sum_{i=1}^{L} E\left\{|z_i|^2\right\} = \min_{\substack{\mathbf{g} \\ \mathbf{1}^T\mathbf{g}=L \\ g_i \geq 0 \ \forall \ i}} \left\{-\mathbf{c}^T\mathbf{g} + \frac{1}{2}\mathbf{g}^T\mathbf{Q}\mathbf{g}\right\}. \qquad [7.46]$$

The minimization then proceeds as it did in the real-valued case (see 4.1.1 or [WAG 09]).

7.3.2. *Implementation*

To find $\widehat{E\left\{z_i\right\}}$ we rewrite the error as $e = \sum_{j=1}^{L} x_j^* z_j + v$ and proceed as in section 4.1.3.

7.4. Complex colored water-filling gain allocation algorithm: one gain per coefficient case

In this section, the complex colored water-filling (cCWF) gain allocation algorithm is proposed. The cCWF extends the cWF gain allocation algorithm to colored input signals with no restrictions on the covariance or pseudo-covariance matrices. The cCWF is derived by minimizing the mean square weight deviation.

7.4.1. *Problem statement and assumptions*

We seek the optimal gain at each time step k. Our approach to this problem is to minimize the MSWD with respect to the gain under two constraints. The two constraints that are to be satisfied are $g_i(k) \geq 0 \ \forall \ i, k$ and $\sum_{i=1}^{L} g_i(k) = L \ \forall \ k$.

Note that in addition to assumptions 2.1, 4.3 and 7.1, we have:

ASSUMPTION 7.3.– The input signal is a stationary Gaussian noise process with zero-mean, covariance $\mathbf{R} = E\{\mathbf{x}\mathbf{x}^H\}$ and pseudo-covariance $\mathbf{T} = E\{\mathbf{x}\mathbf{x}^T\}$. Let $\sigma_x^2 = [\mathbf{R}]_{ii} \ \forall \ i$.

ASSUMPTION 7.4.– $\sum_{l=1}^{L} |x_l|^2 g_l + \delta$ is constant for all times.

This latter assumption is the version of assumption 3.2 for the complex input. For

$$L >> \sqrt{\mathbf{g}^T(\mathbf{R} \odot \mathbf{R}^* + \mathbf{T} \odot \mathbf{T}^*)\mathbf{g}} \Big/ \sigma_x^2 \qquad [7.47]$$

the standard deviation of the term $\sum_{l=1}^{L} |x_l|^2 g_l + \delta$ becomes much smaller than the expected value. It can be shown that a sufficient condition for this to happen is that the support $\mathcal{S}$ satisfies:

$$\mathcal{S} >> \frac{\lambda_{\max}(\mathbf{R} \odot \mathbf{R}^* + \mathbf{T} \odot \mathbf{T}^*)}{\sigma_x^4},$$

where $\mathcal{S}$ is defined by [4.34] and $\lambda_{\max}$ is the largest eigenvalue of $\mathbf{R} \odot \mathbf{R}^* + \mathbf{T} \odot \mathbf{T}^*$. The condition in [7.47] is satisfied for large values of L and $\mathbf{g}$ that is not extremely sparse. Hence we can assume that the denominator term is approximately constant.

By following the steps described in section 7.3.1, we again have [7.39].

7.4.2. *Optimal gain allocation resulting from minimization of MSWD*

The criterion we try to minimize is the mean square weight deviation at time $k+1$. The square weight deviation at time $k+1$ can be represented by:

$$\begin{aligned}
\mathbf{z}^{+H}\mathbf{z}^{+} = {} & \mathbf{z}^H\mathbf{z} - \beta_a \mathbf{z}^H\mathbf{G}\mathbf{x}\mathbf{x}^H\mathbf{z} - \beta_a \mathbf{z}^H\mathbf{G}\mathbf{x}v \\
& -\beta_a \mathbf{z}^H\mathbf{x}\mathbf{x}^H\mathbf{G}\mathbf{z} + \beta_a^2\mathbf{z}^H\mathbf{x}\mathbf{x}^H\mathbf{G}^2\mathbf{x}\mathbf{x}^H\mathbf{z} + \beta_a^2\mathbf{z}^H\mathbf{x}\mathbf{x}^H\mathbf{G}^2\mathbf{x}v \\
& -\beta_a \mathbf{x}^H\mathbf{G}\mathbf{z}v^* + \beta_a^2\mathbf{x}^H\mathbf{G}^2\mathbf{x}\mathbf{x}^H\mathbf{z}v^* + \beta_a^2\mathbf{x}^H\mathbf{G}^2\mathbf{x}|v|^2. \qquad [7.48]
\end{aligned}$$

Next taking the expectation of [7.48] given the prior weight deviation $\mathbf{z}$, and using assumption 4.3 yields:

$$\begin{aligned}
E\left\{\mathbf{z}^{+H}\mathbf{z}^{+}|\mathbf{z}\right\} = {} & \mathbf{z}^H\mathbf{z} - \beta_a\left[\mathbf{z}^H\mathbf{Diag}(\mathbf{R}\mathbf{z}) + \mathbf{z}^T\mathbf{Diag}(\mathbf{R}^*\mathbf{z}^*)\right]\mathbf{g} \\
& +\beta_a^2\sigma_x^2\mathbf{z}^H\mathbf{R}\mathbf{z}\mathbf{g}^T\mathbf{g} + \beta_a^2\sigma_v^2\sigma_x^2\mathbf{g}^T\mathbf{g} \\
& +\beta_a^2\mathbf{g}^T\left[\mathbf{Diag}(\mathbf{R}\mathbf{z})\mathbf{Diag}^*(\mathbf{R}\mathbf{z})\right]\mathbf{g} \\
& +\beta_a^2\mathbf{g}^T\left[\mathbf{Diag}(\mathbf{T}\mathbf{z}^*)\mathbf{Diag}^*(\mathbf{T}\mathbf{z}^*)\right]\mathbf{g}. \qquad [7.49]
\end{aligned}$$

Setting:

$$\mathbf{c}^T = \beta_a\left[\mathbf{z}^H\mathbf{Diag}(\mathbf{R}\mathbf{z}) + \mathbf{z}^T\mathbf{Diag}(\mathbf{R}^*\mathbf{z}^*)\right] \qquad [7.50]$$

$$\begin{aligned}
\mathbf{Q} = {} & 2\beta_a^2\sigma_x^2\mathbf{z}^H\mathbf{R}\mathbf{z}\mathbf{I} + 2\beta_a^2\sigma_v^2\sigma_x^2\mathbf{I} \\
& +2\beta_a^2\left[\mathbf{Diag}(\mathbf{R}\mathbf{z})\mathbf{Diag}^*(\mathbf{R}\mathbf{z})\right] \\
& +2\beta_a^2\left[\mathbf{Diag}(\mathbf{T}\mathbf{z}^*)\mathbf{Diag}^*(\mathbf{T}\mathbf{z}^*)\right]. \qquad [7.51]
\end{aligned}$$

Now the constrained optimization problem can be recast as:

$$\min_{\substack{\mathbf{g} \\ \mathbf{1}^T\mathbf{g}=L \\ g_i \geq 0 \;\forall\, i}} \left(||\mathbf{z}^+||^2 - ||\mathbf{z}||^2\right) = \min_{\substack{\mathbf{g} \\ g_i \geq 0 \;\forall\, i}} \left[-\mathbf{c}^T\mathbf{g} + \frac{1}{2}\mathbf{g}^T\mathbf{Q}\mathbf{g} + \lambda\left(\mathbf{1}^T\mathbf{g} - L\right)\right], \qquad [7.52]$$

where λ is the Lagrange multiplier used to incorporate the constraint that the sum of the gains equal L.

The minimization then proceeds as it did in the real-valued case in section 4.3.1 and results in

$$g_i = \left(\frac{c_i - \lambda}{[\mathbf{Q}]_{ii}}\right)_+. \qquad [7.53]$$

Note that it can be shown that minimizing the MSWD minimizes an upper bound for the MSE, similarly as it is done for the real signal case in section 4.3.2.

7.4.3. *Implementation*

To proceed we need to calculate the terms $\mathbf{Rz}$, $\mathbf{R}^*\mathbf{z}^*$, $\mathbf{z}^H\mathbf{Rz}$ and $\mathbf{Tz}^*$. We propose replacing these quantities with an estimate of their corresponding mean values. Recall also that $\mathbf{R}$ and $\mathbf{T}$ are assumed known.

To find the estimate of $\mathbf{z}$, $\widehat{E\{\mathbf{z}\}}$, we begin with:

$$E\{\mathbf{p}\} = E\{\mathbf{x}e\} = E\{\mathbf{x}(\mathbf{x}^H\mathbf{z} + v)\} = \mathbf{R}E\{\mathbf{z}\} \qquad [7.54]$$

and continue as it is described in section 4.3.1.2.

Now we make three approximations by replacing:

$$\begin{aligned} \mathbf{Rz} &\approx \widehat{E\{\mathbf{p}\}}, \\ \mathbf{z}^H\mathbf{Rz} &\approx \widehat{E\{\mathbf{z}\}}^H \widehat{E\{\mathbf{p}\}}, \\ \mathbf{Tz}^* &\approx \mathbf{T}\widehat{E\{\mathbf{z}\}}^*. \end{aligned}$$

The obtained estimate is good in the transient regime. In the steady-state regime, it is preferable to use uniform gains. One way to implement gradual migration from the different gains to the uniform migration is to use, after replacing squaring with absolute value squaring, the adaptive convex gain combination presented in section 4.1.3.2.

7.5. Simulation results

7.5.1. *cPtNLMS algorithm simulation results*

In this section, we compare the MSE versus iteration for several cPtNLMS algorithms. The real part of the impulse response is given in Figure 6.5, while the imaginary part corresponds to the impulse response in Figure 1.2b shifted by 100 samples to the left. The impulse response has length $L = 512$. The step-size control parameter β was set to a value of 0.1 for all of the cPtNLMS algorithms. The input signal used in the first set of simulations was white, circular, complex, Gaussian and stationary with power $\sigma_x^2 = 1$. The noise used in all simulations was white, circular, complex, Gaussian and stationary with power $\sigma_v^2 = 10^{-4}$. The parameter values $\rho = 0.01$, $\delta = 0.0001$, $\delta_p = 0.01$ and $\mu = 2,960$ (used in cMPNLMS algorithm) were also used.

The MSE learning curve performance for the cNLMS, cPNLMS with one gain per coefficient, simplified cPNLMS with separate gains for the real and imaginary parts, cPNLMS with separate gains for the real and imaginary parts, cMPNLMS with one gain per coefficient, simplified cMPNLMS with separate gains for the real and imaginary parts, cMPNLMS with separate gains for the real and imaginary parts and cWF with one gain per coefficient algorithms are depicted in Figure 7.1. Here we see that the cPtNLMS algorithms outperform the cNLMS algorithm in the transient regime. The simplified algorithms perform virtually the same as the exact separate gain algorithms. In addition, the separate gains for the real and imaginary parts of coefficients versions result in better convergence than the single gain versions. The cWF algorithm with one gain per coefficient has superior convergence performance than all of the algorithms that use only one gain to update the estimated impulse response.

In Figure 7.2, the MSE performance is displayed for a colored input signal. The input signal consists of colored noise generated by a single pole system [4.31], where $n(k)$ is a white, circular, complex, Gaussian and stationary process with power $\sigma_n^2 = 1$, and γ is the complex pole. The value $\gamma = 0.3560 - 0.8266j$ was used in this simulation. The magnitude of γ is equal to 0.9, which implies $\sigma_x^2 = \sigma_\alpha^2/(1 - |\gamma|^2) = 5.263$. Similar trends hold for the colored and white input signal cases. Of course, the convergence rate is lower because of the colored input. The cWF algorithm with one gain per coefficient does not converge. This behavior is not surprising as the cWF algorithm relies on the assumption that the input signal is white.

Now, we are going to assess the performance of the cCWF algorithm. The input signal consists of colored noise generated by a single pole system [4.31] with $n(k) = n_R(k) + jn_I(k)$, where $n_R(k)$ and $n_I(k)$ are white, mutually independent, Gaussian and stationary processes with power $\sigma_{nR}^2 = 1/4$ and $\sigma_{nI}^2 = 3/4$, respectively. This implies that $n(k)$ is non-circular with power equal to one. The algorithm is initialized such that $x(0) = n(0)$. The value of pole $\gamma = -0.5756 + 0.1693j$ is used in this simulation. Hence $|\gamma| = 0.6$ which implies $\sigma_x^2 = \sigma_n^2/(1-|\gamma|^2) = 1.562$. $\mu = 37,291$ is used in the cMPNLMS algorithm. The cCWF algorithm uses values of $\alpha = 0.999$ and $\omega = 2$.

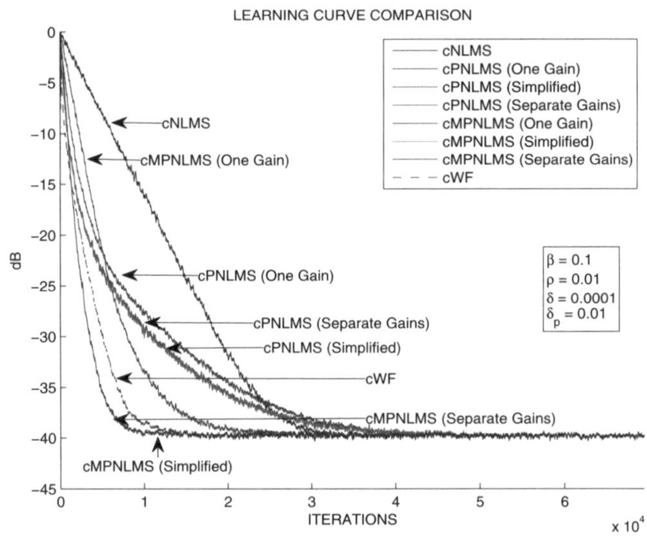

Figure 7.1. *cPtNLMS learning curve comparison with white input*

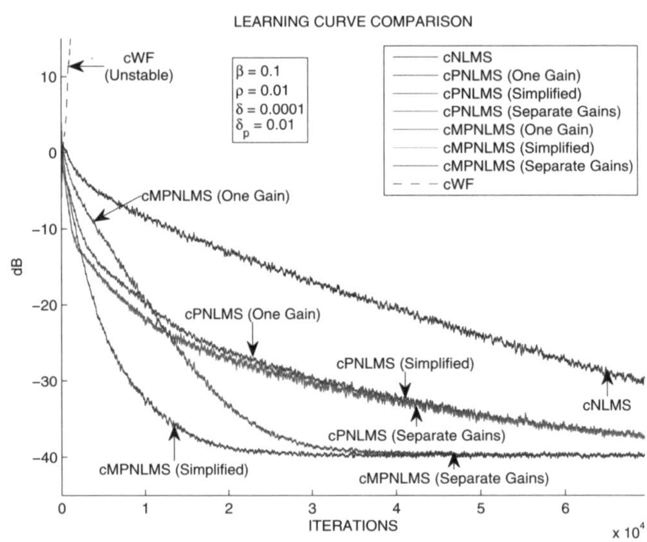

Figure 7.2. *cPtNLMS learning curve comparison with colored input*

The MSE learning curve performance for the cNLMS, cPNLMS with one gain per coefficient, cMPNLMS with one gain per coefficient, cCWF and Ideal cCWF algorithms are depicted in Figure 7.3. The Ideal cCWF uses the true value $\mathbf{w}$ as the input to the cCWF gain allocation algorithm. The Ideal cCWF does not use the adaptive convex gain combination. In Figure 7.3, we see that the Ideal cCWF algorithm has the best performance followed by the cCWF.

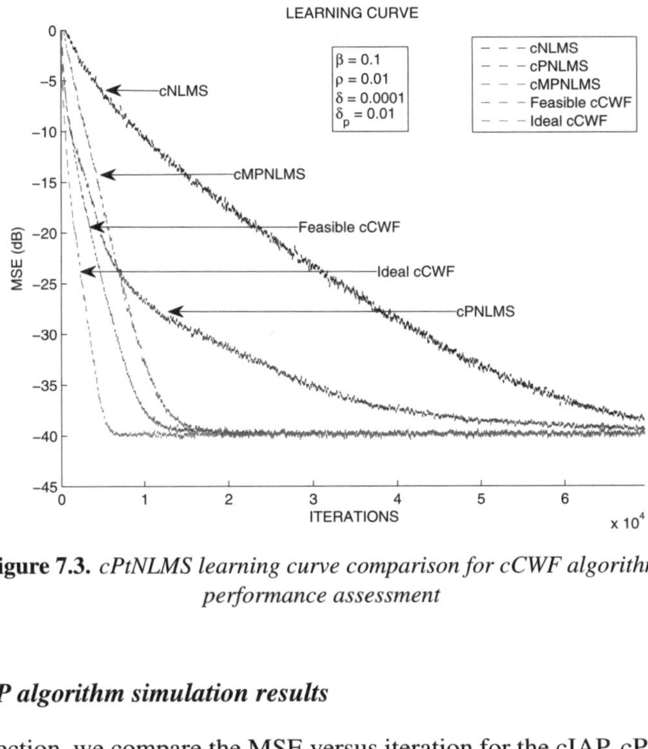

Figure 7.3. *cPtNLMS learning curve comparison for cCWF algorithm performance assessment*

7.5.2. *cPtAP algorithm simulation results*

In this section, we compare the MSE versus iteration for the cIAP, cPAP one-gain, cPAP two-gain and simplified cPAP. For reference purposes, we also plot the MSE versus iteration of the cNLMS and cPNLMS using separate gains to update the real and imaginary coefficients (cPNLMS two-gain).

The colored input signal was generated using the methodology described in section 7.5.1. The following values were used in simulations $\sigma^2_{n_R} = 3/4$, $\sigma^2_{n_I} = 1/4$ and $\gamma = -0.8634 + 0.2540j$. The magnitude of γ is equal to 0.9, which implies $\sigma^2_x = \sigma^2_\alpha/(1 - |\gamma|^2) = 5.263$. The real part of the impulse response is displayed in Figure 6.5 and the imaginary part of the impulse response is displayed in Figure 1.2b. The impulse response used has length $L = 512$ and has separate support for its real and imaginary parts. The noise used in the first simulation was white, circular, complex, Gaussian and stationary with power $\sigma^2_v = 10^{-4}$. The parameter values $P = 5$, $\rho = 0.01$, $\delta = 0.0001$ and $\delta_p = 0.01$ were also used [WAG 12b].

The MSE learning curve performance with colored input and 100 Monte Carlo trials is presented in Figure 7.4. A zoomed-in version of Figure 7.4, focusing on the transient regime of convergence, is displayed in Figure 7.5. The step-size control parameter β was set to a value of 0.5 for the cPtNLMS algorithms, 0.12 for the cIAP algorithm, and 0.072 for the cPAP algorithms. Different values of β were used in each algorithm to ensure the same steady-state MSE was achieved by all of the algorithms. The cPtNLMS algorithms have the slowest convergence. The cIAP algorithm is the first to reach steady-state, however the various cPAP algorithms have a faster initial convergence rate than the cIAP algorithm. These last two trends mimic the trends seen when observing the convergence rates of the NLMS and PNLMS algorithms [DUT 00]. The cPAP two-gain and simplified cPAP algorithms have roughly the same convergence rates. Finally, the cPAP two-gain algorithms have a faster convergence rate than the cPAP one-gain algorithm.

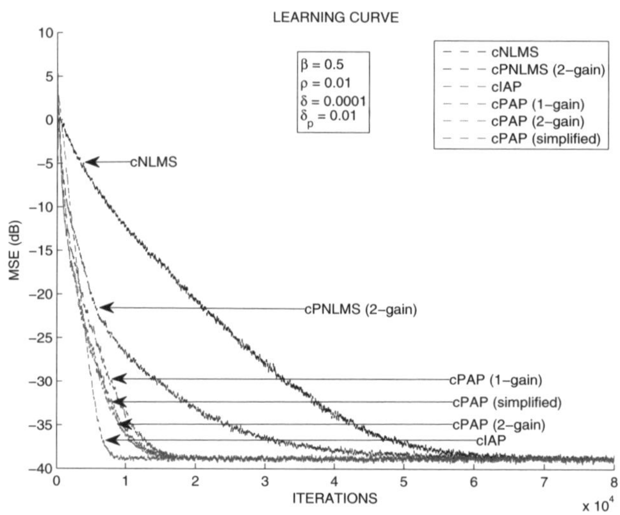

Figure 7.4. *cPtAP learning curve comparison with colored input*

Next, the MSE learning curve performance averaged over 100 uniform shifts of a complex speech input signal is presented in Figure 7.6. The complex speech used in this simulation was obtained by calculating the analytic signal [COH 95] of the real speech depicted in Figure 7.7. The same values of β that were used in the colored input signal simulation were also used in the speech input signal simulation. The parameter P was set to a value of 5. The impulse response was chosen such that $L = 50$. The real and imaginary parts of the impulse response had separate support. No noise was added to this simulation, that is $\sigma_v^2 = 0$. Again, the cPAP two-gain and simplified cPAP algorithms have roughly the same convergence rates. In addition, the cPAP two-gain algorithm has a faster convergence rate than the cPAP one-gain algorithm. In the case of speech input, the cPAP two-gain algorithm outperforms the cPNLMS two-gain algorithm.

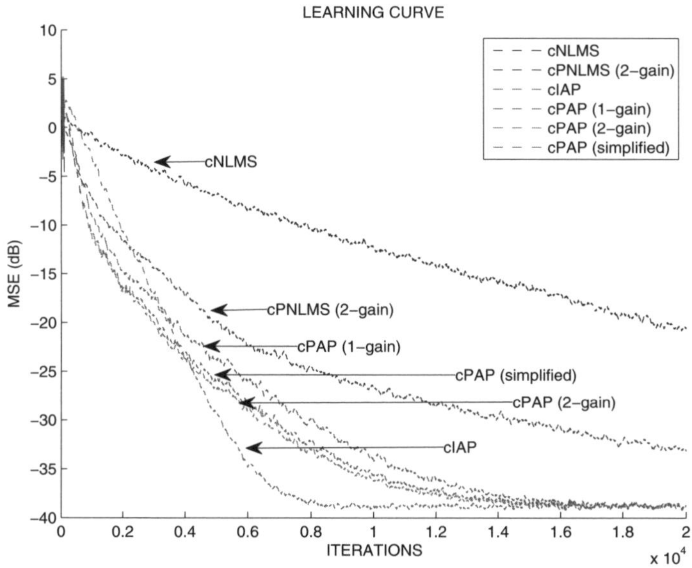

Figure 7.5. *cPtAP learning curve comparison with colored input (zoomed-in view)*

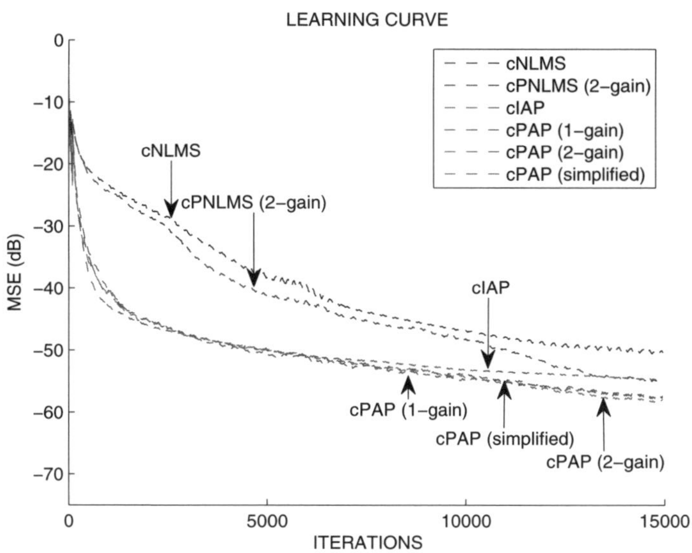

Figure 7.6. *cPtAP learning curve comparison with speech input (averaged over 100 uniform shifts of input signal)*

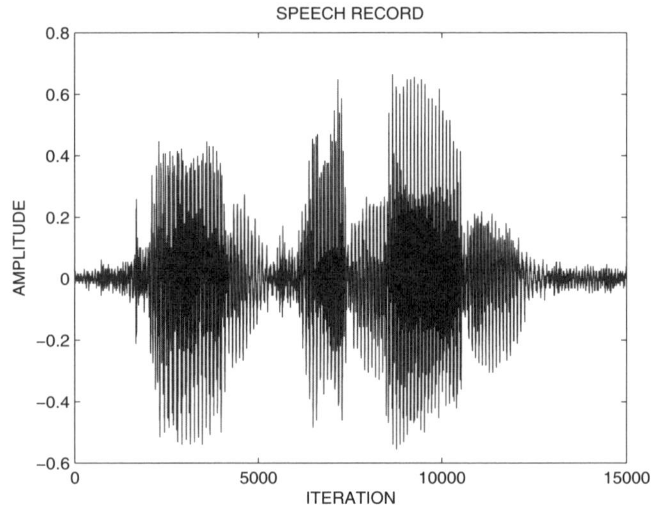

Figure 7.7. *Speech record*

7.6. Transform domain PtNLMS algorithms

The self-orthogonalizing adaptive filter [HAY 02] was originally introduced in an effort to improve the MSE convergence of the LMS [HAY 02] algorithm when the input signal was colored. The original derivation of the self-orthogonalizing filter required knowledge of the covariance matrix. The concept of the self-orthogonalizing adaptive filter was subsequently extended to situations where the covariance matrix was unknown. In this extension, the discrete cosine transform (DCT) matrix was used as an estimate of the Karhunen–Loeve transform (KLT). The DCT–LMS [HAY 02] algorithm was proposed that initially whitened the input signal using the DCT matrix and then applied the LMS algorithm to the whitened input signal. The DCT–LMS algorithm offered improved convergence in colored input signal scenarios at the expense of increased computational complexity.

In this section, the self-orthogonalizing adaptive filter is introduced to the general case of cPtNLMS algorithms for complex colored input signals and complex impulse responses. The self-orthogonalizing cPtNLMS algorithm is derived for an arbitrary gain control matrix. The resulting algorithm is named the TD-cPtNLMS algorithm. Next, the TD-cPtNLMS algorithm is extended to the case of an unknown covariance matrix. The DCT and Haar wavelet transform are proposed as possible substitutes for the unknown eigenvector matrix, which results in the DCT–cPtNLMS and Haar-cPtNLMS algorithms. The trade-off in convergence performance between applying standard cPtNLMS algorithms on the original sparse impulse response and colored input signals as opposed to applying the DCT-cPtNLMS algorithm and Haar-cPtNLMS algorithm on the transformed impulse response (not necessarily sparse anymore) and a whitened input signal is compared through simulation.

This section is organized in the following manner. First, the TD-cPtNLMS algorithm is derived. Next, it follows a discussion on the implementation of the TD-cPtNLMS algorithm when the covariance matrix is unknown. Finally, simulation results are presented and discussed.

7.6.1. *Derivation*

The cPtNLMS algorithm using one real-valued gain to update both the real and imaginary parts of the estimated coefficients is given by [7.22].

To find the cPtNLMS algorithm in the transform domain we first choose the transform matrix $\mathbf{Q}^H$. Now the input signal to the algorithm is:

$$\tilde{\mathbf{x}} = \mathbf{\Lambda}^{-\frac{1}{2}}\mathbf{Q}^H\mathbf{x}.$$

Optimally, that is to get $\tilde{\mathbf{x}}$ white, we would take $\mathbf{Q}$ and $\mathbf{\Lambda}$ such that:

$$\mathbf{R} = \mathbf{Q}\mathbf{\Lambda}\mathbf{Q}^H,$$

where $\mathbf{R}$ is the autocorrelation matrix of $\mathbf{x}$, $\mathbf{Q}$ is the matrix of eigenvectors of $\mathbf{R}$ and $\mathbf{\Lambda}$ is the diagonal matrix of eigenvalues of $\mathbf{R}$. Now we can start by minimizing:

$$(\hat{\mathbf{w}}_T^+ - \hat{\mathbf{w}}_T)^H\mathbf{G}_T^{-1}(\hat{\mathbf{w}}_T^+ - \hat{\mathbf{w}}_T)$$

under the condition:

$$d = \tilde{\mathbf{x}}^H\hat{\mathbf{w}}_T^+,$$

where $\mathbf{G}_T$ is called the step-size control matrix and is a real-valued, non-negative and diagonal matrix with $\mathrm{Tr}[\mathbf{G}_T] = L$.

The method of Lagrange multipliers will be used to cast this constrained minimization problem into one of the unconstrained minimizations. The minimization problem can be rewritten as:

$$\begin{aligned}\min_{\hat{\mathbf{w}}_T^+} J(\hat{\mathbf{w}}_T^+) = {} & (\hat{\mathbf{w}}_T^+ - \hat{\mathbf{w}}_T)^T\mathbf{G}_T^{-1}(\hat{\mathbf{w}}_T^+ - \hat{\mathbf{w}}_T) \\ & +\lambda\left(d - \tilde{\mathbf{x}}^H\hat{\mathbf{w}}_T^+\right) \\ & +\lambda^*\left(d^* - \tilde{\mathbf{x}}^T(\hat{\mathbf{w}}_T^+)^*\right)\end{aligned} \qquad [7.55]$$

Next, taking the derivative of $J(\hat{\mathbf{w}}_T^+)$ with respect to $\hat{\mathbf{w}}_T^+$ and setting the result to zero yield:

$$\frac{\partial J(\hat{\mathbf{w}}_T^+)}{\partial\hat{\mathbf{w}}_T^+} = (\hat{\mathbf{w}}_T^+ - \hat{\mathbf{w}}_T)^H\mathbf{G}_T^{-1} - \lambda\tilde{\mathbf{x}}^H = \mathbf{0}^T. \qquad [7.56]$$

where $\mathbf{0}$ is the column vector of zeros and length L. Taking the conjugate transpose of equation [7.56], multiplying from the left by $\mathbf{G}_T$ and rearranging terms allows us to write:

$$\hat{\mathbf{w}}_T^+ = \hat{\mathbf{w}}_T + \lambda^* \mathbf{G}_T \tilde{\mathbf{x}}. \qquad [7.57]$$

Next we substitute the recursion for the estimated impulse response given in [7.57] into the constraint equation $d = \tilde{\mathbf{x}}^H \hat{\mathbf{w}}_T^+$ to yield:

$$d = \tilde{\mathbf{x}}^H \hat{\mathbf{w}}_T + \lambda^* \tilde{\mathbf{x}}^H \mathbf{G}_T \tilde{\mathbf{x}}. \qquad [7.58]$$

Defining the *a priori* error as $e = d - \tilde{\mathbf{x}}^H \hat{\mathbf{w}}_T$ and rearranging terms in [7.58] allows us to solve for λ^*, which is given by:

$$\lambda^* = \frac{e}{\tilde{\mathbf{x}}^H \mathbf{G}_T \tilde{\mathbf{x}}}. \qquad [7.59]$$

Substituting the solution for λ^* into [7.57] results in:

$$\hat{\mathbf{w}}_T^+ = \hat{\mathbf{w}}_T + \frac{\mathbf{G}_T \tilde{\mathbf{x}} e}{\tilde{\mathbf{x}}^H \mathbf{G}_T \tilde{\mathbf{x}}}. \qquad [7.60]$$

Next, the step-size parameter β is introduced to allow control over the update. The resulting algorithm is called the TD-cPtNLMS algorithm and is given by:

$$\hat{\mathbf{w}}_T^+ = \hat{\mathbf{w}}_T + \beta \frac{\mathbf{G}_T \tilde{\mathbf{x}} e}{\tilde{\mathbf{x}}^H \mathbf{G}_T \tilde{\mathbf{x}}}. \qquad [7.61]$$

In both cases, d is same and given as:

$$d = \mathbf{x}^H \mathbf{w} + v.$$

The optimal (Wiener) weights in the transform domain are:

$$\mathbf{w}_T = \mathbf{\Lambda}^{\frac{1}{2}} \mathbf{Q}^H \mathbf{w}.$$

Note that the optimal weights depend on $\mathbf{\Lambda}$ and $\mathbf{Q}^H$, and therefore on their sparsity property as well.

7.6.2. *Implementation*

If the input signals covariance matrix, $\mathbf{R}$, is not available *a priori* then the TD-cPtNLMS algorithm is not feasible. To overcome this shortcoming we propose the following modification. Choose some orthogonal transformation, such as the DCT, discrete Fourier transform (DFT) or discrete wavelet transform (DWT), for $\mathbf{Q}$.

At this stage we are still left to estimate $\mathbf{\Lambda}$. In practice, the transformed input signal, $\mathbf{x}' = \mathbf{Q}^H\mathbf{x}$, is used to form an estimate of the eigenvalues. The following recursion can be used to estimate the eigenvalues:

$$[\tilde{\mathbf{\Lambda}}]_{ii} = \epsilon[\tilde{\mathbf{\Lambda}}]_{ii} + \frac{1}{k}(|x_i'(k)|^2 - \epsilon[\tilde{\mathbf{\Lambda}}]_{ii}), \qquad [7.62]$$

where $\tilde{\mathbf{\Lambda}}$ is the estimate of the eigenvalue matrix, $\mathbf{\Lambda}$, and $0 \leq \epsilon \leq 1$ is the forgetting factor.

7.6.3. *Simulation results*

In this section, we investigate for sparse unknown systems and the colored inputs the question of whether the convergence of cPtNLMS algorithms is better in the original signal domain or in the transformed signal domain, assuming the same steady-state mean square output error in both cases. The input signal used in all of the simulations was a stationary, real and colored input signal. The input signal consists of colored noise generated by a single pole system [4.31] where $n(k)$ is a white, real, Gaussian and stationary process with power $\sigma_n^2 = 1$. The value of $\gamma = 0.95$ was used, which implies $\sigma_x^2 = \sigma_n^2/(1 - |\gamma|^2) = 10.2564$. The impulse response depicted in Figure 6.5 with length $L = 512$ was used. The measurement noise used in all simulations was white, real, Gaussian, and stationary with power $\sigma_v^2 = 10^{-4}$. The parameter values $\beta = 0.1$, and $\epsilon = 1$ were used. The following parameters related to the NLMS and PNLMS algorithms were also used $\rho = 0.01$, $\delta = 0.0001$, and $\delta_p = 0.01$. The DCT water-filling (DCT-WF) algorithms used the step-size parameter of $\beta_0 = \beta/(\sigma_{\tilde{x}}^2 L) = 1.9^{-4}$ to ensure that the steady-state MSE was the same for all of the algorithms displayed. The term $\sigma_{\tilde{x}}^2 = 1$ is defined to be the variance of $\tilde{x}_i$ for all $i = 1, 2, \ldots, L$. In addition, the self-orthogonalizing water-filling (SO-WF), DCT-WF, and Haar water-filling (Haar-WF) algorithms used the following parameters $(\omega,\alpha) = (2, 0.9999)$, $(\omega,\alpha) = (2, 0.99999)$, and $(\omega,\alpha) = (2, 0.99999)$, respectively. The parameters (ω,α) are related to the implementation of the water-filling algorithm [WAG 11] and have been tuned to increase the convergence speed of the algorithms.

The first set of simulations examined the MSE versus iteration for the NLMS, PNLMS, self-orthogonalizing NLMS (SO-NLMS), self-orthogonalizing PNLMS (SO-PNLMS), and SO-WF algorithms. The self-orthogonalizing algorithms used knowledge of the covariance matrix $\mathbf{R}$. In Figure 7.8, the impulse response in the original domain and the transformed domain is plotted. The transformed impulse response is no longer sparse. Next, the learning curve comparison when using the transformation matrix $\mathbf{Q}^H$ is displayed in Figure 7.9. The SO-NLMS algorithm has the best learning curve performance, followed by the SO-WF and SO-PNLMS algorithms. Because the impulse response is dispersive in the transform domain, the SO-NLMS algorithm outperforms the SO-PNLMS algorithm.

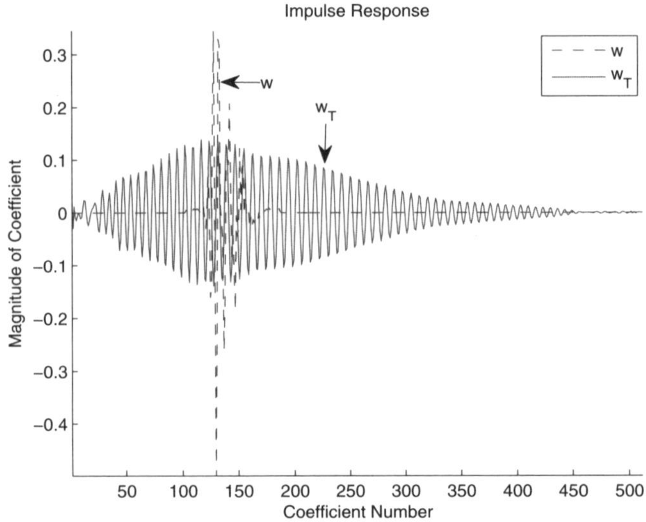

Figure 7.8. *Impulse response in the original domain and transform domain when* $\mathbf{R}$ *is known*

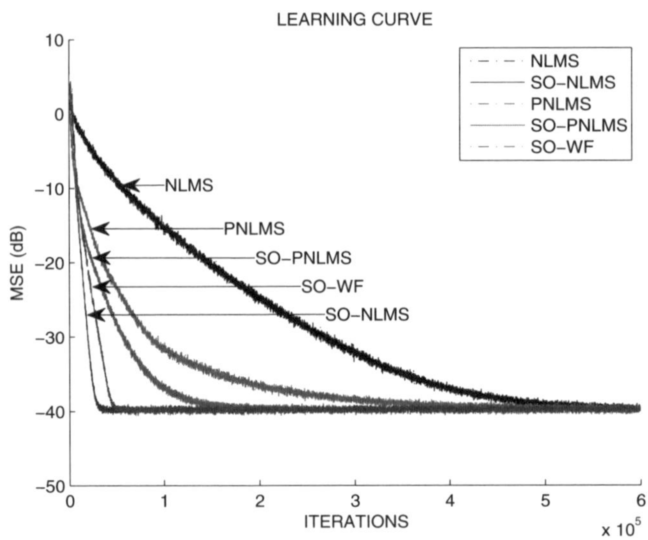

Figure 7.9. *Learning curve comparison when* $\mathbf{R}$ *is known*

The second set of simulations examined the MSE versus iteration for the NLMS, PNLMS, DCT-NLMS, DCT-PNLMS and DCT-WF. The DCT was used as an estimate of $\mathbf{Q}^H$ in the DCT-NLMS, DCT-PNLMS and DCT-WF algorithms. In Figure 7.10, the impulse response in the original domain and the transformed domain is plotted. The transformed impulse response is no longer sparse. Next, the learning curve comparison when using the DCT is displayed in Figure 7.11. Here the DCT-NLMS has the best overall convergence performance followed by the DCT-WF algorithm and then by the DCT-PNLMS algorithm. Note that the DCT-NLMS has better convergence performance than the DCT-PNLMS algorithm because the transform domain signal is no longer sparse. The PNLMS is better than the NLMS algorithm in the original domain because the impulse response is sparse in this domain. The DCT-NLMS and DCT-PNLMS algorithms outperform their counterpart algorithms in the original signal domain. The counterpart algorithm to the DCT-WF is the cCWF [WAG 12a] algorithm. The cCWF is not stable for the value of β chosen in these simulations and has not been included in the figure. Note, the similarity between algorithms using the KLT and DCT is expected, because asymptotically the DCT becomes the KLT in this scenario [HAY 02]. This can be seen further in Figures 7.8 and 7.10 where the transform domain impulse responses are similar.

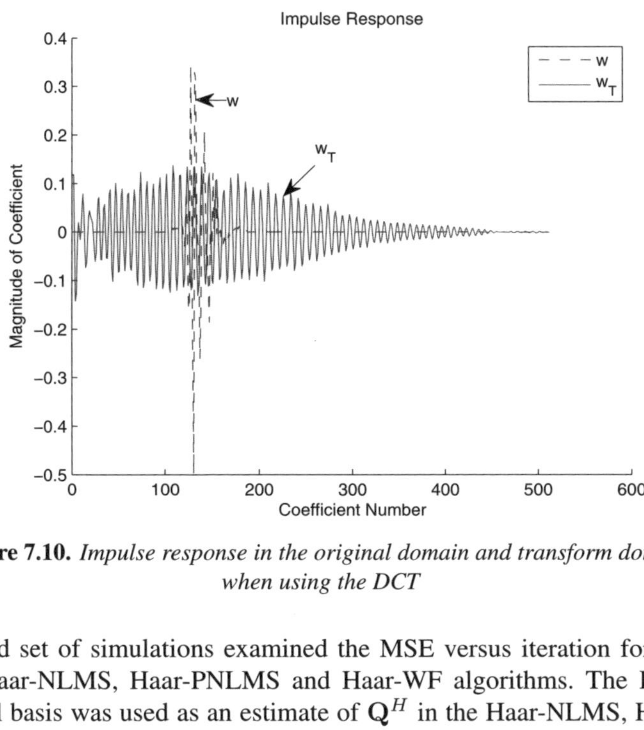

Figure 7.10. *Impulse response in the original domain and transform domain when using the DCT*

The third set of simulations examined the MSE versus iteration for the NLMS, PNLMS, Haar-NLMS, Haar-PNLMS and Haar-WF algorithms. The Haar wavelet orthonormal basis was used as an estimate of $\mathbf{Q}^H$ in the Haar-NLMS, Haar-PNLMS and Haar-WF algorithms. Because $L = 512$, a nine-level Haar wavelet transform was used in these algorithms. In Figure 7.12, the impulse response in the original domain and the transformed domain is plotted. The transformed impulse response is still sparse in this scenario. Next, the learning curve comparison when using the Haar wavelet transform is displayed in Figure 7.13. The Haar-WF has the best overall convergence performance followed by the Haar-PNLMS, PNLMS, Haar-NLMS and, finally, the NLMS algorithm. The Haar-PNLMS algorithm has superior convergence performance relative to the Haar-NLMS algorithm because the impulse response is sparse in the transform domain. The Haar-NLMS algorithm does not converge as quickly as the DCT-NLMS algorithm because the Haar wavelet transform does not whiten the colored input signal as well as the DCT. Hence, there is a trade-off between whitening the input signal and sparsity of impulse response in the transform domain.

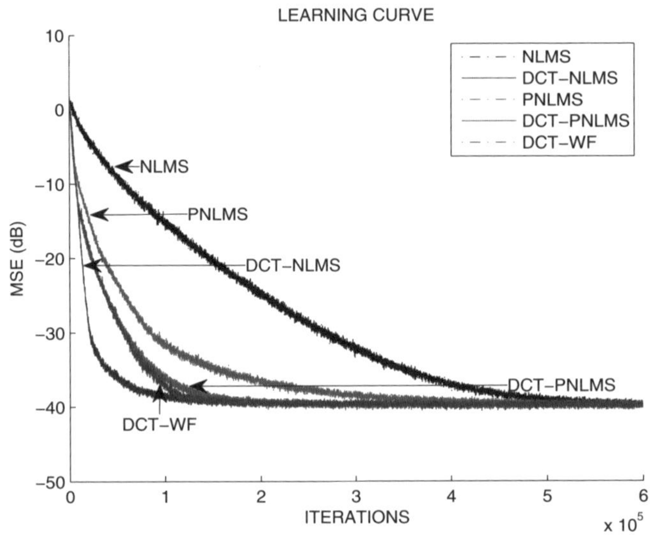

Figure 7.11. *Learning curve comparison using the DCT*

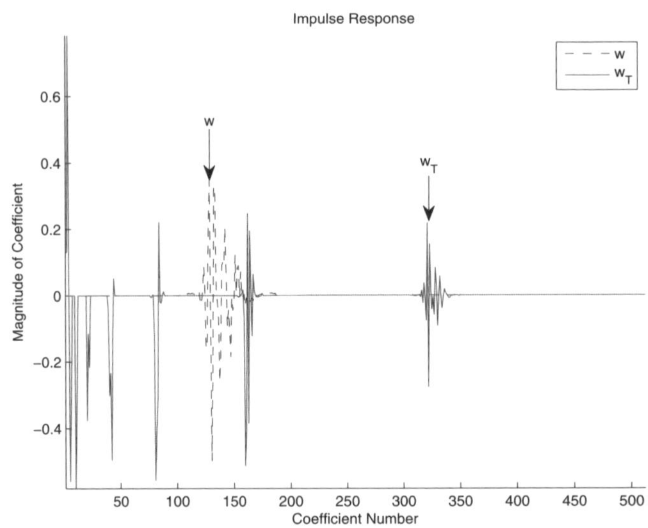

Figure 7.12. *Impulse response in the original domain and transform domain when using the Haar transform*

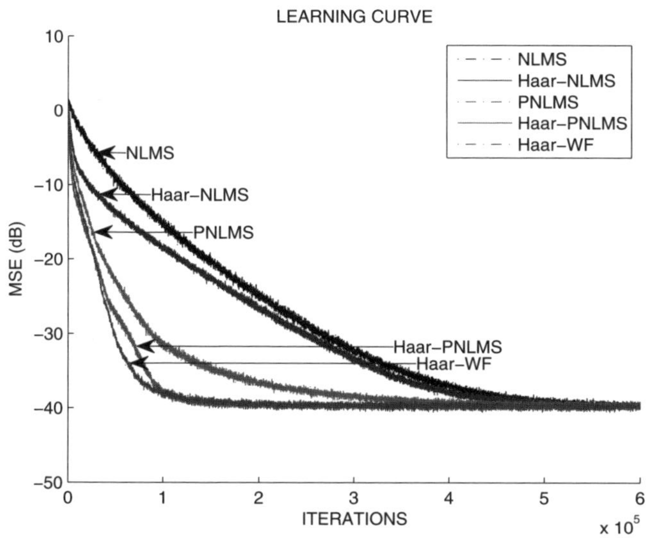

Figure 7.13. *Learning curve comparison using the Haar transform*

7.7. Summary

In this chapter, we have introduced a family of cPtAP algorithms that were derived by minimizing the second norm of the weighted difference between the current estimate of the impulse response and the new estimate under the constraints that at the last P time steps the new adaptive filter output equals the measured output. The cPtNLMS algorithms were also introduced employing a single constraint, or rather by setting $P = 1$. The choice of the step-size control matrix is arbitrary during the derivation that allows the users to design algorithms to suit their needs. Moreover, it can be noted from the simulations that the performances of the complex algorithm with separate gains for the imaginary parts and its simplified version are nearly indistinguishable. The cWF gain allocation algorithms for white and colored input signals were derived. It was also shown through simulation that the cPtAP algorithms offer superior convergence with stationary complex colored inputs and complex speech inputs relative to cPtNLMS algorithms. The usage of separate gains for updating the estimates of the real and imaginary parts provides superior convergence performance relative to using the same gain to update the real and imaginary parts of the estimated impulse response. Finally, the TD-cPtNLMS were derived and it was shown through simulation that in order to improve the MSE convergence performance, the choice of transformation matrix needs to balance the needs for whitening the input signal with the sparsity of the transformed impulse response.

8

Computational Complexity for PtNLMS Algorithms

In this chapter, we present a systematic approach to calculate the computational complexity for an arbitrary PtNLMS algorithm.

8.1. LMS computational complexity

Before examining an arbitrary PtNLMS algorithm, we begin by reviewing the LMS algorithm. The LMS algorithm is repeated here for convenience:

$$\begin{aligned}\hat{y}(k) &= \mathbf{x}^T(k)\hat{\mathbf{w}}(k)\\ e(k) &= d(k) - \hat{y}(k)\\ \hat{\mathbf{w}}(k+1) &= \hat{\mathbf{w}}(k) + \beta\mathbf{x}(k)e(k).\end{aligned}$$

The computational complexity of the LMS algorithm can be calculated in the following steps.

1) Each iteration requires the evaluation of the inner product $\mathbf{x}^T(k)\hat{\mathbf{w}}(k)$. This operation requires L multiplications and $L - 1$ additions.

2) Next, the term "$d(k) - \hat{y}(k)$" is calculated, which needs one addition.

3) Evaluation of the product $\beta e(k)$ requires one multiplication.

4) Multiplication of the scalar $\beta e(k)$ by the vector $\mathbf{x}(k)$ requires L multiplications

5) Finally, the sum of $\hat{\mathbf{w}}(k) + \beta\mathbf{x}(k)e(k)$ requires L additions.

To summarize:

LMS requires $2L + 1$ multiplications and $2L$ additions.

8.2. NLMS computational complexity

Compared to the LMS, the NLMS requires the computation of two additional quantities in the weight update equation given by:

$$\hat{\mathbf{w}}(k+1) = \hat{\mathbf{w}}(k) + \frac{\beta}{\delta + ||\mathbf{x}(k)||^2}\mathbf{x}(k)e(k). \qquad [8.1]$$

1) The inner product $||\mathbf{x}(k)||^2$ requires L multiplications and $L - 1$ additions. However, for tap-delay lines, this can be implemented more efficiently as, $||\mathbf{x}(k)||^2 = ||\mathbf{x}(k-1)||^2 - x^2(k-L) + x^2(k)$, which requires two additions and two multiplications.

2) One addition and one division are needed to evaluate $\beta/(\delta + ||\mathbf{x}(k)||^2)$.

Hence,

NLMS requires $2L + 3$ multiplications, $2L + 3$ additions, and one division.

8.3. PtNLMS computational complexity

Let us begin by assuming that the function $F[|\hat{w}_l(k)|, k]$ is given for all $l = 1, 2, \ldots, L$. Compared to the LMS algorithm, an arbitrary PtNLMS algorithm requires the following additional computations:

1) The term "$\gamma_{\min}(k) = \rho\max\{\delta_p, F[|\hat{w}_1(k)|, k], \ldots, F[|\hat{w}_L(k)|, k]\}$" requires one multiplication and L comparisons to compute.

2) The quantity $\gamma_l(k) = \max\{\gamma_{\min}(k), F[|\hat{w}_l(k)|, k]\}$ needs one comparison to compute.

3) To calculate $g_l(k) = \gamma_l(k) / \left(\frac{1}{L}\sum_{i=1}^{L} \gamma_i(k)\right)$, one multiplication, $L - 1$ additions, and one division operations are needed.

4) The term "$\mathbf{G}(k)\mathbf{x}(k)$" requires L multiplication

5) The calculation of $\beta/[\mathbf{x}^T(k)\mathbf{G}(k)\mathbf{x}(k) + \delta]$ given $\mathbf{G}(k)\mathbf{x}(k)$ requires L multiplications, L additions and one division.

6) Finally, L multiplications are needed to calculate:

$$\beta\mathbf{G}(k)\mathbf{x}(k)/[\mathbf{x}^T(k)\mathbf{G}(k)\mathbf{x}(k) + \delta.$$

Therefore,

PtNLMS requires $5L+3$ multiplications, $4L-1$ additions, 2 divisions, and $L+1$ comparisons, and calculation of $F[|\hat{w}_l(k)|, k]$, $l = 1, \ldots, L$.

8.4. Computational complexity for specific PtNLMS algorithms

The computational complexity of the NLMS, PNLMS, SPNLMS, ASPNLMS, MPNLMS, EPNLMS, AMPNLMS, AEPNLMS, z^2-proportionate, WF, CWF suboptimal gain allocation version 1, CWF suboptimal gain allocation version 2, CWF, cPNLMS and RLS algorithms is listed in Table 8.1 in terms of the total number of additions (A), multiplications (M), divisions (D), comparisons (C), memory words (MW) and logarithms (L) needed per algorithm iteration. All multiplications, additions, divisions, comparisons and logarithms are real-valued operations. Note that the implementation described in section 4.1.3 is included in the computational complexity calculations for the CWF, CWF suboptimal gain allocation version 1 and CWF suboptimal gain allocation version 2 algorithms. Additionally, it is assumed that $\mathbf{R}$ is stationary and known. Therefore, $\mathbf{R}$ and $\mathbf{R}^{-1}$ are precomputed and stored in memory. For cross-referencing purposes, Table 8.3 contains the section numbers where each algorithm is originally discussed.

Algorithm	A	M	D	C	MW	L
NLMS	$2L+3$	$2L+3$	1	0	$4L$+7	0
PNLMS	$4L+2$	$5L+4$	2	$2L$	$8L$+11	0
SPNLMS	$4L+2$	$6L+4$	2	$3L$	$9L+12$	0
ASPNLMS	$4L+3$	$6L+8$	2	$3L$	$9L+18$	0
MPNLMS	$5L+2$	$6L+4$	2	$2L$	$9L+12$	L
EPNLMS	$4L+2$	$6L+4$	2	$3L$	$9L+12$	L
AMPNLMS	$5L+3$	$6L+6$	3	$2L$	$9L+18$	L
AEPNLMS	$4L+3$	$6L+6$	3	$3L$	$9L+18$	L
z^2-proportionate	$6L+2$	$9L+2$	2	1	$10L$+11	0
Water-filling	$\mathcal{O}(L^2)$	$13L+3$	2	$\mathcal{O}(L\ln L)$	$13L$+11	0
CWF suboptimal 1	$\mathcal{O}(L^2)$	$\mathcal{O}(L^2)$	1	1	$\mathcal{O}(L^2)$	0
CWF suboptimal 2	$6L+3$	$13L+7$	1	1	$10L$+11	0
CWF	$\mathcal{O}(L^2)$	$\mathcal{O}(L^2)$	2	$\mathcal{O}(L\ln L)$	$\mathcal{O}(L^2)$	0
cPNLMS	$\mathcal{O}(100L)$	$\mathcal{O}(100L)$	2	2L + 2	$16L+22$	0
RLS	$\mathcal{O}(L^2)$	$\mathcal{O}(L^2)$	1	0	$\mathcal{O}(L^2)$	0

Table 8.1. *Computational complexity of algorithms – addition (A), multiplication (M), division (D), comparison (C), memory words (MW) and logarithm (L)*

The NLMS algorithm requires the least number of computations. The CWF algorithm requires the highest number of operations due to the sort operation needed to find the optimal value of λ. Based on standard sort algorithms, we estimate that the sort operation requires $L \ln L$ comparison operations [HOA 62]. With regard to memory requirements, the NLMS algorithm requires the least number of words. The CWF suboptimal gain allocation version 1, CWF and RLS algorithms require the maximum amount of words. The cPNLMS algorithm requires twice as many memory words as the real-valued PNLMS algorithm.

In Table 8.2, we display the average computation time in microseconds per algorithm iteration for the NLMS, PNLMS, SPNLMS, ASPNLMS, MPNLMS, EPNLMS, AMPNLMS, AEPNLMS, z^2-proportionate, WF, CWF suboptimal gain allocation version 1, CWF suboptimal gain allocation version 2, CWF, cPNLMS and RLS algorithms. These simulations were performed on a 2.30 GHz quad-core AMD Opteron processor with an impulse response of length L = 512. We can see that the NLMS algorithm has the fastest simulation time, while the PNLMS and the CWF suboptimal gain allocation version 2 algorithm have comparable simulation times. The RLS algorithm takes significantly longer to operate. The cPNLMS algorithm takes approximately twice as long as the PNLMS algorithm.

Algorithm	Simulation time per iteration (μs)	Relative time w.r.t. NLMS
NLMS	28.8	1.00
PNLMS	46.1	1.60
SPNLMS	89.6	3.10
ASPNLMS	91.7	3.18
MPNLMS	108.8	3.77
EPNLMS	113.9	3.95
AMPNLMS	111.7	3.87
AEPNLMS	125.9	4.37
z^2-proportionate	48.8	1.69
Water-filling	268.6	9.33
CWF suboptimal 1	442.4	16.24
CWF suboptimal 2	56.2	2.07
CWF	2,000.0	72.02
cPNLMS	110.3	3.83
RLS	35,800.0	1,243.00

Table 8.2. *Algorithm simulation times relative to NLMS*

Algorithm	Section number
NLMS	1.3
PNLMS	1.4.2
SPNLMS	6.2
ASPNLMS	6.2
MPNLMS	1.4.7
EPNLMS	1.4.8
AMPNLMS	6.1
AEPNLMS	6.1
z^2-proportionate	4.1.2
Water-filling	4.1.1
CWF suboptimal 1	4.4
CWF suboptimal 2	4.4
CWF	4.3
cPNLMS	7
RLS	4.1.4.1

Table 8.3. *Algorithm description location*

8.5. Summary

In this chapter, the methodology used to calculate the computational complexity of PtNLMS algorithms has been presented. The computational complexity for a variety of algorithms has been shown.

Conclusion

There are many opportunities to extend the results presented in this book further. Keeping that in mind, this section presents several open questions that are not addressed in this book as well as ideas for future extensions of the work presented here.

A closed-form solution for the joint probability density function of the weight deviation at any time is an open area of research. The assumption that the weight deviations are Gaussian seems to be satisfactory, at least for simple gain control laws such as the NLMS and PNLMS algorithms. However, this assumption quickly leads to erroneous results when examining more complex gain control laws such as the MPNLMS algorithm. Besides allowing the analysis of existing algorithms, knowledge of the joint probability density function would allow the user to design new algorithms by choosing gains that manipulate the joint probability density function. A future area of work could be to find a closed-form representation of the joint probability density function in some specific cases.

Due to the lack of finding a closed-form solution for the joint probability density function at all times, further applications and examples that manipulate the conditional probability density function of the weight deviations, given the previous weight deviations, could be studied. For instance, this book gives one- and two-dimensional examples of numerically finding the steady-state joint probability density function of the weight deviations using the conditional probability density function. An extension of this would be numerically finding the steady-state joint probability density function of the weight deviation for an arbitrary dimension problem. In addition, gain allocation algorithms, which maximize the conditional probability density function for the true weights, could be derived.

Another area of future work is choosing optimal gains that minimize the mean square output error for colored input signals. The work presented in this book finds optimal gains for minimizing the mean square weight deviation. It was shown that minimizing the mean square weight deviation minimizes an upper bound for the mean square error. Minimizing the mean square weight deviation resulted in gains that depended only on corresponding weight deviations. This means that the ith gain depends only on the ith weight deviation. Minimizing the mean square output error results in a problem where the ith gain depends on all the weight deviations. There is currently no solution for this problem.

In addition, transient analysis of PtNLMS algorithms is an open question when the input signal is colored. Also, an extension of white-input analysis to the segmented PNLMS and MPNLMS can be considered. Similarly, transient and steady-state analyses could be extended to the cPtNLMS algorithm. Finally, there is the possibility of finding more computationally efficient implementations of the algorithms presented.

Appendix 1

Calculation of $\boldsymbol{\beta}_i^{(0)}$, $\boldsymbol{\beta}_{i,j}^{(1)}$ and $\boldsymbol{\beta}_i^{(2)}$

A1.1. Calculation of $\beta_i^{(0)}$ term

We assume δ is very small and we can write:

$$\beta_i^{(0)} \approx E\left\{ \frac{\beta x_i^2(k)}{g_i(k)x_i^2(k) + \sum_{j \neq i} g_j(k)x_j^2(k)} \middle| \mathbf{z} \right\}.$$

When all $g_i(k)$, for $i = 1, 2, \ldots, L$, are equal or when all but one of these gains are equal, it is possible to calculate the above expectation [TAR 88]. But, in general, the expectation is difficult to calculate and we proceed by assuming that we are trying to calculate the following (where for notational simplicity we consider the time indexing):

$$\beta_i^{(0)} \approx E\left\{ \frac{\beta x_i^2}{g_i x_i^2 + E\{\sum_{j \neq i} g_j x_j^2 | \mathbf{z}\}} | \mathbf{z} \right\},$$

where $E\{\sum_{j \neq i} g_j x_j^2 | \mathbf{z}\} = \sum_{j \neq i} g_j E\{x_j^2\} = \sigma_x^2(L - g_i)$. This was calculated using the fact that $E\{x_i^2\} = \sigma_x^2$, $\sum_{i=1}^{L} g_i = L$, and that x_i, $i = 1, 2, \ldots, L$ are independent of $\mathbf{z}$.

Now, we define $a^2 = \sigma_x^2(L - g_i)$ and calculate the initial expectation as:

$$\beta_i^{(0)} \approx E\left\{ \frac{\beta x_i^2}{g_i x_i^2 + a^2} | \mathbf{z} \right\} = \frac{\beta}{g_i} E_{x_i}\left\{ \frac{x_i^2}{x_i^2 + a^2/g_i} \right\}. \qquad \text{[A1.1]}$$

The expectation in [A1.1] uses the conditional PDF of x_i.

Next, we define $b^2 = a^2/g_i$ and note that $b \geq 0$. Now, we need to find the expectation:

$$E_{x_i}\left\{\frac{x_i^2}{x_i^2+b^2}\right\} = E_{x_i}\left\{\frac{x_i^2+b^2-b^2}{x_i^2+b^2}\right\} = E_{x_i}\left\{1-\frac{b^2}{x_i^2+b^2}\right\}$$
$$= 1 - b\sqrt{\frac{\pi}{2\sigma_x^2}}e^{\frac{b^2}{2\sigma_x^2}}\operatorname{erfc}\left(\frac{b}{\sqrt{2\sigma_x^2}}\right). \qquad [A1.2]$$

Therefore, we have:

$$\beta_i^{(0)} \approx E\left\{\frac{\beta x_i^2}{g_i x_i^2 + \sum_{j\neq i} g_j x_j^2}|\mathbf{z}\right\} \approx \frac{\beta}{g_i}\left[1 - b\sqrt{\frac{\pi}{2\sigma_x^2}}e^{\frac{b^2}{2\sigma_x^2}}\operatorname{erfc}\left(\frac{b}{\sqrt{2\sigma_x^2}}\right)\right]. \qquad [A1.3]$$

We show $\beta_i^{(0)}$ versus gain in Figure A1.1.

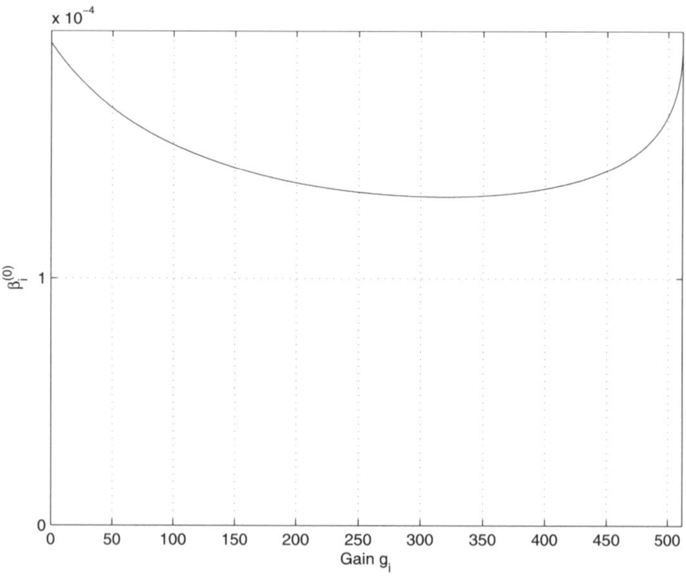

Figure A1.1. $\beta_i^{(0)}$ *versus gain for* $\sigma_x^2 = 0.01$, $L = 512$ *and* $\beta = 0.1$

A1.2. Calculation of $\beta_{i,j}^{(1)}$ term

We assume that δ is very small and we can write:

$$\beta_{i,j}^{(1)} \approx E\left\{\frac{\beta^2 x_i^2 x_j^2}{(g_i x_i^2 + \sum_{j\neq i} g_j x_j^2)^2}|\mathbf{z}\right\}.$$

Again, we make the assumption:

$$\beta_{i,j}^{(1)} \approx E\left\{\frac{\beta^2 x_i^2 x_j^2}{(g_i x_i^2 + E\{\sum_{j\neq i} g_j x_j^2|\mathbf{z}\})^2}|\mathbf{z}\right\}.$$

A1.2.1. *Case 1:* $i = j$

The expression for $\beta_{i,i}^{(1)}$ becomes:

$$\beta_{i,i}^{(1)} \approx E\left\{ \frac{\beta^2 x_i^4}{(g_i x_i^2 + E\{\sum_{j \neq i} g_j x_j^2 | \mathbf{z}\})^2} | \mathbf{z} \right\}.$$

Using the same constants where $b^2 = a^2/g_i$ and $a^2 = \sigma_x^2(L - g_i)$, we can rewrite:

$$\begin{aligned} \beta_{i,i}^{(1)} &\approx \frac{\beta^2}{g_i^2} E\left\{ \frac{x_i^4}{(x_i^2 + b^2)^2} | \mathbf{z} \right\} \\ &= \frac{\beta^2}{g_i^2} \left[1 - E_{x_i}\left\{ \frac{2x_i^2 b^2}{(x_i^2 + b^2)^2} \right\} - E_{x_i}\left\{ \frac{b^4}{(x_i^2 + b^2)^2} \right\} \right]. \end{aligned} \quad \text{[A1.4]}$$

We can calculate these expectations as follows:

$$\begin{aligned} I_1 &= E_{x_i}\left\{ \frac{1}{(x_i^2 + b^2)^2} \right\} \\ &= \frac{1}{2b^2} \left[\sqrt{\frac{\pi}{2\sigma_x^2}} e^{\frac{b^2}{2\sigma_x^2}} \operatorname{erfc}\left(\frac{b}{\sqrt{2\sigma_x^2}} \right) \left(\frac{1}{b} - \frac{b}{\sigma_x^2} \right) + \frac{1}{\sigma_x^2} \right]. \end{aligned} \quad \text{[A1.5]}$$

$$\begin{aligned} I_2 &= E_{x_i}\left\{ \frac{x_i^2}{(x_i^2 + b^2)^2} \right\} \\ &= \frac{1}{2} \left[\sqrt{\frac{\pi}{2\sigma_x^2}} e^{\frac{b^2}{2\sigma_x^2}} \operatorname{erfc}\left(\frac{b}{\sqrt{2\sigma_x^2}} \right) \left(\frac{1}{b} + \frac{b}{\sigma_x^2} \right) - \frac{1}{\sigma_x^2} \right] \end{aligned} \quad \text{[A1.6]}$$

and this leads to:

$$\beta_{i,i}^{(1)} \approx \frac{\beta^2}{g_i^2} \left[1 - 2b^2 I_2 - b^4 I_1 \right]. \quad \text{[A1.7]}$$

The calculation of I_1 and I_2 results in large numerical errors for large values of b. Knowing that the $\operatorname{erfc}(x)$ function [ABR 72] is bounded from below and above as:

$$\frac{2}{\sqrt{\pi}} \frac{e^{-x^2}}{x + \sqrt{x^2 + 2}} < \operatorname{erfc}(x) < \frac{2}{\sqrt{\pi}} \frac{e^{-x^2}}{x + \sqrt{x^2 + \frac{4}{\pi}}}$$

we resort to the calculation of the lower and the upper bound in place of $\operatorname{erfc}(x)$ itself. In Figure A1.2, we plot the ensemble averaged value of $\beta_{i,i}^{(1)}$ as well as its bounds when the upper and the lower bounds on the $\operatorname{erfc}(x)$ function are used.

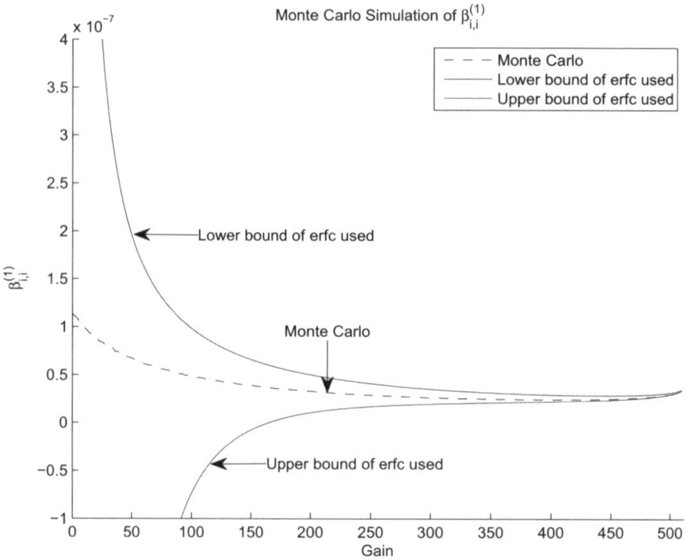

Figure A1.2. $\beta_{i,j}^{(1)}$ *versus gain for* $\sigma_x^2 = 0.01$, $L = 512$, 10^5 *Monte Carlo trials and* $\beta = 0.1$

A1.2.2. *Case 2: $i \neq j$*

We start with:

$$\begin{aligned}\beta_{i,j}^{(1)} &\approx E\left\{\frac{\beta^2 x_i^2 x_j^2}{(g_i x_i^2 + E\{\sum_{j\neq i} g_j x_j^2|\mathbf{z}\})^2}|\mathbf{z}\right\}\\ &= E\left\{\frac{\beta x_i^2}{(g_i x_i^2 + E\{\sum_{l\neq i} g_l x_l^2|\mathbf{z}\})}\frac{\beta x_j^2}{(g_j x_j^2 + E\{\sum_{l\neq j} g_l x_l^2|\mathbf{z}\})}|\mathbf{z}\right\}\\ &= E\left\{\frac{\beta x_i^2}{(g_i x_i^2 + a_i^2)}|\mathbf{z}\right\}E\left\{\frac{\beta x_j^2}{(g_j x_j^2 + a_j^2)}|\mathbf{z}\right\}\\ &= \beta_i^{(0)}\beta_j^{(0)},\end{aligned} \quad [A1.8]$$

where we let $a_i^2 = \sigma_x^2(L - g_i)$.

A1.3. Calculation of $\beta_i^{(2)}$ term

We assume that δ is very small and we can write:

$$\beta_i^{(2)} \approx E\left\{\frac{\beta^2 x_i^2}{(g_i x_i^2 + \sum_{j\neq i} g_j x_j^2)^2}|\mathbf{z}\right\}.$$

Again, we make the assumption:

$$\beta_i^{(2)} \approx E\left\{\frac{\beta^2 x_i^2}{(g_i x_i^2 + E\{\sum_{j\neq i} g_j x_j^2|\mathbf{z}\})^2}|\mathbf{z}\right\}.$$

Using the same constants where $b^2 = a^2/g_i$ and $a^2 = \sigma_x^2(L - g_i)$, we can rewrite:

$$\beta_i^{(2)} \approx \frac{\beta^2}{g_i^2} E\left\{\frac{x_i^2}{(x_i^2 + b^2)^2}|z_i\right\}.$$

We can calculate this expectation (same expectation as A1.6) that gives us

$$\beta_i^{(2)} \approx \frac{\beta^2}{2g_i^2}\left[\sqrt{\frac{\pi}{2\sigma_x^2}} \exp(\frac{b^2}{2\sigma_x^2})\mathrm{erfc}(\frac{b}{\sqrt{2\sigma_x^2}})(\frac{1}{b} + \frac{b}{\sigma_x^2}) - \frac{1}{\sigma_x^2}\right]. \quad \text{[A1.9]}$$

The ensemble averaged $\beta_i^{(2)}$ is shown in Figure A1.3.

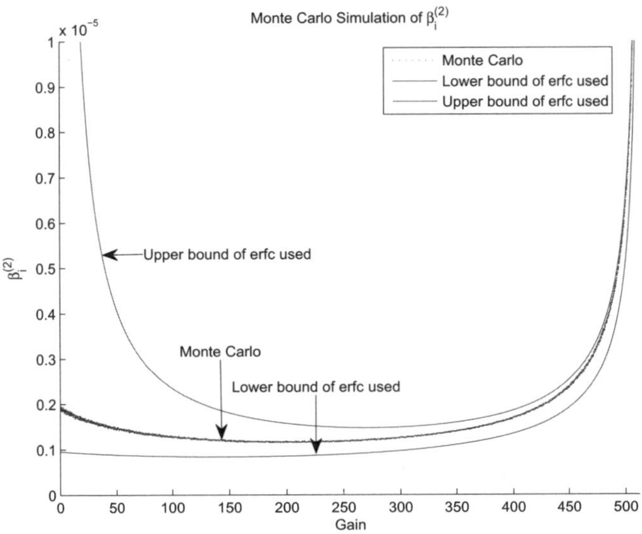

Figure A1.3. $\beta_i^{(2)}$ *versus gain for* $\sigma_x^2 = 0.01$, $L = 512$, 10^4 *Monte Carlo trials and* $\beta = 0.1$

Appendix 2

Impulse Response Legend

A wide variety of impulse responses are used to generate the simulation results discussed in this book. In this section, the reader can find a description of impulse response that was used in each figure. The description of each impulse response shown in Table A2.1 includes the name of an impulse response, the length of the impulse response L, the figures in which the impulse response is shown, whether the impulse response was fabricated data or real-world data, a description of the impulse response sparseness such as sparse and dispersive, and a list of figures in which the impulse response was used.

Name	L	Figure presenting impulse response	Source	Sparsity	Figure presenting performance
Sparse1	512	1.2b	Real world	Sparse	2.1, 2.2, 2.3, 3.1, 3.2, 3.8, 3.10, 3.12, 3.13, 3.14, 3.16, 3.18, 3.19, 4.4, 4.7, 7.1, 7.2, A1.1, A1.2, A1.3
Sparse2	512	4.2b	Real world	Sparse	4.2a, 4.4, 4.5, 4.7, 4.8, 4.9, 4.13, 5.7, 5.8, 6.2, 6.3
Sparse3	512	6.5	Real world	Sparse	6.6a, 6.6b, 6.6c, 6.7a, 6.7b, 6.7c, 6.8, 6.9, 7.1, 7.2
δ-Impulse	50	Not shown	Simulated	Sparse	3.3, 3.4, 3.5, 3.6, 3.7
Dispersive1	512	1.2a	Real world	Dispersive	
Dispersive2	512	4.3b	Simulated	Dispersive	4.3a, 4.6
Exponential	50	4.12	Simulated	Sparse	4.10, 4.11, 4.14b, 4.15, 6.4b

Table A2.1. *Impulse response legend*

Bibliography

[ABR 72] ABRAMOWITZ M., STEGUN I., *Handbook of Mathematical Functions with Formulas, Graphs, and Mathematical Tables*, 9th ed., Dover, New York, 1972.

[BEN 80] BENVENISTE A., GOURSAT M., RUGET G., "Analysis of stochastic approximation schemes with discontinuous and dependent forcing terms with applications to data communication algorithms", *IEEE Transactions on Automatic Control*, vol. 25, no. 6, pp. 1042–1058, December 1980.

[BEN 02] BENESTY J., GAY S., "An improved PNLMS algorithm", *2002 IEEE International Conference on Acoustics, Speech, and Signal Processing (ICASSP)*, vol. 2, Orlando, FL, pp. 1881–1884, May 2002.

[COH 95] COHEN L., *Time-Frequency Analysis*, Prentice Hall, 1995.

[CON 80] CONOVER W., *Practical Nonparametric Statistics*, 2nd ed., John Wiley & Sons, Inc., New Jersey, 1980.

[CUI 04] CUI J., NAYLOR P., BROWN D., "An improved IPNLMS algorithm for echo cancellation in packet-switched networks", *IEEE International Conference on Acoustics, Speech, and Signal Processing, 2004 (ICASSP '04)*, vol. 4, Montreal, Quebec, Canada, pp. 141–144, May 2004.

[DEN 05] DENG H., DOROSLOVAČKI M., "Improving convergence of the PNLMS algorithm for sparse impulse response identification", *IEEE Signal Processing Letters*, vol. 12, no. 3, pp. 181–184, March 2005.

[DEN 06] DENG H., DOROSLOVAČKI M., "Proportionate adaptive algorithms for network echo cancellation", *IEEE Transactions on Signal Processing*, vol. 54, no. 5, pp. 1794–1803, May 2006.

[DEN 07] DENG H., DOROSLOVAČKI M., "Wavelet-based MPNLMS adaptive algorithm for network echo cancellation", *EURASIP Journal on Audio, Speech, and Music Processing*, vol. 2007, pp. 1–5, March 2007.

[DOO 53] DOOB J., *Stochastic Processes*, Wiley, 1953.

[DOR 06] DOROSLOVAČKI M., DENG H., "On convergence of proportionate-type NLMS adaptive algorithms", *IEEE International Conference on Acoustics, Speech and Signal Processing, 2006 (ICASSP '06)*, vol. 3, Toulouse, France, pp. 105–108, May 2006.

[DUT 00] DUTTWEILER D., "Proportionate normalized least-mean-squares adaptation in echo cancellers", *IEEE Transactions on Speech and Audio Processing*, vol. 8, no. 5, pp. 508–518, September 2000.

[FAN 05] FAN L., HE C., WANG D., *et al.* , "Efficient robust adaptive decision feedback equalizer for large delay sparse channel", *IEEE Transactions on Consumer Electronics*, vol. 51, no. 2, pp. 449–456, May 2005.

[GAY 98] GAY S., "An efficient, fast converging adaptive filter for network echo cancellation", *Conference Record of the 32nd Asilomar Conference on Signals, Systems and Computers*, Pacific Grove, CA, vol. 1, pp. 394–398, November 1998.

[HAY 91] HAYKIN S., *Adaptive Filter Theory*, 2nd ed., Prentice Hall, Upper Saddle River, NJ, 1991.

[HAY 02] HAYKIN S., *Adaptive Filter Theory*, 4th ed., Prentice Hall, Upper Saddle River, NJ, 2002.

[HOA 62] HOARE C., "Quicksort", *Computer Journal*, vol. 5, no. 1, pp. 10–16, 1962.

[KUS 84] KUSHNER H., *Approximation and Weak Convergence Methods for Random Process with Applications to Stochastic System Theory*, MIT Press, Cambridge, MA, 1984.

[LI 08] LI N., ZHANG Y., HAO Y., *et al.*, "A new variable step-size NLMS algorithm designed for applications with exponential decay impulse responses", *Signal Processing*, vol. 88, no. 9, pp. 2346–2349, September 2008.

[LIL 67] LILLIEFORS H., "On the Kolmogorov-Smirnov test for normality with mean and variance unknown", *Journal of American Statistical Association*, vol. 62, no. 318, pp. 399–402, June 1967.

[LIU 09] LIU L., FUKUMOTO M., SAIKI S., *et al.*, "A variable step-size proportionate affine projection algorithm for identification of sparse impulse response", *EURASIP Journal on Advances in Signal Processing*, vol. 2009, pp. 1–10, September 2009.

[LOG 09] LOGANATHAN P., KHONG A., NAYLOR P., "A class of sparseness-controlled algorithms for echo cancellation", *IEEE Transactions on Audio, Speech, and Language Processing*, vol. 17, no. 8, pp. 1591–1601, November 2009.

[MEC 66] MECHEL F., "Calculation of the modified Bessel functions of the second kind with complex argument", *Mathematics of Computation*, vol. 20, no. 95, pp. 407–412, July 1966.

[MIN 06] MINTANDJIAN L., NAYLOR P., "A study of synchronous convergence in μ-law PNLMS for voice over IP", *Proceedings of the European Signal Processing Conference*, Florence, Italy, September 2006.

[NAY 03] NAYLOR P., SHERLIKER W., "A short-sort M-max NLMS partial-update adaptive filter with applications to echo cancellation", *IEEE International Conference on Acoustics, Speech, and Signal Processing, 2003 (ICASSP '03)*, Hong Kong, China, vol. 5, pp. 373–376, April 2003.

[OMU 65] OMURA J., KAILATH T., Some useful probability distributions, Report No. 7050–6, Stanford Electronics Laboratories, 1965.

[PAL 05] PALOMAR D., FONOLLOSA J., "Practical algorithms for a family of waterfilling solutions", *IEEE Transactions on Signal Processing*, vol. 53, no. 2, pp. 686–695, February 2005.

[SAY 03] SAYED A., *Fundamentals of Adaptive Filtering*, John Wiley & Sons, New Jersey, 2003.

[SCH 95] SCHREIBER W.F., "Advanced television system for terrestrial broadcasting: some problems and some proposed solutions", *Proceedings of the IEEE*, vol. 83, no. 6, pp. 958–981, June 1995.

[SHI 04] SHIN H.-C., SAYED A.H., SONG W.-J., "Variable step-size NLMS and affine projection algorithms", *IEEE Signal Processing Letters*, vol. 11, no. 2, pp. 132–135, February 2004.

[SON 06] SONDHI M.M., "The history of echo cancellation", *IEEE Signal Processing Magazine*, vol. 23, no. 5, pp. 95–102, September 2006.

[SOU 10] DAS CHAGAS DE SOUZA F., TOBIAS O., SEARA R., *et al.*, "A PNLMS algorithm with individual activation factors", *IEEE Transactions on Signal Processing*, vol. 58, no. 4, pp. 2036–2047, April 2010.

[SPI 96a] SIGNAL PROCESSING INFORMATION BASE, October 1996. Available at: http://spib. rice.edu/spib/cable.html.

[SPI 96b] SIGNAL PROCESSING INFORMATION BASE, October 1996. Available at: http://spib. rice.edu/spib/microwave.html.

[STO 09] STOJANOVIC M., PREISIG J., "Underwater acoustic communication channels: propagation models and statistical characterization", *IEEE Communications Magazine*, vol. 47, no. 1, pp. 84–88, January 2009.

[SYL 52] SYLVESTER J., "A demonstration of the theorem that every homogeneous quadratic polynomial is reducible by real orthogonal substitutions to the form of a sum of positive and negative squares", *Philosophical Magazine*, vol. 4, pp. 138–142, 1852.

[TAN 02] TANRIKULU O., DOGANCAY K., "Selective-partial-update proportionate normalized least-mean-squares algorithm for network echo cancellation", *IEEE International Conference on Acoustics, Speech, and Signal Processing, 2002 (ICASSP '02)*, vol. 2, pp. 1889–1892, Orlando, FL, May 2002.

[TAR 88] TARRAB M., FEUER A., "Convergence and performance analysis of the normalized LMS algorithm with uncorrelated Gaussian data", *IEEE Transactions on Information Theory*, vol. 34, no. 4, pp. 680–691, July 1988.

[WAG 06] WAGNER K., DOROSLOVAČKI M., DENG H., "Convergence of proportionate-type LMS adaptive filters and choice of gain matrix", *40th Asilomar Conference on Signals, Systems and Computers, 2006 (ACSSC '06)*, Pacific Grove, CA, pp. 243–247, November 2006.

[WAG 08] WAGNER K., DOROSLOVAČKI M., "Analytical analysis of transient and steady-state properties of the proportionate NLMS algorithm", *42nd Asilomar Conference on Signals, Systems and Computers, 2008*, Pacific Grove, CA, pp. 256–260, October 2008.

[WAG 09] WAGNER K., DOROSLOVAČKI M., "Gain allocation in proportionate-type NLMS algorithms for fast decay of output error at all times", *IEEE International Conference on Acoustics, Speech and Signal Processing, 2009 (ICASSP '09)*, Taipei, Taiwan, pp. 3117–3120, April 2009.

[WAG 11] WAGNER K., DOROSLOVAČKI M., "Proportionate-type normalized least mean square algorithms with gain allocation motivated by mean-square-error minimization for white input", *IEEE Transactions on Signal Processing*, vol. 59, no. 5, pp. 2410–2415, May 2011.

[WAG 12a] WAGNER K., DOROSLOVAČKI M., "Complex colored water-filling algorithm for gain allocation in proportionate adaptive filtering", *46th Asilomar Conference on Signals, Systems and Computers*, Pacific Grove, CA, November 2012.

[WAG 12b] WAGNER K., DOROSLOVAČKI M., "Complex proportionate-type normalized least mean square algorithms", *IEEE International Conference on Acoustics, Speech and Signal Processing, 2012 (ICASSP '12)*, pp. 3285–3288, Kyoto, Japan, March 2012.

[WEI 77] WEINSTEIN S., "Echo Cancellation in the telephone network", *IEEE Communications Society Magazine*, vol. 15, no. 1, pp. 8–15, January 1977.

[WID 75] WIDROW B., MCCOOL J., BALL M., "The complex LMS algorithm", *Proceedings of the IEEE*, vol. 63, no. 4, pp. 719–720, April 1975.

[WOO 50] WOODBURY M., Inverting modified matrices, Memorandum Report no. 42, Statistical Research Group, Princeton University, Princeton, NJ, 1950.

Index

D

E

G